Bathudi and Sounti Tribes
A Bio-Anthropological Profile

BATHUDI AND SOUNTI TRIBES

A Bio-Anthropological Profile

SWARAN SINGH

GYAN PUBLISHING HOUSE
NEW DELHI-110 002

Bathudi and Sounti Tribes
A Bio-Anthropological Profile

(Anthropology, Tribal Studies, Ethnology)

The opinions expressed in the book are those of the author and not necessarily of the Anthropological Survey of India.

ISBN : 81-212-0466-6
Library of Congress Card No. 93-900321

Published in 1994 by
Gyan Publishing House
5 Ansari Road
New Delhi - 110002

Composed by Ideal Computers Pvt. Ltd., Delhi-110007 and printed at Goyal Offset Works, Delhi

Dedicate most respectfully

to

Baba Gajjan Shahji

of

Phalound Kalan

ACKNOWLEDGEMENTS

I am grateful to the Director General Anthropological Survey of India for giving me the permission to publish the official data and providing me the facilities for the present research study.

I am indebted to Prof. Ajit Kumar Danda, Ph.D. (Cornell University, U.S.A.) for his most invaluable guidance and supervision. I express my gratitude with deep and sincere regards to Prof. Danda.

I express my sincere gratitude for invaluable suggestions & encouragements to Prof. S.R.K. Chopra, Sh. T.N. Pandit, Prof. R.S. Mann, Prof. A.R. Banerjee, Prof. V. Bhalla, Prof. K.C. Malhotra and late Shri H.K. Rakshit. I am indebted to Shri V. Saha and R.B. Bhale who assisted in working out Statistical reduction of the data, Shri Swapan Saha helped in tracing the graphs and Shri Indranil Pal typed out the manuscript. I express my sincere appreciation to all of them. I am specially thankful to all the Government Officials of Mayurbhanj District, Orissa State; specially the District Magistrate, Additional District Magistrate, Sub-divisional Magistrate (Civil), Panchpir Sub-division, Karanjia and the Block Development Officers of Jashipur, Karanjia, Thakumunda and Sukruli Blocks and the members of their staff.

I am also grateful to the Sarpanches, members of Panchayat, Secretary, Mahila Samitees, Headmasters of different schools of Karanjia Tehsil, Officials of forest Department, interpreter-cum-field guides for their extra-ordinary and ungrudging Co-operation. I express my deep regards to my parents and relatives for their encouragement and blessings and specially my uncle Shri Bachittar Singh for his inspirations. I sincerely thank my wife Mrs Gur Sharan Kaur son Sundeep Singh and daughter Amrita Kaur for their co-operation.

I shall remain indebted to all my subjects specially the ladies without whose invaluable co-operation the present book could not have been written, once again sincerely thanks to all my friends both in my office and in the field, who extended their co-operation and invaluable suggestions and the Gyan Publishing House for bringing out the present book.

SWARAN SINGH

LIST OF TABLES

LIST OF FIGURES

CONTENTS

1

INTRODUCTION

1.0 According to Census of India (1981) 51,628,638 individuals are scheduled tribes and they constitute 7.76% of the total Indian population. The scheduled tribes in India are mainly concentrated in the North Eastern States such as Manipur, Meghalaya, Nagaland, Tripura, Mizoram, Arunachal Pradesh, Assam, Sikkim and Central and Eastern States such as Orissa, Madhya Pradesh and Bihar, West Bengal and Western States such as Rajasthan and Gujarat. The tribes have always attracted the adequate attention of the Anthropologists, Social Scientists and administrators alike, as they still maintain their age old traditions, customs, social organisations, culture, language, dress, mating pattern, etc. In due course of time various Indian tribal populations may also be effected by various micro evolutionary factors such as isolation, migration, inbreeding and hybridization which are operating at different levels. Due to the various Government developmental programmes such as education, better medium of communication, industrialization, employment opportunities including job reservations for the scheduled tribes have also resulted in their occupational mobility. Those tribals, who are educated and are immigrants in distant places in India from their native places for better employment opportunities, the various evolutionary factors are likely to operate more in their cases as compared to the past, when such facilities were not available. This situation may create a crises of the loss of their tribal identity. There are several research studies on the various cultural aspects of the Indian tribal populations. However, similar comprehensive and comparative research exercises on the Bio-Anthropological aspects of tribes are lacking, but similar studies among the tribal females have not yet been attempted. The present research exercise is a similar attempt of a case study among the Bathudi and Sounti scheduled tribes from Mayurbhanj district of Orissa which borders with Madhya

Pradesh, Bihar, West Bengal having high concentration of the tribal populations.

1.1 LOCATION OF ORISSA

Orissa, Kalinga or Utkal is situated between 17° 48′ to 20° 34′ North latitude and 81° 24′ to 87° 29′ East longitude. It comprises an area of 155,842 square kilometers. The total population of Orissa is 26,272,054 individuals, including 13,253,523 males and 13,018,531 females (according to Census of India, 1981). Orissa has four physiogeographical divisions, two of which are hilly, the northern plateau and the eastern ghats. Two other divisions are more or less plain, the coastal plain and the central tract. Most of the rivers flow from north-west to south-east. Orissa mostly has tropical climate. All the geographical divisions do not offer equal opportunity for human habitation. There are 13 districts of Orissa including Mayurbhanj. The density of population is not equally distributed in all the districts. Coastal divisions are more densely populated than the interior divisions. Cuttack district is most thickly populated, while the Phulbani district is least populated (Census of India, 1961).

1.2 LOCATION OF MAYURBHANJ DISTRICT

Mayurbhanj district with its boundaries reaching the northern most point of Orissa lies between 20° 61′ North and 22° 34′ North latitude and between 85° 40′ East and 87° 11′ East longitude. It is bounded in the North by Midnapur district of West Bengal and Singhbhum district of Bihar, in the South by Keonjhar and Balasore districts of the same states in the West by Singhbhum and Keonjhar districts and in the East by Balasore districts. The district is divided into four sub-divisions that is Sadar, Bamanghaty, Panchpir and Kaptipada with their respective headquarters at Baripada, Rairangpur, Karanjia and Udala. Baripada is the district headquarters of Mayurbhanj (Census of India, 1961). (Fig. 1.2)

1.2.1 Physical Features of Mayurbhanj

The physical features of Mayurbhanj district are characterised by groups of hills which are extended over an area of 600 square miles, known as *Simlipal Hills*. Simlipal hills are situated in the central part of Mayurbhanj district and run from North to South direction with the result there are three natural divisions of this district namely:

1. Eastern division forms the Sadar and Kaptipada sub-divisions,
2. North-western division forms the Bamanghaty sub-division, and
3. South-west division forms the Panchpir sub-division.

The eastern division gradually slopes from the foot of the Simplipal hills towards the way of Bengal and forms several stream. Two other divisions are mainly undulating slopes. Burabalanga and Salandi are two main rivers arising from the hills of the district. These two rivers are joined by a large number of hill streams. Baitarani river flows along the western border of Mayurbhanj district for a short distance and later on enters the neighbouring district of Keonjhar. Most part of this district has red soil and belt of laterites. There are large deposits of iron ore and china clay in the rocks (Census of India, 1961).

1.2.2 Flora and Fauna

Forests cover about 1481 square miles and mostly have northern tropical semi evergreen species such as Sal, Piasal, Sisu, Kurum, Bandhan, Gambhari, Kendu, Mahua, Asan and Mango. Important forest products are Tusser, Cocoon, lac, myrobalan, Sunari bark, arrowroot, etc. The above flora has the following fauna in large number : Elephants, bison, sambar, tiger, panther, spotted deer, barking deer, peacock, green pigeon, grey patridges, painted patridges, cobra, python and many others. Crocodiles are found in Burabalanga and Deo rivers (Census of India, 1961).

1.2.3 Environment of the District

Mayurbhanj has a hot summer with high humidity from March to May, the rains are well distributed during the monsoon period which lasts from June to September. The average rain fall during the year is about 1650 millimeters. October to November is the post monsoon period. Winter season is from December to

February and December is usually the coldest month (Census of India 1971).

1.3 MAYURBHANJ UNDER VARIOUS RULERS

In ancient times Mayurbhanj district formed a part of Utkala which was founded by Prince Utkala, the son of Sudyumna. This area formed the southern part of present Chotanagpur and was extended over the present Mayurbhanj and parts of Balasore district. This area including Mayurbhanj formed a part of Kalinga under Ashoka and Kharvela. During earlier christian centuries Murunda family ruled Mayurbhanj. The history of this territory when Guptas ruled northern India is not known. But in the post-Gupta period the Mana and Bhanjas came to power. During medieval period Bhanjas ruled over Khijjinga Mandala territory. It was comprised of the present Mayurbhanj district and part of Keonjhar district with its capital at Khijjinga Kotta, the present Khiching. In the beginning of 12 century A.D. the Bhanjas became subordinate to the Imperial Ganga powers. In 1361 Orissa was invaded by the Sultan of Delhi Firoj Shah Toghulak, who marched through Manbhum, Singhbhum and Mayurbhanj. He is believed to have destroyed Khijjinga Kota the capital of Bhanjas. In 1568, the Afghans occupied Orissa and Moghuls took possession of the area and ruled from 1592-1751 A.D. By the end of 18th century East India Company made diplomatic relations with the ruling family of Mayurbhanj. On first January 1949, Mayurbhanj princely state was merged with Orissa and formed into a district (Census of India, 1961).

1.4 POPULATION OF MAYURBHANJ DISTRICT

Mayurbhanj district covers an area of 10,416.6 square kilometers which forms 6.68 percent of the Orissa State. There are altogether 1,434,200 individuals in the district including 1,394,249 individuals in rural and 39,951 individuals in urban areas, who constitute 6.54 percent of the State's population with density of 141 individuals per square kilometer. The sex ratio is 987 females per 1000 males. The populations of scheduled tribes and scheduled castes are 58.6 percent and 7.2 percent respectively of the total population of this district. In other words about 66 percent of the population of Mayurbhanj is scheduled population (Census of India, 1971).

1.5 VARIOUS MAJOR SCHEDULED POPULATIONS OF MAYURBHANJ

According to Scheduled Caste and Scheduled Tribe List (modification) order 1956, one tribe namely Gorait was excluded from 1951 list and 21 new tribes were included in the list namely Bhottada, Bhumia, Bhumij, Bhunjia, Desua Bhemij, Dharua, Didayi, Gandia, Halva, Kandha Gauda, Kol, Kotia, Lodha, Madia, Matya, Omanatya, Parenga, Pentia, Rajuar, Shabar and Sountia. This has resulted in the increase of tribal population of Mayurbhanj during 1951 to 1961 (Census of India 1961).

Table 1.1
Distribution of Scheduled Tribe and Scheduled Caste populations of Mayurbhanj District (Census of India 1961)

Sl. No.	*Name of the Scheduled Tribe*	*Population*	*Sl. No.*	*Name of the Scheduled Caste*	*Population*
1.	Bathudi	59,377	1.	Amanator or Amat	6,939
2.	Bhuiya	29,616	2.	Bariki	1,674
3.	Bhumij	79,394	3.	Chamar	1,203
4.	Gond	16,659	4.	Dhoba	14,757
5.	Ho	27,090	5.	Dom	7,580
6.	Kharia	10,090	6.	Ghasi	4,441
7.	Kolho	119,136	7.	Hari	3,764
8.	Mahali	3,891	8.	Karua	1,715
9.	Munda	4,727	9.	Pan	11,174
10.	Mundari	8,292	10.	Pantanti	8,547
11.	Orson	1,783	11.	Patratanti	26,094

(Contd.)

(Contd.)

12.	Pentia	3,853	12.	Tamudia	6,839
13.	Santal	340,327	13.	Ujia	1,299
14.	Saora	2,087			
15.	Shabar	5,128			
16.	Sounti	11,450			

Some of the major Scheduled Tribe and Scheduled Caste population of Mayurbhanj district are given in Table 1.1. Santal, Kolho, Bhumij and Bathudi are some of the highly concentrated scheduled tribe populations. Dhoba, Patra-tanti and Pantanti, Pan and Dom are the largest scheduled caste populations of this district (Census of India 1961).

1.6 CRITERIA OF SELECTION OF POPULATIONS UNDER STUDY

In Mayurbhanj District the Scheduled Castes constitute only 7.2 percent, where as the proportion of Scheduled tribes is about 59 percent (Census of India, 1971). Since for our study it was decided to concentrate our attention to the hitherto unknown population of the less known areas, selection of Scheduled Tribes from Mayurbhanj District of Orissa became more or less the automatic choice, the purpose of the present exercise was modest, to fill up to the extent possible the major information gaps. At the out set therefore, it become necessary to have an evaluation of the existing level of knowledge about the area as well as the population.

Among the 16 major Scheduled tribes of Mayurbhanj District, there are several, the maximum concentration of whom are not only outside the district but sometimes from outside the state. The Bhumij are highly concentrated in the State of West Bengal. The Ho, Kharia, Kolho, Mahji, Munda, Oraon, and Santal are found mostly in Bihar. The Gonds have their maximum concentration in Madhya Pradesh (Census of India, 1971). The Bhuiya have been well studied by Risley (1891), Roy (1935), and Basu (1929). The Juangs of Keonjhar district of Orissa were studied by Rout (1948, 1969/70), Sarkar *et. al.* (1959/60), Banerjee (1956) and Ray (1958). The Khonds of Koraput district were investigated by De (1967), Ray (1949), Das (1966), Deka (1991) and Sharma (1979). The Pentia have been investigated by Deka (1991) and have been further investigated by a researcher of Anthropological Survey of India (R.K.Kundu). The Rajuar were studied by Mahalanobis *et al* (1949) and are being further investigated by another colleague from the Survey (N.K.Das). Saora-Savara or Sahara were investigated by Rao *et al.* (1963), and Tripathy (1963), while Banerjee (1956) and Sarkar (1956-57) studied the Sabhar. In contrast, the Bathudi and Sounti tribes hardly received any major attention from researchers yet.

1.7 PUBLISHED LITERATURES ON THE BATHUDI AND SOUNTI

Since Mayurbhanj District of Orissa from the ethonographic point of view, is still largely unknown and even less we know about its populations like the Bathudi and Sounti particularly about the physical anthropological parameter of the populations. The obvious choice of the author is to focus attention to these two populations for specific study. Nevertheless, at the out set an appraisal of the published literatures on these two populations as such is considered important.

1.7.1 Bathudi

Dalton (1872), Risley (1891), O'Malley (1911), Russel and Hiralal (1916) were among the earlier to make references to the Bathudi Chatterjee (1929) referred to the Physical features of the Bathudi while making special mention about the marriage ceremony of these peoples. Laccquidin (1931) published some ethnographic details of the Bathudi in the Census of Mayurbhanj State in 1931, Vol. I. Roy (1935), Prasad (1961) and Chowdhury (1963) also published short notes on the Bathudi. Satpathy *et al.* (1968) mentioned about some of the demographic aspects of the Bathudi, while describing the living conditions of the tribes of Similipal hills. Gupta (1962) carried out investigations on ABO Blood groups on the Bathudi of Dalbhum, Bihar. Thus, although some literatures exit on this population, there is hardly any major work on various physical Anthropological parameters.

1.7.2 Sountis

The Sountis are less covered as compared to the Bathudis. O'Malley (1911), Grierson (1931), Shoobert (1931). Laccquidin (1931) and Roy (1935) referred to the Sountis in their respective publications though, there is practically little published materials about the various physical anthropological parameters of the people.

1.8 AIMS AND OBJECTIVE OF THE STUDY

The following are some of the main objectives of the present investigations :

1. In the past various authors have investigated a tribe for various physical anthropological parameters. Some authors have investigated a particular tribal population from the same area or different areas for a specific parameter, sometimes over a period of time in order to investigate the nature of variations manifested in time and space. We have information for specific tribal populations which have been intensively studied by various authors on different occasions. Although such studies are valuable in their own context, they are not likely to project any comprehensive picture about the population as a whole. Therefore, we do not find information on many aspects of the people. As different authors have investigated the same different important populations on separate occasions with their respective specific objectives in view, there is a wide variety in the extent of coverage. As-a result chances of reflection of personal bias becomes conspicuous. In the present investigation an attempt has been made to study the morphological and genetical composition and the variations, if any, among the Bathudi and Sounti both males and females for all the major attributes for example, the Blood groups (A_1A_2BO system), Anthropometric measurements, Dermatoglyphics, Demographic aspects, some of morphogenetic traits and anthroposcopic observations. As the data have been gathered by a single hand, the likelihood of bias due to human factor seems minimum.

2. Very few research informations are available on the female populations. Among the tribal populations in particular the study on females are still insignificant. Due to certain cultural reasons such information on their physical measurements are even less. Some of the females have been examined for a particular parameter but there is perhaps none to provide field data on all the important parameters. The present investigation being an attempt to examine both the males and females of the Bathudi and Sounti tribes for a

specified set of parameters is certain to be relatively more comprehensive one.

3. In the present study an attempt will be made to study the sex variations between the Bathudi and Sounti populations for the various characters as mentioned above to make the investigations comprehensive and relatively more meaningful. Due to practical considerations and paucity of data, no such major attempt has been made so far.

4. The Bathudi and Sounti are endogamous populations. But according to O'Malley (1911) the Sountis are originally the peoples who were outcasted from their Oriya caste background. As stated, under such circumstance Shri Joygobind Das of Puri formed this new caste. The only qualification prescribed for admission to this caste was that the newcomers must have belonged to some caste from whom Brahmins would take water. This proposes a possible heterogenous origin of the Sountis. Now after about four hundred years, whether the Sountis still have intra-group variations as compared to the Bathudi for various morphogenetic attribute could be an important by product of this study.

5. The present study will also fill the information gap about the populations under study, belonging to both the sexes.

6. An attempt will be made to evaluate the biological relationship of the two populations with the Bhuiya, of whom they are considered as an offshoots.

7. An attempt will also be made to determine the extent of variation of the Bathudi and Sounti males as well as females with the other tribal populations of the neighbourhood, particularly from Orissa.

8. The present study may throw some more light on the migration history of the populations of the region.

On the whole the objective of the study is extremely modest, to elicit physical anthropological data of the two populations, the Bathudi and Sounti of Orissa about whom very little systematic study has been made and there is hardly any existing literature. As information have been gathered both from males and females of the concerned tribes, they provide scope for comparison at different levels through which we are likely to get some picture, their nature and extent of variation. Systematic comparison, together with appropriate analysis are expected to throw some light on the migration history of the populations of the neighbourhood and their biological proximity.

1.9 PEOPLE

1.9.1 Bathudi

The Bathudi are scheduled tribes and mainly found in Orissa and Bihar with 130,792 individuals and 880 individuals respectively (Census of India 1971). In Orissa the Bathudi are mostly concentrated in Mayurbhanj and Keonjhar districts and specially in their bordering areas on both sides of Baitarani river. Laeequidin (1937), in the Census of Mayurbhanj State 1931, volume I has given a fairly good ethnographic account of the Bathudis. According to Satpathy (1968), the Bathudi came in search of Ramachanda during the reign of Bharat from their ancestral home in Oudh and as these people could not find Ramachandra, instead of returning to their native place they prefered to settle down at Chotanagpur plateau. They later on migrated to Singhbhum as they were told about the availability of land in Jamuna-Bardanda of Similipal.

According to Census of Mayurbhanj, 1931, the Bathudis first came to 'Simplipal hills' in the course of their migration to Mayurbhanj. In Mayurbhanj they defeated the king Chandrasen of Simplipal hills, selected twelve valleys (Barthali), and established themselves there. The so called Talmal, present Joshipur was ruled by Kharia chief, Dassu Khardia. Bathudis under the leadership of Nand Das defeated the Kharia chief and captured the Joshipur fort. The Bomanghaty, under the control of Gond King, was also annexed by the Bathudis. So the Bathudis became chief of Adipur, Jamuna Bardanda, Karanjia and Jashipur in due course of time. During a famine, some Bathudis migrated to the adjoining area of Keonjhar and Sukinda. The Bathudis established the Jashipur math and installed the Raghunath jiu their tutelar deity. The Bathudi are endogamous people but marriage within the same clan is prohibited. The Bathudi speak about their intimate connections with the Bhuiya and the Sounti. It is said that there were intermarriage among the three tribes with a condition that after marriage the whole family of the girl had to leave its own community to join that of bridegroom. But this practise has now become very rare (Census of Mayurbhanj State, 1931).

Chatterjee (1929) mentioned that the marriage of the Bathudi among the blood relation is prohibited upto 3 generations that is it will remain in force from the son and his grand son (his grand son can marry his grand daughter's daughter, i.e., daughter's daughter's daughter). The consent of boy's or girl's parents and maternal uncle is essential. Although earlier child marriage is said to be in practice, at present they marry adults. There is no professional middleman to conduct the marriage. The male can marry as many times as he likes depending upon his economic status but the girl ordinarily can marry only once. The payment of bride price is the general custom on the occasion of marriage among the Bathudi but the amount of bride price varies. If a boy takes fancy of a girl he communicates it to the girl as well as to his parents. His parents propose the marriage to the girl's family. In case the girl disagrees, the parents of the girl convince her to marry him and she generally gives her consent. But in case she refuses, the proposal is dropped. This procedure also applies in case a girl takes fancy to a boy. Marriage by capture is non-existent now. In case of divorce, the parents of the girl consult the council of village elders presided over by the pradhan and seek their permission for "Mukti'. If the "Mukti" is granted the girl can marry under the "Saga" form only. If the village elders are not convinced with the cause of the divorce and girl is charged with adultery of misbehaviour, she is not granted "Mukti" and hence marriage even by "Saga" form is disallowed.

Bathudi are mostly land owners and engage themselves in agriculture. Those who do not have sufficient land to cultivate also engage themselves as labourers for the local cultivators. They take clean food and some of them also take "Handia"' Kalci and Kurkuti (termites and red ants). Rice is their staple food, they frequently take fowl. In Panchpir sub-division they have the status of *Jalachalaniyas* and have the services of Brahman, barbar and washerman. Thus they are considered Hindus as they worship Hindu Gods. The Bathudi either cremate or bury their dead. The mourning period lasts for ten days.

1.9.2 Sounti

The Sountis constitute a Scheduled Tribe and comparatively a smaller population than the Bathudi. The concentration of the

Sounti is maximum in the Orissa State. According to Census of India 1971, there are 55,178 Sounti individuals in Orissa. The Sountis are mostly concentrated in Keonjhar and Mayurbhanj districts and specially in the adjoining parts of these two districts of Orissa. According to Census of India 1961, the populations of the Sounti in Keonjhar and Mayurbhanj districts is 30,891 individuals and 11,450 individuals respectively.

Origin of Sountis

O'Malley (1911) and Laeequidin (1937) has mentioned in detail about the Ethnohistory of the Sounti. As already indicated, Shri Joygobind Das was Khandait and come to Keonjhar in 1603 A.D. (1010 Oriya Sal) from Puri. He organised the people, who were outcasted from various Oriya castes and became their leader. The number of such individuals was sufficiently large and gave them the name Sounti, meaning *'gathered-in'*. The meaning of the title Berdhajal that the headman of the Sounti bears is 'Surrounded by net' also supports about the nature of group of this population. The chief of Keonjhar allowed them to settle at one of his villages Mananta. The headquarters of the Sountis is at Musakhuri in Keonjhar and this village is about 15 kilometers from Karanjia. In consideration of special services rendered by the Sounti in Keonjhar the Berdhajal is allowed to bear the following title:

"Guman Ganjan Singh Berdhajal Mahapatra Patajamindar".

In course of time title "Raj Kumar" was added to this title, when Ramgobinda Singh was recognised as a founder of the special branch of the Sounti. The members of this family in Keonjhar and Mayurbhanj bear the title 'Singh' and 'Raj Kumar' respectively.

About a century ago, due to certain unknown reasons, the Senior branch of the Berdhajal family shifted from Keonjhar to Thakurmunda area of Panchpir Sub-division of Mayurbhanj. Raj Kumar Mardaraj came to Mayurbhanj and served the state as one of its Sardars. His son 'Chakradhar Das Raj Kumar Guman Ganjan Berdhajal Bhuyan Mahapatra' obtained from the Maharaja Jadunath Bhanj and his son Shrinath Bhanj Sanad Dutta Jagir and Datta Mahatran (quit rent grants) with a total area of about 100 acres in the Baliposi, Bansdiha and Thakurmunda villages. The descendants of Chakradar Das still have the possession of these Lakhraj grants. The Sountis of Mayurbhanj bear the title of 'Das' presently instead of 'Berdhajals'. The Sountis received various titles on the basis of services rendered by them to the rulers and the Zamindars. These titles became territorial and functional later on. There are 97 titles of *Khilis* recorded among the Sountis but they have one Nagaswar gotra. Marriage within the same Khili is prohibited. There is no restriction among them about taking more than one wife and there are reports stating that the Bathudi and Bhuiya family were seen living with the Sounti people as their wives. But no such case has been observed during the present investigation. With the sanction of the caste council divorce and widow remarriage is permitted. Sountis are mostly landless labourers and are 'Jalachalaniys' in Panchpir and are employed as personal servants by the caste Hindus. They do not take unclean food. They take fowl, red ants and termites. They take the services of Brahmans, Barbar and Washermen. Earlier they were having their tutelar deity as 'Raghunath jiu' but subsequently they accepted their tutelar deity 'Tarini Thakurani'. They observe mourning for 10 days and the purification or Sudhi Kriya is done on the 11th day. On the occasion of birth day, the purification is done on the 7th day. They mostly bury, their dead but cremation is not uncommon. (Census of Mayurbhanj State, 1931.)

1.10 METHOD AND MATERIALS

1.10.1 Field work

(*a*) Bathudi and Sounti of both sexes were investigated for the following parameters from the Panchpir Sub-division, Mayurbhanj District:

1. Demographic aspects;
2. (a) Anthroposcopic observations,
   (b) Behavioural and other genetic parameters;
3. Anthropometric characters;
4. Finger and Palmar Dermatoglyphics;
5. A_1Q_2 BO Blood groups; and
6. Colour vision deficiency.

Field investigations were carried out during the following two field trips:

(1) May to October, 1978, (2) October 1979 to February 1980. Apart from these, a short trip for a period of about a fortnight was also made together some additional information during December, 1981.

Before proceeding to field the District Magistrate, Mayurbhanj was approached for necessary help and co-operation to the investigator. As the area and language was not known local persons, who were well conversant with the area and language were engaged as guide-cum-interpreters.

(*b*) *Selection of samples*

Random sampling as a technique is generally considered the best. But it is very difficult to follow due to various practical reasons. In view of the modest scope and specific objectives of this study, a special sampling procedure was adopted for the purpose of the present study.

In the present study unrelated adult males (20-45 years) and adult females (18 to 45 years) of Bathudi and Sounti tribes were the subjects. Closely related subjects have not been included in the present study. Depending upon the population 5 to 10 subjects were measured and examined from the sixty villages covered by this study. All the subjects were studied in their respective villages (Table 1.2). Before undertaking the investigations, details related to age, name and tribe were ascertained from each subjects in the presence of Sarpanch/Village elders/Secretary, Mahila Samity/Elderly relatives. Subjects were measured between 8 A.M. to 11 A.M. and preference was given to the husband and wife being the subjects of present investigations and togather as much information from them as possible. However, closely related individuals such as father and son, brother and brother/sister/sister were not included in the present study. Unrelated male students between 10-22 years of age group were the subjects for the incidence of colourblindness and their samples were drawn from various school of Karanjia tahsil.

(*c*) *Age estimation*

In biological studies age is one of the very important factors. As most of the Bathudis and Sountis are non-literates, they do not maintain proper records of their age. For the present investigations, extra care was taken to record the age with minimum error of each subject. In case of doubt, the age was cross examined by referring to the major historical events, checking the age with contemporary subjects of neighbourhood. Any error in recording or hearing the name of the subjects and their age was also avoided.

(*d*) *Area of study and extent of coverage*

Field investigations were carried out in the following four out of five blocks of Panchpir sub-division, with its head office at Karanjia.

1. Jashipur, 2. Karanjia, 3. Sukruli, and 4. Thakurmunda.

Karanjia tahsil is bounded in the North by Singhbhum and Midnapore Districts of Bihar and West Bengal States respectively, in the West by Singhbhum and Keonjhar Districts of Bihar and Orissa, in the East by its Balasore District. Panchpir has two regions, one is hilly region called as 'Simlipal hills' and the other undulating ground. May is the hottest month and temperature during this month varies between 110°F to 120°F. Minimum temperature during winter is 57°F. During rainy season, it becomes impossible to approach the hilly areas. According to Census of India (1971), 63.4 percent and 7.7 percent of the total population of the Panchpir sub-division belongs to scheduled tribes and scheduled castes respectively.

Table 1.3 presents the extent of coverage for various parameters among the Bathudi and Sounti of both sexes. One hundred and two Bathudi and one hundred Sounti families are also covered for Household Census in order to know their fertility performance.

Table 1.2
Villages of investigations among Bathudi and Sounti of Panchpir Sub-division

Sl. No.	*Block*	*Name of the Location*
1.	Jashipur	Basantpur, Badapahar, Balijudi, Banapangandi, Baunsanali, Bhonda, Champabalda, Chakidi, Digposi, Jamkeshwar, Jashipur, Jamda, Kapand, Kajala, Kumbharpandugandi, Maharda, Nebda, Padampur, Rugudi and Singarpur.

(Contd.)

(Contd.)

2.	Karanjia	Aukura, Bala, Baddeuli, Batpalsa, Bhadubeda, Bhanra, Beuria, Bisipur, Ghatiali, Jumkakudar, Kerkera, Kalakad, Kunjia, Kenjara, Mandua, Pingu, Patbil, Rasamtala, Radang, Saradha, Sounti Sahi (Karanjia) and Tato.
3.	Sukruli	Ghagi, Haldia, Sarubali and Sunaposi.
4.	Thakurmunda	Baliposi, Chamakpur, Digdhar, Guhaldiha, Handifuta, Khamdiha, Khuntaposi, Mituani, Nihangandi, Raipada, Rugudibeda, Thakurmunda and Tikerpada.

Table 1.3

Extent of coverage for various parameters among the Bathudi and Sounti of both sexes

Sl. No.	Characters	Bathudi		Sounti	
		Males	Females	Males	Females
1.	Anthroposcopic Characters	109	110	106	105
2.	Morpho-genetic traits	109	110	106	105
3.	Anthropometric Characters	109	110	106	105
4.	Finger and Palmar dermatoglyphic	110	109	108	106
5.	Blood groups [A_1A_2BO]	109	110	111	109
6.	Colourvision	154		114	

Demographic information was gathered from each couple or the wife/husband of the study village and the details of particulars were further confirmed from the village elders/neighbours. Univeriate analysis has only been applied for population and sex comparisons of the Bathudi and Sounti.

1.10.2 Methodology

(*a*) *Anthroposcopic observations:*

Anthroposcopic observations have been used in Anthropological investigations in the past for the classification of man into different races. In the present study the following qualitative observations were made using the standard technique:

1. Skin colour, 2. Hair colour, 3. Hair forms, 4. Hair texture, 5. Hair quantity on head, 6. Beard and moustache, 7. Eye colour, 8. Eye fold, 9. Eye slits, 10. Sclera, 11. Eye brow, 12. Supraorbital ridges, 13. Fore head height, 14. Forehead slope, 15. Nasion depression, 16. Nasal bridge, 17. Nasal septum, 18. Lip thickness, 19. Chin, 20. Prognathism, 21. Incisor fold, and 22. Body musculature.

Other traits:

23. Hand clasping : It is recorded as R and L type according to the upper most position of Right and Left thumb respectively.
24. Handedness : It is recorded as R and L type depending upon the use of Right and Left hand for various activities such as eating, writing, etc. respectively.
25. Arm folding : It is recorded as R and L type depending upon the upper most position of right and left arm respectively.
26. Tongue rolling : It is recorded as folders and non-folders.
27. Tongue folding : It is recorded as folders and non-folders.
28. Occipital hair whorl : It is recorded as single, double and triple. The single may be clockwise (+), Anticlock wise (-). The double occipital hair whorl may be clockwise - clockwise (++), clockwise-anticlockwise (+-), Anticlockwise-clockwise (-+), and Anticlockwise-Anticlockwise (- -).
29. Earlobe attachment : It is classified as completely free, completely attached and intermediate.
30. Digital formulae : It is recorded as 2 > 4 (when the index finger is greater than the ring finger, 2 < 4 (when the index finger is less than the ring finger and 2=4 (When the index finger is less than the ring finger and 2=4 (when the index finger is equal to the ring finger).

31. Mid phalangeal hair : The quality and density of hair on the middle phallanges was recorded as 01234 of both the hands.
32. Darwin's tubercle : It is recorded as present, Absent.
33. Cleft chin : It is recorded as present, absent.

(*b*) *Anthropometric characters*

Metric characters have been preferred to the qualitative observation and as these can be easily quantified and subjected to rigorous statistical analysis. Martin's (1928) definition of various land marks and technique for measuring the following characters was strictly followed :

1. Stature, 2. Sitting height , 3. Thoracic Circumference, 4. Foot length, 5. Foot breadth, 6. Weight, 7. Head length, 8. Head breadth, 9. Head Circumference, 10. Auricular height, 11. Minimum frontal breadth, 12. Bizygomatic breadth, 13. Bigonial breadth, 14. Total facial height, 15. Upper facial height, 16. Nasal height, 17. Nasal breadth, and 18. Nasal depth.

On the basis of above measurements the following indices were also worked out: 1. Ponderal Index, 2. Relative sitting height index, 3. Cephalic index, 4. Length height index, 5. Breadth height index, 6. Morpho-facial index, 7. Upper facial index, 8. Fronto-parietal index, 9. Fronto-Zygomatic index, 10. Tran-Cephalo facial index, 11. Zygomandibular index, 12. Nasal index, 13. Foot index, and 14. Pignets constitutional index (Vallois, 1965).

Measurements were taken with the help of standard swiss anthropometric, sliding caliper, spreading caliper and steel tape as recommended by Martin (1928). The Auricular height was measured with Schultz's parallelometer and the average of the two reading was considered. The weight was recorded with the portable weighing machine in kilograms. In the present samples the mean age of the Bathudi males is 29.51 + 0.82 years, while among Bathudi females it is 29.82 +0.58 years respectively. The Sounti males and females have mean age of 27.56 + 0.63 years and 28.58 ± 0.58 years respectively. Thoracic circumference has been recorded only among the males. As the investigator is a male, it was not possible to take up such measurements among the females. For the males, however, it was recorded midway between the inspiration and expiration. As commended by Majumdar and Rao

(1960) median values of the various indices have been calculated. As pointed out by Rao (1948) no test of significance has been used for the indices because there is no theoretical justification for treating an index as a separate character.

(c) Finger and Palm Dermatoglyphics

The value of dermatoglyphics as markers in population studies has been realised for many years. Dermatoglyphics have so far been proved to be an effective tool fulfilling all the necessary qualifications for ascertaining ethnic relationships. The only short coming of dermatoglyphics was limited to its genetical background (Boyd, 1940). Dermatoglyphics is a faithful tool which provides a model of unique importance for population genetics (Rife, 1954). Regional and local variation, urban and rural populations variations in dermatoglyphics have been observed by Galton (1895), and Poll (1937). Dermal ridges and its configurations are not effected developmentally by age, throughout post-natal life and they are not affected by environment. Detailed structures of individual ridges are extremely variable. Patterns formed by the ridges vary in size, shape and detailed structure, they can be classified into several main types. All these characters make the dermal ridges important not only for personal identifications but for human biology studies (Holt, 1968).

The digital and palmar impressions were collected according to the method suggested by Cummins and Midlo (1943). The impressions of finger and palm prints were taken on slightly glazed paper sheet of size 15″x10″. This sheet was specially designed for the palmar prints on its centre and the rolled digital prints on its margin. Relevant additional information about the subject was also collected on it. The following equipments were used for taking the impressions :

(*a*) Printers ink, (*b*) Printers roller (3″ size),

(*c*) Glass slab of 6″ x 10″ size.

Before taking impressions, the subjects were asked to wash their hands throughly with soap and dry them with towel. As the tribals of Central India by and large engage themselves as manual workers, it is rather difficult to have good prints of their hands which are often interrupted with scar marks or rigidity of fingers. In the present case, however, impressions except that of a single individual were very good and the people extended excellent cooperation.

The palmar and finger prints are analysed following the methods suggested by Cummins and Midlo (1943), Holt (1968), Penrose (1965, 1968), Mukherjee (1966, 1967, 1974, 1980) before statistical analysis.

The following characters have been analysed on the finger and palm prints :

Finger

1. *Pattern type*

Whorl, Radial loop, Ulnar loop, Tented arche and plain arche patterns are identified following the method of Galton (1892), Mukherjee (1967) and Penrose (1968).

2. *Total finger ridge counts*

As suggested by Holt (1961) the sum of ridges counts on all the ten fingers, but only the large of the two counts of whorls is included.

3. *Total number of triradii on finger*

It is obtained by counting two triradii in whorls, one triradii in loop or a tented arch on the finger and suming up over ten fingers. This is nearly equal but not exactly the pattern intensity index (Cummins and Midlo, 1943). The pattern intensity index does not count the triradii of tented arches or a loop with zero ridge counts (Mukherjee, 1966).

4. *Monomorphic hands*

When a hand has same pattern on all the 5 digits, it is recorded as monomorphism.

5. *Symmetry and Asymmetry*

When both the hands of an individual has indentical patterns, and one hand is the mirror image of other. This phenomenon of occurence of like finger pattern on both the hands were recorded as symmetrical hands. The occurence of different types of pattern on various digits which are not symmetrical is observed as asymmetrical.

Palm

1. In the present study as suggested by Mukherjee (1966, 1967), Penrose (1968) and Mukherjee *et. al.* (1980) loops and whorls have been taken into account as the pattern types on different areas of palm.

2. *'a-b' ridge count*

It is obtained by counting the number of ridges between the palmar triradii 'a and b' (Fang, 1950).

3. *Number of Palmar triradii*

It is obtained by adding 4 to the no. of loops and tented arches on a palm and summing up the scores of both palms of a individual (Mukherjee, 1966) and Mukherjee and Sirajuddin (1974).

4. *D, B and C line endings*

Main line D and B endings have been formulated according to the method of Cummins and Midlo 1943, Plato's (1970) method has been used for grouping of the ending of C-line.

5. *Main line index*

Main line index is a summation of various courses of main line D and A ending. It is obtained by deducting five from the sum of D and A line endings and adding one more for the endings for 5" upwards.

Indices

1. *Pattern intensity index*

The value of the pattern intensity index is expressed as a number of triradii per finger (Cummins and Stegarda, 1935). It is obtained either from the individual records or from the data of total frequencies of patterns. The total is then divided by the number of individuals or by ten when the absolute or percentage frequencies are calculated respectively.

2. *Furuhata (1927) index* is calculated by dividing the total frequencies of whorls by the total number of loops (Radial and ulnar loops combined) and multiplying the quotient by one hundred.

3. *Dankmeijer (1934) suggested* Arch/whorl index. It is obtained by dividing the total frequency of Arches by the total frequency of whorls and multiplying the quotient by 100.

(d) ABO Blood group

ABO Blood groups were discovered by Landsteiner (1900). Epstein and Ottenberg (1908) suggested about the inheritance of ABO blood groups, Dungern and Hirszfeld (1910) proved the inheritance of the ABO blood groups. Sub-groups of A were first explained by Dungern and Hirszfeld (1911). Hirszfeld and Hirszfeld (1919) discovered that human populations had different ABO groups distribution and they used this system for classifying the human populations on the basis of their variation in allele frequencies. Boyd (1939,1950), Mourant (1954), Mourant *et. al.* (1958), Kopec (1970) Bhalla (1966), and Mourant (1976) made collection of published results on large scale. Distribution of various alleles has been used for assessing the extent and direction of gene flow in different continents by Mourant *et. al.*, (1976).

Blood groups are discontinuous characters and are determined at conception and remain fixed for life. There is very little chance of personal error in the observation and Blood groups are direct consequence of the genetic constitution (Mourant *et. al.*, 1976).

There is little doubt about the fact that the observations of the serologists have by now contributed as much information to the classification of human population as those of the Anthropometrists. Morever, the rate of accumulation of Serological data within the larger known genetical systems, together with the constant finding of new system makes it certain that very soon Serology will have made a far greater contribution than anthropometry to human taxonomy, if it has not done so already (Mourant *et. al.*, 1976).

Technique of Blood analysis

Small amount of blood samples (5-7 drops) were collected in the normal salines solution from the left ring finger tip by giving a prick after sterilization with alcohol. The samples from the subjects were collected in their respective villages and were analyzed on the same day in the laboratory set in the field. Washed Red Blood Corpusles in appropriate suspension were used for carrying out the tests with the help of high titre Anti-A, Anti A_1 and Anti-B sera. Testing of Blood samples was performed in small microtubes. Observation was recorded with the assistance of magnifying lens after about half an hour. Controls for every series of tests were included through out the investigations. Gene frequencies were estimated by the maximum likelihood method as suggested by Bhale (1970).

Colour Vision

It is a sex-linked character (Gates, 1952). Hypothesis of 'Selection relaxation and positive selection of colour Blindness (Post, 1962;

Pckford, 1963; Neel and post, 1963) was reviewed, re- examined and supported in the Indian context (Mukherjee, 1963; Dutta, 1966, Malhotra *et. al.*, 1974, Deka *et. al.*, 1977) but Negi *et. al.* (1977) Goud *et. al.*, (1981) and Singh (1982) proposed to examine the above hypothesis carefully in more details.

Unrelated male students between 10-22 years of age from different schools of Karanjia sub-division were the subject for colour vision test. Ishihara Charts (1968) were used for testing the colour vision test. In case of doubt or when the subjects were unable to read the numerals, Plates 26 to 38 with marked lines on them were used. Otherwise plates 1 to 25 for other subjects who were literates were used.

Statistical formulae

Chamber (1955) has been consulted for the calculation of mean, standard deviation and co-efficient of variation along with their respective standard errors. The Anthropometric characters are subjected to t-test (Fisher, 1930) for testing the homogeneity of the two samples. Mean and standard deviations along with their respective standard errors for the quantitative dermatoglyphic finger and palmer configurations have been calculated. The qualitative characters were subjected to chi-square (X^2) homogeneity test.

1. Standard error of Mean (SE) $= \frac{SD}{\sqrt{N}}$

2. Standard deviation $= \sqrt{\frac{1}{n-1} \times (X-\overline{X})^2}$

3. Co-efficient of variation (CV) $= \frac{\text{SD}}{\text{Mean}} \times 100$

4. Fishers modified t-test $= \frac{M_1 - M_2}{\sqrt{SE_1^2 + SE_2^2}}$

Where M_1 and M_2 are the means of population 1 and 2, SE_1 and SE_2 are their respective standard errors respectively.

5. $X^2 = \frac{(O-E)^2}{E}$

Where O is the observed frequency and E is the expected frequency.

1.11 MORPHOLOGICAL VARIATIONS

Dixon (1923), Haddon (1924), Garn (1961), Coon (1963) and others have attempted for taxonomic classification of various races and sub-races. While Thurston (1909), Risley (1915), Eickstedt (1934), Guha (1935), Sarkar (1954) and others have approached the problem of ethnic affinities. Gupta and Dutta (1966) compiled the available material on various metric characters to study the morphological variations. Sanghvi *et. al.*, (1981) attempted to study the migration history and biology of Tamil Nadu populations.

1.11.1 Risley (1915) divided the people of Indian sub-continent into 7 main physical types, such as

I. *The Turko-Iranian Type*

II. *The Indo-Aryan Type*

III. *The Scytho-Dravidian Type*

IV. *The Aryo-Dravidian Type*

V. *The Mongolo-Dravidian Type*

VI. *The Mongoloid Type*

VII. *The Dravidian type*

There are other existing racial classifications of Indian population among whom Dr. B.S.Guha's classification is considered the most important. Based on the physical anthropological data gathered as part of the 1931 census. Guha divided the populations of India into the following categories:

There are six main races with nine sub-types and are as follows:

1. The Negrito
2. The Proto-Australoid
3. The Mongoloid, consisting of (i) Palae-Mongoloids of: (a) long headed, and (b) broad-headed types. (ii) Tibeto-Mon-goloids
4. The Mediterranean, comprising.
   (i) Palae-Mediterranean,
   (ii) Mediterranean, and
   (iii) the so called oriental type.
5. The Western Brachycephals, consisting of :
   (i) The Alpinoid, (ii) The Dinaric, and (iii) The Armenoid.

6. The Nordic

Since a critical evaluation of various racial classifications is not within the scope of the present exercise, in order to provide only a substantive background of the populations of India, passing references have been made on the major two racial classifications of this country. Since migration had an important role in making the populations as they are, we also make a brief reference to the migration history of the people of the area which is also likely to throw light on the social composition of the populations.

1.12 MIGRATION HISTORY OF THE PEOPLE

According to Census of Mayurbhanj State 1931 the following account has been given regarding the origin and migration of the various populations of the area.

1.12.1 Santal, Kol (Ho), Munda, Bhumij, Tamaria, Kharia, Mahali and Karua

All the tribes of this group are Kolaria

(*a*) *Santals*:

It is supposed that Santals were called Kherwars or Kherwals (Santal puritan) before they settled in the country around a place called Soant in Midnapur. There seems to be good reasons to hold that the Santals are only a branch of the Kols or Mundas. Their customs and traditions have been modified either by large separation from the Mundas of Chhotanagpur or by contact with Hindu influences. Santali and Mundari, according to the account of Sir George Grierson, shows that the two dialects closely resemble each other. The Principal deity of the Santals, Marang Buru (Big hill) is a Munda God. According to Sir H.Risley: Santals, Hos, and Mundas are local branches of the same tribe. There is also inter-marriage between the two communities, though with certain restrictions. For all these reasons observed above, there seems good reasons to hold that the Santals are only a branch of the Kols or Mundas. In 1891 only 91,490 Santals were returned from Mayurbhanj.

(*b*) *Kol (Ho)*:

The majority of Kol immigrants come as it appears from the four adjoining pirs of the Kolhan estate of Singbhum, viz., Anla, Lalgarh, Thoi, and Bharbharia, which formed an integral part of the territory of Mayurbhanj till 1837. When their administration went over to the British Government, the migration mostly took place to the adjoining parts of Bamanghati and Panchpir sub-divisions and to a particular part in Kaptipada sub-division adjoining Panchpir. Migration is influenced by the feeling among the Singhbhum Kols, as they prefer to be called in Mayurbhanj, that Mayurbhanj was their original home where they have still their relations and Kinsmen with whom they freely unite. The Kol tribe has given its name to the territory where it has made its home (Kolhan) and to the Kolarian family of the tribes and languages. In 1891, the number of Kols was 57,685.

(*c*) *Munda* :

In Chhotanagpur, those Kols who have partly adopted Hinduism and have become to some degree civilized are commonly known as Mundas. In fact, the Munda is the common term employed by the Kols to refer to the headman of a village.

The Hos are believed to be only a sub-division of the Mundas though they claim superiority over the Mundas of Ranchi. There is good reason to believe from the names and from local traditions that the Munda tribe was once spread over Bihar and parts of the Gangetic Valley and it is presumed that the advance of the Aryans or the Hindus from the north drove the Mundas from the open country to the seclusion of hills and forests. The Mundas now appear to be a very mixed group. It is possible that the village headman of various tribes having adopted the designation "Munda" by inter-marriage with the families of other headman, brought into being a superior group which identified itself as the Munda tribe and has since come to be known as belonging to that tribe. Unlike the Hos, the Mundas have always moved from place to place, without rigidly confining themselves to any particular part of Mayurbhanj and have not yet permanently settled over there.

(*d*) *Bhumij* :

In Mayurbhanj, a Bhumij is called a Munda. The Santals hardly call a Bhumij, "Bhumij". They call him by the other name. In fact Bhumij of which Tamaria is a sub-section, is a more Hinduised section of the Munda tribe. Sir H. Risley states that the Bhumij are closely allied to, if not identical with the Munda. In some localities inter-marriage with the Mundas and are known as Bhumij-Munda. Of all the other Munda tribes, the Hinduisation of Bhumij tribe is proceeding apace.

1.12.2 Gond, Khond, Dharua, Oraon

All the tribes in this group belong to the Dravidian family. Gond is the principle tribe of this family and is considered to be the most important non-Aryan or forest-tribe in India. The Oraon are no less an important tribe of this family.

(*a*) *Gond:*

The Gond dynasty possessed a great part of the territory of the central provinces formerly known as Gondwana or the country of the Gonds comprised of the Satpura plateau and a section of the Nagpur plain and Narbudda Valley to the South and West. The Gonds are believed by some as a section of Konds or Kandhs (Khonds) of the Khondmal. The former call themselves "Kui", while the latter call themselves "Ku". The Telgu people call the Khonds "Gonds". The Gonds speak a language of the same family as Tamil, Canarese, and Telgu. The name "Gond" is believed to have been modified into "Khond" in Orissa. The language of the Gonds, that is Gondi, is more nearly allied to Tamil, while that of the Khonds to the Telgu.

Various parts of the Central provinces were under the rule of the Rajput dynasty from about 6th to 12th century, after the fall of which Gond kingdom were found established in different centres in the said provinces. This became possible on account of the fact that the Mohammadan invasion of northern India by that time had weakend or destroyed the Central authority of the Hindus and prevented any assistance being afforded to the outlying settlements. After having established themselves there, the Gonds succeeded in governing the province for three centuries and became known for the spacious forts they built with masonary tanks and wells inside them. They were known for their tolerance and beneficence towards the Hindu immigrants. But the weak point about the Gond rulers was that they had no strength for defence of which the Maratha chiefs of the 18th centuary took advantage after having acquired some knowledge of the art of war and military training by their war against the Mughals. The country fell before the Maratha army almost without a struggle. The Gonds were badly treated which made them soon lose every vestige of their civilization. Under the British rule the Gonds became the timid and inoffensives people. The Gonds of Mayurbhanj call themselves Raj Gonds probably under the impression that they are descendents of the rulers of Gondwana.

(*b*) *Oraon* :

In the Central provinces, the Oraons are commonly known as Dhongard. In Chhotanagpur, Dhangard means a farm servant. The Mundas being earlier settlers are employed by the Oraons as priests of the village God, which is a function regularly assigned to the earliest settlers of a place. The Oraons in Mayurbhanj are generally earth-diggers and growers of vegetables.

1.12.3 Bhuiya, Bhanjpurans, Bathudi, and Rajuars

The tribes of this group are completely Hinduised, all of them having long abandoned their original language, if they had any.

(*a*) *Bhuiya*

According to Sir H. Risley, in most parts of Chhotanagpur, there is a well known distinction between a Bhuiya by tribe and Bhuiya by title. The Bhuinyas of Bonai and Keonjhar according to description given by Col. Dalton belong to the former category, while the Bhuiya, Mundas and Oraons to the latter. In Orissa, high land-owning class of the Khandaits also bear the Bhuinya title. The Chutias and Bhuinyas were once dominant in the country of Assam prior to its conquests by the Ahoms in the 13th Century. Sir Edward A.Gait who refers to this fact in his 'History of Assam' considers that these Chutias gave their name to Chutia or Chhotanagpur. The Bhuiyas who form the first batch of the Munda immigrants in Chhotanagpur, became greatly or completely Hinduised. The Bhuiyas in Mayurbhanj were once the sub- proprietors or Zamindars in Pergannah uperbhag in Sadar and Ratanpur in Pandapir. They appear to have degenerated to a noticeable extent and are now a lazy and indolent people.

(*b*) *Bhanja purans*

They are believed to be very nearly allied to the Bhuinyas, like the Bhiyas and Bathuris they wear sacred thread and consider themselves to be of Kshatriya origin.

(*c*) *Bathudi*

Among the different sub-castes of the Bhuinyas, found in different places like Singhbhum, Manbhum and North Bihar, Sir Edward A. Gait put down Bathuris as one of them. Mr. Russell makes a similar record in his tribes and castes of the Central provinces. According to him, the Bathuria, sub-division of the

Bhuiyas as he calls them, form an inferior group who are said to be looked down upon, because of having taken food from other low castes.

(*d*) *Rajuars*

The Rajuars are a low cultivating caste of Bihar and Chhotanagpur, who are probably an offshoot of the Bhuiyas. In the central provinces the Bhuiyas have a sub-caste called Rajuar. The Rajuars of Bengal give a different story, admitting that they are the descendants of mixed unions between Kurmis and Kols. In Chhotanagpur, the Rajuars, like the landholding branches of other forest tribes, claim to be a inferior class of the Rajputs.

1.12.4 Lodha and Lodhi

(*a*) *Lodh*

Lodh, Lodha or Nodh is the name of an aboriginal tribe of Angul and the Orissa State. Their headquarters are in the Central provinces where they have become land-holders, and are addressed by the honorific title of "Thakur", ranking with the higher cultivating castes. They are also found in Midnapore where to they migrated from Singhbhum and Mayurbhanj, and in Midnapore, they are considered as allied to Sabars and Sahars. In Mayurbhanj, they are considered to be a criminal tribe and one of the oldest tribes of the state. They are sometimes called Lodha Kharia.

1.12.5 Sahar and Sabar

The Sabars and Sahars are separate branches of the same tribe though sometimes a line of distinction has been drawn between them. Sir E.A.Gait, observe that Sahars are said to be different from the Sabars. But Mr O'Malley is of opinion that in some parts it is impossible to distinguish the two, "Those who have come in contact with the Hindus and have adopted Hindu customs being called Sahars and those who have not yet reached that Stage, Sabars". In Mayurbhanj persons belonging to this tribe have returned themselves more as Sabars than as Sahars though practically it is difficult to make any hard and fast distinction between them. In some parts as in Panchpir, members of the Sahars branch have become Jalachalaniya, while in other parts they have not yet reached that stage. Orissa is the principle home of the tribe. The Sabars are believed by some authorities to be formerly the dominent branch of the great Kolarian family.

1.12.6 Jona Pan and Pan tanti

The pans are mainly divided into two branches, *viz.*, Jena Pan and Pan Panti or Patar Tanti. The former is a clean Caste, while the later have become clean Sudras. Sir Edward A.Gait states that in the Orissa states "the pans ranks higher; he is there largely employes as a weaver and calls himself patra pan or Buna pan". The Patras are a sub-castes of the Tantis of Oriya Origin. They weave silk or tassar cloth, as opposed to the Ranginis, who weave only cotton fabrics.

1.12.7 Dom, Ghasi, Hari, Mathuria, Kandra

This group consists of the lowest castes who are scavengers or the like.

1.12.8 Muchi, Chamar, Pasi

Muchi is a cobbler, while the Chamar in Orissa and the Pasi in Bengal and Bihar are toddy-drawers. In upper India, Cobblers are called chamars. The Muchis cobble shoe and are admittedly descended from the Chamars. The Chamars were formerly tanners which occupation they seem to have given up in Orissa. According to Nesfield, "The industry of tanning is preparatory to and lower than that of Cobblery and hence the caste of Chamar ranks decidedly below that of Muchi". In Mayurbhanj as in the rest of Orissa, the Chamars have given up tanning.

1.12.9 Amata, Baghuti, Baiti, Dandachhatra Majhi, Ghani, Gokha, Jhara, Kent, Mahisya, Malo, Tiyar and Ujia

The tribes or castes of this group are connected with fishing and boating, though some of them have given up their traditional occupation in favour of cultivation. All of them are more or less completely Hinduised. The relation between some of these castes is so close that in Mayurbhanj some Amatas make no distinction between themselves and the Dandachhatra Majhi or Ujias.

1.12.10 Sadgop, Gohala (Goala), Ahir Gaura, Bagal, Gaura, Kahar and Gareri

The castes mentioned in this group are the milk-man, cattle herd or Shepherd castes. Different communities of them occupy different position in society. Some have altogether given up their traditional occupation.

(a) Sadgop

The Sadgop claim to be vaisyas and are commonly refered as purified sub-caste of Goala, who are also known as Gohala in Mayurbhanj. They have succeeded in obtaining a higher position then the rest by adopting agriculture as their occupation and by acquiring proficiency in it. West Bengal is their principal home.

(b) Gohala (Goala)

The two names are interchangeable in the same way as Goala is interchangeable with Ahir. Various aboriginal tribes in the Chhotanagpur Plateau have gradually come to be known as Goala though they do not belong to the true Goala Caste.

(c) Ahir Gaura

According to Mr. Russell, the Ahirs of Central provinces are largely recuited from the Gonds and other tribes. They do not tend cattle or cultivate land. They are acrobats, jugglers and exhibiters of puppets. Some of them have taken to herding cattle and cultivation.

(d) Bagal

They are cattle-herds and herding of cattles is their principle occupation. Bagals of Mayurbhanj are really of aboriginal descent. They agree in their manners and customs with the Bhumijs from whom they take food.

(e) Gaur

The Gaura is the Goala caste of Orissa. The Mathurapuri or Mathurabasi sub-caste ranks highest in Balasore as in Mayurbhanj. Though the tradition of the Gauras is cow-keeping and dealing in Milk and other products from it, in Mayurbhanj they have completely forgotten that occupation, having made themselves prominent in cultivation and other means of livelihood.

(f) Kahar

They are palkibearers but are now, frequently domestic servants.

(g) Gareri

They are immigrants from Bihar, where they are shepherds, goatherds and blanket weavers. The correct name is Gadaria.

1.12.11 Kamar and Kumbhar

There are 7 different classes of Kamars, *viz.*, Astalohi, Chapua, Bathuri, Hatua, Bindani, Bangala and Nahura and four different classes of Kumbhars, *e.g.* Hatua, Jharua, Maghia and Dandapatia.

The constitution of the Kamar caste is of heterogenous nature Chapu, Bindhani and Nahara Kamars are probably Kol Kamars, who are recent accretions from the rank of the Kols. Bathuri Kamars are accretions for the rank of the Bathuri, Bangla Kamar, are immigrants from Bengal. Hatua Kamars are the true Kamars of Orissa.

The name of Kumbhars is derived from the Sanskrit term "Kumbha" a water pot. It is ancient as caste. The Kumbhars have a number of sub-castes many of which are a territorial type and indicate the different localities from which they migrated. The Hatua section is a Nai of aboriginal heritage, while Jharua Kumbhars are those who belong to the forest. The Maghias are immigrants from Bihar.

1.12.12 Dhoba and Bhandari

The Dhobi and Bhandari are in one sense key castes in as much as their attitude towards other castes in the exercise of their own vocation, indicates the status and position in society of the later. Thus the castes for which the Dhoba will not do washing and the Bhandari will not do shaving, must be very low or must have been put outside the pale of the society. When the person is out caste for some social offence, the services of the Dhoba and the Bhandari are denied to him and they would again be made available to him, only if and when he is readmitted to caste.

1.12.13 Vais, Vais Bania, Agarwal, Khandelwal, Gandha, Banik Subara Banik, Mahuri, Noniar and Mahesri

The Occupational castes of bankers, money-landers and dealers in grain, groceries and spices are collected together in this group. The members of Subarna Banik or Sunar caste make ornaments of silver or gold. The generic name for all these castes is Bania, which is derived from the Sanskrit work Ḅanija a merchant. The main sub-castes of Banias may be classified roughly into 3 groups coming from Rajputana, Bundelkhand and United provinces.

1.12.14 Teli, Tambuli, Baroi and Guria

The castes of the group are of different origins but their services to the community is a matter of every day necessity. The Teli presses oil, the Guria is a confectioner, while the Tambuli and Baroi grow and sell betel leaf.

1.12.15 Chasa, Khandait and Karan

(a) Chasa

The Chasa is a great cultivating caste of Orissa. It is known to be recruited originally from various aboriginal tribes. Many Chasa prefers to be called Khandaits. According to Sir H.Risley the Chasa are said to be for the most part of non-Aryan descent. Loose organisation of the caste system made it possible on one hand for outsiders to be admitted into the caste and on the other hand to assume the respectability title of Mohanty which Mr.Russel observes was a "broader term than Karan or Oriya Kayastha" the Word Chasa has a generic meaning of cultivator. They take food from Rajputs and Brahmans.

(b) Khandait

They are practically confined to Orissa. There is some difference of opinion says Sir Edward A.Gait as to the origin of the word Khandait. The general view is that it means a "Swordsman" Another explanation which has been put forward and with much plausibility is that Orissa was formerly divided into Khandas or groups of villages, corresponding to the perganas of Mohemmadan times and their was over each a headman called Khandpati, which was subsequently corrupted to Khandait. The Khandaits form the military caste of Orissa.

(c) Karan

Other names for the caste are Karnam and Mahanti. The Origin of the word Karan is said to be the Hindi word "Kerani" which means a clerk or writer. The caste fulfils the same function in Orissa as the Kayastha do elsewhere and it is said that their original ancestors were brought from Northern India by Yayati Kesari, King of Orissa (A.D.447 to 526) to supply the demands of writers and clerks. There are two sub-castes, *viz.*, the Jharna and Jungli Karan and the Utkali or Ariya Karan. The caste has a high social position.

1.12.16 Kayastha, Vaidya and Sinduria

The Kayasthas claim to be Kahatriyas and say that they have aboundoned the sword for the pen. Vaidyas commonly practise medicine. The Sindurias are sellers of Sindur (Vermillian) and claim to be Kayasthas, but the genuine Kayasthas deny all connections with them.

1.12.17 Brahmans

Brahmans is the well known priestly caste of India and the first among the four traditional varnas of the Hindu scriptures. The Brahman caste has ten main territorial divisions forming two groups. *The Panch Gaura*: (a) Saraswat, (b) Gaura, (c) Kanuji, (d) Maithil, (e) Utkal, and *the Panch-Dravida*: (a) Maharastra, (b) Andra, (c) Dravida, (d) Karnata, and (e) Gurjara.

The Brahmans commonly met within Mayurbhanj are Utkal Brahmans. They are divided into two groups. The Dakshinatya or the Southern and the Jajpuratraya or the Northern clan. The Utkal Brahmans who first settled in Sambalpur are known as Jharna or Jungli and form a separate sub-caste. Another group of Orissa Brahmans have taken to cultivation and are known as *Halua* (from-bal, a plough). The third group of the Orissa Brahmans are the Pandas, who beside serving as priests and cooks, travel all over India touting for pilgrims to visit the Jagannath temple at Puri. Besides all these, Andhra Brahmans of somewhat lower rank and known as "Banchua" and "Jaya" are found both in Mayurbhanj and Keonjhar states. Raja Narasingh Bhanj of Keonjhar (1479-1504 A.D.) is said to have brought these classes of Brahmans, where he joined the battle of Kanchi. From Keonjhar these Brahmans came over to Mayurbhanj in the time of Maharaja Jadunath Bhanj. There is another class of Brahmans known as Atharvavedi Brahmans, who are found both in Mayurbhanj other parts of Orissa.

2

DEMOGRAPHIC CHARACTERS

The caste system determines the main structure of Hindu society and in this context the tribals occupy rather a peripheral position of the Hindu dominated society. The various Indian populations including the tribals are basically endogamous in Character. In addition to caste groups, the linguistic groups and religious groups also constitute important denominations. Indian society can also be arranged according to social distance. There are horizontal as well as vertical divisions of the society. According to hierarchical traditions, the Brahmans occupy the highest position and the lowest position is occupied by some scheduled castes and tribes depending on the area. Mates for individuals within a breeding isolate are selected from within the same group. Selection of a mate is controlled by the nature of endogamous social groupings.

The mating pattern controls the gene flow which in turn determines the physical characters of a individual of a specific endogamous population. Demography has attracted the attention of Anthropologists. Chatterjee and Kumar (1950) studied some tribes from Kerala, Sen (1953) studied the reproductive life of some Indian women belonging to the caste populations, Rakshit and Dasgupta (1971), Basu and Guha (1973) and Rakshit (1972) concentrated on the populations of Nagpur and Madhya Pradesh for the demographic studies. Basu (1972), Devi (1975), Chatterjee (1975), Kumar and Maitra (1965-66), Kumar (1970), Lal (1968-70), Guha (1960-61, 1962-63) and Ray (1965) studied some tribal and caste populations for demographic studies. Following the leads of the given studies, in the present chapter demographic details with special reference to the fertility performance of the Bathudi and Sounti are discussed. The author has presented the results of Demo- genetic study among the Bathudis and Sountis elsewhere [Singh, 1985].

2.1 CLAN

According to Chatterjee (1929):

"The Bathudis are divided into several clans of which I have been able to collect 8 names:

1. Kargali or Kaga,
2. Dahukcharai,
3. Kurgotra,
4. Khandan,
5. Panipak,
6. Hasti,
7. Lalsaluk, and
8. Naga."

The Census of Mayurbhanj (1931) however, states : "........ Bathudis have a number of different Gotras such as: 1. Parasara, 2. Nageswaware, 3. Sailya, 4. Ganeswara, 5. Kashyapa, 6. Dhanphula, 7. Bhardwaja, etc.....while the Sountia have one gotra namely Nagasa." The Buthudi and Sounti are endogamous populations and are divided into different exogamous sections, called Khilis. The names of various Khilis titles were awarded by the rulers or Zamindars to the ancestors of the tribes for the distinguished services rendered by them. Out of 126 and 56 Sounti and Bathudi titles as mentioned in census of Mayurbhanj 1931, 36 Sounti and 50 Bathudi titles have appeared in the 100 families covered from each tribe (Table 2.1). As expected not a single case of marriage between the same Khili among either of the tribe has been observed. Name of various Khilis appeared in the present sample are shown in Table 2.1.

Table 2.1

Names of various Khilis observed among the Bathudi and Sounti

Bathudi :	Badnaik, Bahbalinder, Bansalia, Bargaian, Bhulo, Biswal, Das, Dalbehera, Dalahi, Danik, Dhola, Dehuri, Giri, Gurgaian, Jharial, Kabata, Kapandia, Khalpadia, Khatua, Khondai, Kotie, Kuabasia, Kumar, Kusamalia, Manik, Matiana, Mirdia, Modhai, Naik, Nimbal, Padhuria, Padhial, Paida, Palasia, Palia, Pandiki, Patra,

	Patulia, Raithia, Ramjudia, Ranthania, Raransia, Rout, Sankhamalia, Sankhial, Salkho, Sarpadia, Senapati, Simnikhia, Sulia.
Sounti :	Ankulia, Baghsingh, Babhalinder, Balaria, Banpaida, Bansalia, Bisainaik, Biswal, Chattarpania, Chipindia, Choudhuri, Das, Daldasia, Dalhai, Dandapat, Danakulia, Dehuri, Giri, Kapandia, Karjee, Kulapadia, Kusmalia, Mirikhia, Mundlana, Naik, Paida, Palia, Palta, Parmanik, Punjia, Putlia, Sankhamalia, Sarpuria, Singh, Talosudia and Tarania.

Bahabalinder, Bansalia, Biswal, Das, Dehuri, Giri, Kapandia, Kusmalia, Naik, Paida, Palai, Putlia, Sankhamalia and Sarpuria are some of the common Khilis of the Bathudi and Sounti.

2.2 MARRIAGE

Marriage is mostly monogamous among the people. Polygeneous unions are permitted though, seldom found. Marriages usually takes place across Khili and sometimes with in same village. In certain rare cases marriage within the Khili has been reported to be possible. There are instances where the Bathudi and the Sounti married within the same village and also in a village as far as 70 kilometers. Most of the marriages, however, took place with villages located within 20 kilometers radius. The mean marriage distance among the Bathudi is 19.52 ± 1.54 kilometers, while among the Sounti the marriage distance is 16.87 ± 1.39 kilometers.

Most of the Bathudi and Sounti males get married around twenty two years of their age. The average age at marriage among the Bathudi and Sounti females is about 18 years of age. Out of 102 Bathudi and 100 Sounti ever married females two Bathudi and six Sounti females have never conceived. Out of two Bathudi females one belongs to the age-group 25-34 years and the other to 65-74 years. Out of six Sounti females, one female belongs to the age group 15-24 years, four females belong to the age group of 25-34 years and one female belongs to the age group 55-64 years. The females who have crossed the child bearing age of 45 years are considered by the villagers as sterile. But Biologically the reasons for not having children could be something else.

The average age of fatherhood of the Bathudi and Sounti is about 24 years while most of the Bathudi and Sounti ever married females become mothers at the age of 21 years. The mean age at the birth of the last child among the Bathudi and Sounti females, who have completed their reproductive cycle is worked out to be 35.58 years and 37.5 years respectively. Reproductive life span of such females has been found to be slightly higher among the Sounti (13.69 years) as compared to the Bathudi (13.37).

2.3 FAMILY SIZE

The members of a unit residing under a common roof and sharing a same kitchen are referred to in the present study as family. Immediately after the marriage the couple tries to build its own house or hut. Husband and wife both contribute to the economic support of their family. The average size of the Bathudi family is 5.25 individuals. While the Sounti family size is 5.03 individuals. The family size has been compared with some other tribal population in Table 2.2.

Table 2.2

Percentage family size among some other populations and the Bathudi and Sounti

Number of persons	*Bathudi (102)%*	*Sounti (100)%*	*Population Irula%*	*Dorla%*	*Dhurwa %*
1–3	16.67 (17)	19.00 (19)	33.8	31.6	19.2
4–6	58.82 (61)	61.00 (61)	48.5	52.7	44.8
7–9	22.55 (23)	20.00 (20)	16.2	15.2	22.7
10–13	1.96 (2)	–	1.5	0.4	13.3

Figures in brackets are absolute numbers.

2.4 OCCUPATION

Bathudis and Sountis are mostly engaged in the agriculture. The wives equally assist their husbands in the economic development of their family by either working as daily labourers or working in their own agricultural fields and also attending to their house hold activities. The individuals who has sufficient land for cultivation do not work as labourers for other cultivators, but in case the land is not adequate to produce sufficient grains for the maintenance of a family in that case either the husband or both the husband and wife work as labourers for the local cultivators. About 40 percent Bathudi and 20 percent Sountis have their own land for cultivation. About 35 percent Sountis have cultivable land but it is not adequate for their maintenance and hence these individuals also engage themselves as labourers. About 54 percent Bathudis and 44 percent Sountis are engaged as daily labourers either with the local land owners, forest department, or local business men. About seven percent Bathudi and one percent Sounti are in government service and one percent each in business. Individuals who are either in service or business are economically better off and their wives only attend to the household activities. The percentage, distribution of males and females of both populations engaged in different occupations are presented in Table 2.3.

Table 2.3

Percentage distribution of occupational status among the Bathudi and Sounti of Both sexes

Sl. No.	*Occupational status*	*Bathudi*		*Sounti*	
		Male (102) %	*Female (102) %*	*Male (100) %*	*Female (100) %*
1.	Labourer	53.92 (55)	54.90 (56)	44.00 (44)	51.00 (51)
2.	Owner and Cultivators	38.24 (39)	36.28 (37)	19.00 (19)	22.00 (22)
3.	Cultivators and labourers	–	–	34.00 (34)	25.00 (25)
4.	Service	6.86 (7)	–	1.00 (1)	–
5.	Business	0.98 (1)	–	1.00 (1)	–
6.	Household	–	8.82 (9)	–	2.00 (2)

Figures in brackets are absolute numbers.

2.5 LITERACY POSITION

The Sountis are mostly concentrated in the villages which are isolated and there are very few schools as compared to the areas where the Bathudis are found. The Sountis sent their children to the forest for collection of wood, forest produce or for catching fish in order to sell these item in the weekly markets. But the Bathudi, who are more conscious about the role of education and are more economically better off as compared to the Sounti, prefer to send their male children to schools. School going female children are far less in number. None of the females has passed Class X. None of the males belonging to the Sounti have passed Class X standard. Percentages of literacy among the Bathudi and Sounti of both sexes have been shown in Table 2.4.

Table 2.4

Literacy position among the Bathudi and Sounti of both Sexes

Sl. No.	*Educational status*	*Bathudi*		*Sounti*	
		Male (102) %	*Female (102) %*	*Male (100) %*	*Female (100) %*
1.	Non-literate	65.69 (67)	89.22 (91)	73.00 (73)	99.00 (99)
2.	Upto class IV	7.85 (8)	5.88 (6)	15.00 (15)	1.00 (1)
3.	V-VIII class	14.71 (15)	4.90 (5)	6.00 (6)	—
4.	IX—X	6.86 (7)	—	6.00 (6)	—
5.	Undergraduates	2.94 (3)	—	—	—
6.	Graduate	1.96 (2)	—	—	—

Figures in brackets are absolute numbers.

2.6 ANNUAL INCOME

Most of the Bathudi and Sounti are not land owner and at the same time they are also non-literate. In order to maintain and fulfill their daily requirements, they engage themselves as labourers during sowing, weeding and harvesting seasons, but during the rest of the period and specially during the rainy seasons, when the job opportunities are comparatively less, most of the individuals find it difficult to make the two ends meet. All the persons do not get the job opportunities. Sometimes husband gets job and on certain occasion his wife is employed as a labourer. It is very rare when both the husband and wife get job opportunities. The annual income of a family is shown in table 2.5. Most of the families have their annual income between Rs. 501 to Rs.1000. About four percent Bathudis, who have engaged themselves in government service, or business have annual income between Rs. 4001 to Rs. 5000. While among the Sountis one percent of the persons engaged in business have annual income between Rs. 3501 to Rs. 4000.

The tribal people do not maintain records of their daily income. Therefore, care was taken to collect the annual income from families with minimum error. Still what is presented here in this (Table 2.5) respect is nothing but mere estimation.

Table 2.5

Percentage frequency distribution of Annual income among the Bathudi and Sounti

Sl. No.	*Range (in Rupees)*	*Bathudi %*	*Sounti %*
1.	400—500	1.96	2.00
2.	501—1000	51.96	54.00
3.	1001—1500	26.47	39.00
4.	1501—2000	9.80	3.00
5.	2001—2500	2.94	1.00
6.	2501—3000	2.94	—
7.	3001—3500	—	—
8.	3501—4000	—	1.00
9.	4001—4500	1.96	—
10.	4501—5000	1.96	—

2.7 AGE-STRUCTURE AND SEX RATIO

The sex ratio has been calculated as number of females per hundred males. The Bathudi and Sounti population has been arranged in the age groups of 5 years interval. There are 535 Bathudi and 503 Sounti individuals, with higher sex ratio among the Bathudi as compared to the Sounti. The Bathudi have been found with higher frequency of individuals in the age group 15-49 years by about 8 percent. While the Sounti have preponderance of individuals of about six percent and two percent in the age group categories of 0-14 years and 50 years and above respectively. This has resulted in the higher child depending ratio (Number of individuals in the age group 0.14 years divided by number of individuals in the age group of 15-64 years and multiplied by (100) (Bopegamage, 1959) among the Sounti (72.06) as compared to the Bathudi (57.22). Bathudi has greater sex ratio in the preadolescent (0-14) age but among the Sounti the number of males and females does not exceed each other. In the adolescent and post adolescent period (15-49 years) the number of females has been found to be higher than the males among the Bathudis. But among the Sountis with successive increase of age in the post adolescent period the number of females as compared to the males has been found to be less than the Bathudi. The Bathudi and Sounti have over all sex-ratio of 108 and 93 respectively. Table 2.6 presents the age structure and sex ratio among the Bathudi and Sounti, while Figure 2.1 shows the population Pyramid among there two populations.

2.8 FERTILITY

Birth of a child in a family is always welcome and it has a special significance, if it is the first issue of a couple. There can not be a better opportunity for joy in ones life than be a father/mother. Fertility of women has always attracted the attention of administrators and planners. Sounti mothers have been found to have a higher rate of pregnancies than that the Bathudi. Average number of pregnancies per mother among the Sounti is 4.22 and 4.02 among the Bathudi. Birth wastage has been 4.5 percent and 1.5 percent among the Sounti and Bathudi mothers. The number of females has been observed to be higher at birth among the Bathudi than the males. This has resulted in higher sex ratio. The sex ratio among the Bathudi and Sounti of live born child is 110 and 91

Table 2.6

Age structure and sex ratio among the Bathudi and Sounti

Sl. No.	Age group (years)	Bathudi Percentage Frequency			Sex Ratio	Sounti Percentage Frequency			Sex Ratio
		Male	Female	Total		Male	Female	Total	
1.	0—4	2.80 (15)	3.74 (20)	6.54 (35)	133	4.58 (23)	6.16 (31)	10.74 (54)	135
2.	5—9	5.80 (31)	8.22 (44)	14.02 (75)	141	9.54 (48)	99.96 (35)	16.50 (83)	73
3.	10—14	8.41 (45)	7.10 (38)	15.51 (83)	84	6.56 (33)	7.75 (39)	14.31 (72)	118
4.	0—14	17.01 (91)	19.06 (102)	36.07 (193)	112	20.68 (104)	20.87 (105)	41.55 (20)	101
5.	15—19	6.17 (33)	7.85 (42)	14.02 (75)	127	4.57 (23)	4.18 (21)	8.75 (44)	91
6.	20—24	3.74 (20)	5.42 (29)	9.16 (49)	145	3.98 (20)	4.37 (22)	8.35 (42)	110
7.	25—29	3.18 (17)	4.11 (22)	7.29 (39)	129	5.96 (30)	5.37 (27)	11.33 (57)	90
8.	30—34	3.36 (18)	4.49 (24)	7.85 (42)	133	3.98 (20)	2.98 (15)	6.96 (35)	75
9.	35—39	4.49 (24)	3.92(21)	8.41 (25)	87	2.98 (15)	3.58 (18)	6.56 (33)	120
10.	40—44	3.18 (17)	2.62 (14)	5.80 (31)	82	2.58 (13)	1.79 (9)	4.37 (22)	69
11.	45—49	2.80 (15)	2.62 (14)	5.42 (29)	93	1.99 (10)	1.99 (10)	3.98 (20)	100

12.	15—49	26.92 (144)	31.03 (166)	57.95 (310)	115	26.04 (131)	24.26 (122)	50.30 (253)	93
13.	50—54	1.87 (10)	0.75 (4)	2.62 (14)	40	1.79 (9)	1.79 (9)	3.58 (18)	100
14.	55—59	1.31 (7)	0.93 (5)	2.24 (12)	71	1.59 (8)	0.99 (5)	2.58 (13)	62
15.	60—64	0.56 (13)	0.19 (1)	0.75 (4)	33	0.99 (5)	0.20 (1)	1.19 (6)	20
16.	65—69	0.19 (1)	0.18 (1)	0.37 (2)	100	0.40 (2)	0.20 (1)	0.60 (3)	50
17.	70 +	—	—	—	—	0.20 (1)	—	0.20 (1)	—
18.	50 +	3.93 (21)	2.05 (11)	5.98 (32)	52	4.97 (25)	3.18 (16)	8.15 (41)	64
19.	Total	47.86 (256)	52.14 (279)	100.00 (535)	108	51.69 (260)	48.31 (243)	100.00 (503)	93

Figures in brackets are absolute numbers.

Table 2.7

Reproductive history according to the age groups of the Bathudi and Sounti mothers

Age group in years	Population	No. of mother	No. of conception	Total number of live births			Birth wastage	Live born dead			Live born living			Twin births					
														Alive			Dead		
				M	F	Total		M	F	Total	M	F	Total	M	F	T	M	F	T
15–19	Bathudi	1	1	1	—	1	—	—	—	—	1	—	1	—	—	—	—	—	—
	Sounti																		
20–24	Bathudi	7	10	5	5	10	—	—	—	—	5	5	10						
	Sounti	10	21	8	11	19	2	2	—	2	6	11	17						
25–29	Bathudi	12	29	14	15	29	—	3	—	3	11	15	26						
	Sounti	21	66	32	28	60	6	3	2	5	29	26	55						
30–34	Bathudi	22	80*	43	34	77	2	9	7	16	34	27	61	—	1	1	—	1	1
	Sounti	13	54	24	27	51	3	2	8	10	22	19	41						
35–39	Bathudi	20	86	33	52	85	1	7	6	13	26	46	72						
	Sounti	16	73	36	35	71	2	6	3	9	30	32	62						
40–44	Bathudi	14	67*	28	38	66	—	1	6	7	27	32	59	—	—	—	2	—	2
	Sounti	8	42	18	23	41	1	2	3	5	16	20	36	—	—	—	—	—	—
45 +	Bathudi	24	129	63	62	125	3	9	7	16	54	55	99	—	—	—	2	—	2
	Sounti	26	141	80	57	137	4	21	18	39	59	39	98	—	—	—	—	—	—
Total	Bathudi	100	402*	187	206	393	6	29	26	55	158	180	338	—	1	1	4	1	5
	Sounti	94	397	198	181	379	18	36	36	70	162	147	309						

* Twins not included.

respectively. Reproductive history of the Bathudi and Sounti mothers, according to their age groups is presented in table 2.7. The average number of live born children among the Bathudi and Sounti mothers (of all ages) is 3.93 and 4.03 respectively, and are comparable with the Maler, Dhurwa, Konds and Dorla (Table 2.8). The completed fertility of women belonging to the Bathudi and Sounti who are 45 years of age and above has been found to be 5.21 and 5.27 children per women respectively and are comparable with the Dhurwa, Konds, Dorla and Kanikkar womens (Table 2.9). Average fertility rate has been found to be higher in all the different age groups among the Sounti as compared to the Bathudi as presented in Table 2.10.

Table 2.8

Number of Children born per mother (all ages) of different tribal population

Sl. No.	*Population*	*Locality*	*Number of Mothers*	*Children ever born per mother*	*Author*
1.	Maler	Bihar	69	4.30	Sarkar, 1944
2.	Dorla	Bastar (M.P.)	231	3.36	Rakshit, 1959
3.	Dhurwa	Bastar (M.P.)	296	3.86	do
4.	North Andamanese	Andaman Island	25	2.36	Sarkar, 1953
5.	South Andamanese	-do-	32	2.81	-do-
6.	Pahira	Bihar	101	3.01	Ray, 1954
7.	Kond	Orissa	157	3.64	Devi, 1975
8.	Kond	-do-	50	3.58	Sharma, 1979
9.	Bathudi	-do-	100	3.93	Present Study
10.	Sounti	-do-	94	4.03	-do-

Table 2.9

Number of Children born per mother of age 45 years of age and above

Sl. No.	*Population*	*Locality*	*Number of mothers*	*Children ever born per mother*	*Author*
1.	Maler	Bihar	10	5.8	Sarkar, 1944
2.	Santal	Bihar	10	6.1	-do-
3.	Kanikkar	Kerala	31	4.74	Nag, 1954
4.	Dorla	Bastar (M.P.)	43	4.86	Rakshit, 1959
5.	Dhurwa	Bastar (M.P.)	54	5.17	-do-
6.	Kond	Orissa	31	4.61	Devi, 1975
7.	Kond	Orissa	11	5.36	Sharma, 1979
8.	Irula	Tamil Nadu	37	6.55	Basu, 1967
9.	Bathudi	Orissa	24	5.21	Present Study
10.	Sounti	Orissa	26	5.27	-do-

Table 2.10

Average fertility rate according to different age groups of the Bathudi and Sounti mothers

Sl. No.	*Age group (in years)*	*Population*	*Total Number of mothers*	*Total Number of births*	*Average fertility rate*
1.	15—19	Bathudi	1	1	1.00
		Sounti	—	—	—
2.	20—24	Bathudi	7	10	1.43
		Sounti	10	19	1.90
3.	25—29	Bathudi	12	29	2.42
		Sounti	21	60	2.86
4.	30—34	Bathudi	22	77	3.50

(Contd.)

(Contd.)

		Sounti	13	51	3.92
5.	35—39	Bathudi	20	85	4.25
		Sounti	16	71	4.43
6.	40—44	Bathudi	14	66	4.71
		Sounti	8	41	5.12
7.	45 +	Bathudi	24	125	5.21
		ounti	26	137	5.27
8.	All ages	Bathudi	100	393	3.93
		Sounti	94	379	4.03

2.9 SEX-RATIO AND BIRTH ORDER

Table 2.11 presents sex-wise distribution of live births according to birth orders alongwith their sex ratio. It may be observed that the frequency of births which is maximum for the first birth order shows a trend of decrease in the number of live births with the increase of birth orders. Except birth orders IV and VII, the Bathudis have greater sex ratio than Sountis for all the corresponding birth orders. The average sex ratio of the Bathudi indicate higher frequency of females and it is attributed to the fact that except birth order III and IV the females are born more than males in all the birth orders. Contrary to it, a large number of males are born than females in all the birth orders from I to IV among the Sountis. From birth order V to VIII the number of females are born in higher frequency among the Sountis. This has resulted in the overall less number of females then males among the Sounti (Table 2.11).

Table 2.11

Distribution of live birth (dead and alive) and sex ratio according to birth orders of the Bathudi and Sounti mothers

Sl. No.	*Birth orders*	*Bathudi*				*Sounti*			
		Male	*Female*	*Total*	*Sex Ratio*	*Male*	*Female*	*Total*	*Sex Ratio*
1.	I	50	50	100	100	48	46	94	96

(Contd.)

(Contd.)

2.	II	39	51	90	130	46	43	89	96
3.	III	42	38	80	90	41	32	73	78
4.	IV	34	26	60	76	30	25	55	83
5.	V	11	24	35	218	17	18	35	106
6.	VI	5	11	16	220	10	10	20	100
7.	VII	3	3	6	100	4	5	9	125
8.	VIII	2	3	5	150	2	2	4	100
9.	IX	1	—	1	—	—	—	—	—
10.	Total	187	206	393	110	198	181	279	91

2.10 MULTIPLE BIRTHS

Multiple births or litter size in one of the very important factors in demographic studies and it has been neglected on most of the occasions. We can explore further studies in demography by knowing the frequency, sex and the rate of survival of the multiple births. Multiple births have not been reported among the Sounti. Three out of 402 pregnancies have resulted in twin birth of 0.75 percent among the Bathudi. Three twins includes four males and two females. All four males and one female have died and one female has survived. Twins and general population of the Bathudi are compared in Table 2.12. The death rate has been observed to be higher among the males of both twin and general population. In the general population the females are born in higher frequency but in case of twins, males have been found in greater frequency. The rate of survival of males born as twin birth is zero, while half the females born out of twin birth have survived.

The male twins are born in the let and III birth orders, and the females twin in the II birth orders. The frequency of twins among the Bathudi is 1 : 134 and it can be compared with the Irule of Tamil Nadu as observed by Basu (1967) with its frequency as 1 : 142.

Table 2.12

Comparison of twin and general population of the Bathudi

	Males			*Females*		
	Dead %	*Alive* %	*Total* %	*Dead* %	*Alive* %	*Total* %
Twin population	4 (100)	0 (0)	4 (100)	1 (50)	1 (50)	2 (100)
General population (Twin not included)	29 (15.51)	158 (84.49)	187 (100.00)	26 (12.62)	180 (87.38)	206 (100.00)

2.11 MORTALITY

Mortality is equally important for the demographic studies as the fertility is. Man has been trying to control the various diseases that causes death, through the magicians, priests and medicine man. The comparison to deaths and births give an idea about the decline or increase in growth of a population. The Bathudi are comparatively literate, economically better off and concentrated in areas, where the medical facilities are easily available as compared to the Sounti. This may possibly be the reason of higher death percentage among the Sounti (18.47%), than the Bathudi (13.99%). First birth order experiences maximum mortality among both the populations and with successive birth orders it goes on decreasing, till V and VII birth orders among the Bathudi and Sounti respectively. The mortality again increases from VI and VIII birth orders among the Bathudi and Sounti respectively (Table 2.13). The trend is graphically represented as an U shaped curve in Fig. 2.3. Similar observations regarding the birth order and mortality have been made by Podder (1975), Datta Banik *et. al.* (1975) and Barua (1982). The prenatal and post natal mortality (Figure 2.2) also depicts the similar trends as observed in case of post natal mortality except the rate of pre and post natal mortality is higher than the corresponding post natal mortality from I to III birth orders of the Bathudi and from I to VI birth orders of the Sounti. The Birth wastage has been observed to be highest in the first birth order and it decreases with the subsequent birth order among both the populations.

Table 2.13

Mortality according to birth orders among the Bathudi and Sounti

Birth order	Number of mothers		Number of pregnancies (live birth & birth, wastage)		Number of live births		Prenatal and post natal mortality		Post natal mortality	
	Bathudi	Sounti	Bathudi	Sounti	Bathudi	Sounti	Bathudi %	Sounti %	Bathudi %	Sounti %
I	100	94	106	102	101	94	22.64	31.37	18.81	25.53
II	90	89	92	94	91	89	18.48	20.21	17.58	15.73
III	80	73	75	75	81	73	12.34	21.33	12.35	19.18
IV	60	55	56	56	60	55	10.00	21.43	10.00	20.00
V	35	35	36	36	35	35	8.57	16.67	8.57	14.28
VI	16	20	21	21	16	20	12.50	9.57	12.50	5.00
VII	6	9	9	9	6	9	33.33	–	33.33	–
VIII	5	4	4	4	5	4	20.00	25.00	20.00	25.00
IX	1	–	–	–	1	–	–		–	–

2.12 AGE SPECIFIC MORTALITY

It is calculated by dividing the number of death in a specific age category by the total number of deaths and multiplying it by 100. Mortality has been found to be highest within a year of birth of a child among both the populations. During first two years the mortality has been found to be the highest among the Bathudi females than males. From third year onwards the mortality has been found in higher frequency among the Bathudi males. Among the Sounti mortality occurs in higher frequency among the males in the pre adolescent period except 2nd year, when the females show an increase in mortality. About seven percent females of Sounti tribe die in the adolescent period is however attributed to the pregnancy complications (Table 2.14).

Table 2.14

Age specific mortality among the Bathudi and Sounti

Died within	*Bathudi*			*Sounti*		
	Male %	*Female* %	*Total* %	*Male* %	*Female* %	*Total* %
1st year	14.55	23.64	38.18	18.57	10.00	28.57
2nd year	3.64	7.24	10.91	1.43	10.00	11.43
3rd year	10.90	3.64	14.54	1.43	10.00	21.43
5th year	14.55	7.27	21.82	5.71	2.86	8.57
10th year	7.27	5.45	12.73	8.57	8.57	17.14
15th year	—	—	—	2.86	4.28	7.14
Adults	1.82	—	1.82	2.86	2.86	5.72

The highest frequency of first born dead is within the first year among both the groups. Females have the highest mortality among the Bathudi with in first year, while the males have been reported with greater mortality among the Sounti. Males are more prone to death than the females of both the populations (Table 2.15).

Table 2.15

Mortality of first born among the Bathudi and Sounti

	Bathudi			*Sounti*		
	Male %	*Female* %	*Total* %	*Male* %	*Female* %	*Total* %
1st year	15.38	38.46	53.85	30.00	20.00	50.00
2nd year	—	7.70	7.69	20.00	20.00	40.00
3rd year	23.08	—	23.08	10.00	—	10.00
5th year	15.38	—	15.38	—	—	—
Total	53.84	45.10	100.00	60.00	40.00	100.00

3

QUALITATIVE OBSERVATIONS (ANTHROPOSCOPIC CHARACTERS AND OTHER MORPHO-GENETIC TRAITS)

ANTHROPOSCOPIC CHARACTERS

Anthroposcopic characters have long been used by the anthropologists for the classification of races of man. Various authors have used different observations but colour of skin, hair and eye, shape of the nose, form, texture of hair are some of the very important anthroposcopic observations which are often been used for racial classification. In the absence of any mechanism to quantify them these characters are subjected to visual observations or chart comparison for the skin colour, hair colour and eye colour. According to Gulati *et. al.* (1981) "Although there are sharp differences of opinion among scholars in respect of the utility of these characters in interpreting biological affinities between populations in restricted region, the relative group discriminatory property of scopic characters, particularly pigmentation of skin, hair and eye could even be better than some of the metric characters in some situations, as it exists in India in general and in South India in particular". According to Mourant *et. al.* (1976) in addition to the contribution of anthropometrist and serologist for the classification of human population "it would clearly be wrong for anthropologists to neglect just those characters of individuals and populations by which they are indentified in every day life". In the present chapter some of the qualitative characters have been discussed among the Bathudi and Sounti tribes, both populationwise and sexwise. These will throw light on inter-tribal and intratribal variations and thus indicate the approximate positions the tribes occupy in the community composition of the area under observations. The author has reported the results of Anthroposcopic investigations elsewhere.

3.1 SKIN COLOUR (FOREHEAD)

Dark shades of skin colour have been found in higher frequency among the Bathudi and Sounti of both sexes. Females of both the populations are characterised by the lighter shades of skin colour than the males. Some what over 29 percent of the Bathudi and 11.3 percent Sounti males have light brown skin colour. Lighter shades of skin colour have preponderance among the males and females of Bathudi, while the Sounti males and females have been characterised by the relatively darker shades. About 70 percent Bathudi and 80 percent Sounti males have been found with dark shade of skin complexion. About 73 percent Bathudi females are characterised by dark skin complexion, similarly about 92 percent of the Sounti females have dark skin colour. It may be observed that Bathudi and Sounti females assist their husbands equally in the outdoor activities in the agricultural fields and are preferred as labours also. This, to some extent, may account for their dark complexion. Table 3.1 presents the percentage frequency distribution of skin colour among the Bathudis and the Sountis.

Table 3.1

Skin Colour of the Bathudi and Sounti of both sexes

Sl. No.	*Skin Colour*	*Bathudi*		*Sounti*	
		Males	*Females*	*Males*	*Females*
		N = 109	*N = 110*	*N = 106*	*N = 105*
		%	%	%	%
1.	Blackish Brown	25.7	10.9	35.8	11.4
2.	Dark Reddish Brown	18.3	0.9	1.9	4.8
3.	Reddish Brown	11.0	8.2	14.2	37.1
4.	Brown	14.7	52.7	36.8	39.1
5.	Light Brown	29.4	25.5	11.3	7.6
6.	Olive Yellow	0.9	—	—	—
7.	Yellowish	—	1.8	—	—

3.2 HAIR COLOUR

Black followed by dark brown shades of hair colour have been found in higher frequency among the Bathudi and Sounti of both sexes. Females of both sexes have preponderance of black hair colour as compared to the males of both populations. However, the males of both the populations have been found with higher frequencies of Dark brown hair colour than their respective female populations. Reddish brown hair colour has been found among the Bathudi males only but in low frequencies (3.7%). Percentage frequency distribution of hair colour is presented in table 3.2.

Table 3.2

Hair colour among the Bathudi and Sounti of both sexes

Sl. No.	*Hair Colour*	*Bathudi*		*Sounti*	
		Males	*Females*	*Males*	*Females*
		N = 109	*N = 110*	*N = 106*	*N = 105*
		%	%	%	%
1.	Black	56.9	80.9	73.6	78.1
2.	Dark Brown	39.4	19.1	26.4	21.9
3.	Reddish Brown	3.7	—	—	—

3.3 HAIR FORM

Bathudi and Sounti males and females are characterised by the highest frequency of straight followed by low wavy hair. Deep wavy hair have been observed in low frequency among the Bathudi (2.7%) and Sounti (0.9%) males only. Frequency of straight hair have been found in greater frequency among the females of both the populations. It may also be observed that the low wavy hair are found in greater frequency among the males of both populations as compared to their respective female populations. Table 3.3 presents the frequency distribution of hair form.

Table 3.3

Hair form among the Bathudi and Sounti of both sexes

Sl. No.	*Hair form*	*Bathudi*		*Sounti*	
		Males	*Females*	*Males*	*Females*
		N = 109	*N = 110*	*N = 106*	*N = 105*
		%	%	%	%
1.	Straight	62.4	91.8	65.1	85.7
2.	Low wavy	34.9	8.2	34.0	14.3
3.	Deep wavy	2.7	—	0.9	—

3.4 HAIR TEXTURE

Most of the Bathudi and Sounti males and females have medium hair texture. Medium hair texture has been found in greater frequency among the Bathudi, when compared to the Sounti. It is also observed that the Bathudi and Sounti males have higher frequency of medium hair texture than their respective female populations. Fine hairs have been found to occur in great frequency among the females of the Sounti (20.0%) and Bathudi (14.5%). Table 3.4 presents the percentage frequency distribution of hair texture.

Table 3.4

Hair texture among the Bathudi and Sounti of both sexes

Sl. No.	*Hair texture*	*Bathudi*		*Sounti*	
		Males	*Females*	*Males*	*Females*
		N = 109	*N = 110*	*N = 106*	*N = 105*
		%	%	%	%
1.	Coarse	20.2	18.2	10.4	18.1
2.	Medium	76.2	67.3	89.6	61.9
3.	Fine	3.7	14.5	—	20.0

3.5 QUANTITY OF HEAD HAIR

Bathudi and Sounti of both sexes have been found with preponderance of thick followed by medium growth of head hair.

The occurrence of baldness has not been observed. Sometimes individuals in their late fifties have been found with thick growth with very less, and sometime the absence of grey hair on their head. Table 3.5 presents the distribution of quantity of head hair.

Table 3.5

Quantity of head hair among the Bathudi and Sounti of both sexes

Sl. No.	*Quantity*	*Bathudi*		*Sounti*	
		Males	*Females*	*Males*	*Females*
		N = 109	*N = 110*	*N = 106*	*N = 105*
		%	%	%	%
1.	Medium	31.2	27.3	47.2	47.6
2.	Thick	68.8	72.7	52.8	52.4

3.6 BEARD AND MOUSTACHE : QUANTITY

This is a sex linked trait and found among the males only. Bathudi and Sounti males have preponderance of scanty distribution of beard and moustaches. Among five per cent of the Bathudis it has been observed to be absent. Medium growth of beard has been reported in low frequency among the Bathudi and Sounti. There is no thick growth of beard and moustaches among the people. Table 3.6 presents the percentage distribution of beard and moustache.

Table 3.6

Quantity of beard and moustache among the Bathudi and Sounti males

Sl. No.	*Quantity*	*Bathudi*	*Sounti*
		N = 109	*N = 106*
		%	%
1.	Scanty	79.8	87.7
2.	Medium	14.7	12.3
3.	Thick	0.9	—
4.	Absent	4.6	—

3.7 EYE COLOUR

Dark brown followed by brown eye colour has been found to occur in greater frequency among the Bathudi and Sounti of both sexes. Light brown character of eyes have been observed among the Bathudi males (21.1%) and Bathudi females (5.4%), and this is nearly non-existant among the Sounti males and absent among the Sounti females. Black eyes occur in low frequency except among the Sounti females, who do not have black eyes. Tablè 3.7 presents distribution of eye colour among Bathudi and Sounti.

Table 3.7

Eye colour among the Bathudi and Sounti of both sexes

Sl. No.	*Eye colour*	*Bathudi*		*Sounti*	
		Males	*Females*	*Males*	*Females*
		N = 109	*N = 110*	*N = 106*	*N = 105*
		%	%	%	%
1.	Black	5.5	4.5	3.8	—
2.	Dark Brown	52.3	65.4	77.4	60.0
3.	Brown	21.1	24.6	17.9	40.0
4.	Light Brown	21.1	5.4	0.9	—

3.8 EYE FOLD

Mongoloid type of epicanthus fold has not been found among the Bathudi and Sounti of both sexes, though its traces have been observed in low frequency among the Bathudi (5.9%), Sounti (2.8%) males and Bathudi females (0.9%). Table 3.8 presents the distribution of eye fold among the Bathudi and Sounti.

Table 3.8

Eye fold among the Bathudi and Sounti of both sexes

Sl. No.	*Eye hold*	*Bathudi*		*Sounti*	
		Males	*Females*	*Males*	*Females*
		N = 109	*N = 110*	*N = 106*	*N = 105*
		%	%	%	%
1.	Absent	94.5	99.1	97.2	100.00
2.	Traces	5.5	0.9	2.8	—

3.9 EYE SLITS

Straight eye slits have been observed and the obliquity of eye opening has been found to be absent among the Bathudi and Sounti of both the sexes.

3.10 SCLERA

Males of Bathudi (43.1%) and Sounti (56.6%) have higher frequency of yellow sclera. The Bathudi (50.9%) and Sounti (36.2%) females have preponderance of clear sclera. The yellow colour of sclera may possibly be attributed to the consumption of 'handia', a local liquor prepared from rice, by the males in huge quantity. Nevertheless, the variations are worth mentioning. Table 3.9 presents the distribution of sclera among the Bathudis and Sountis.

Table 3.9

Sclera among the Bathudi and Sounti of both sexes

Sl. No.	*Sclera*	*Bathudi*		*Sounti*	
		Males	*Females*	*Males*	*Females*
		N = 109	*N = 110*	*N = 106*	*N = 105*
		%	%	%	%
1.	Clear	24.8	50.9	26.4	36.2
2.	Yellow	43.1	17.3	56.6	32.4
3.	Dull	32.1	31.8	17.0	31.4

3.11 EYE BROWS

Bathudi males are characterised by medium, followed by thin eye brows. The Sounti of both sexes and Bathudi females have preponderance of thin followed by medium eye brows. But the thin eye brows have been found more among the females than males of both the populations. Thick eye brows have been observed only among the male individuals but its frequency is very low. Table 3.10 presents the distribution of eye brows among the Bathudis and Sountis.

Table 3.10

Eye-brows among the Bathudi and Sounti of both sexes

Sl. No.	*Eye brows*	*Bathudi*		*Sounti*	
		Male	*Female*	*Male*	*Female*
		N = 109	*N = 110*	*N = 106*	*N = 105*
		%	%	%	%
1.	Thin	44.0	60.00	71.7	94.3
2.	Medium	55.0	40.00	26.4	5.7
3.	Thick	1.0	—	1.9	—

3.12 SUPRA-ORBITAL RIDGES

Supra-orbital ridges are absent among the females. Traces of supra-orbital ridges are present among the males of Bathudi (53.2%) and Sounti (44.4%). Moderate to pronounced supra-orbital ridges are not found among the individuals of the present series. Table 3.11 presents the distribution of supra-orbital ridges among the Bathudis and the Sountis.

Table 3.11

Supra-orbital ridges among the Bathudi and Sounti of both sexes

Sl. No.	*Supra-oribital ridges*	*Bathudi*		*Sounti*	
		Males	*Females*	*Males*	*Females*
		N = 109	*N = 110*	*N = 106*	*N = 105*
		%	%	%	%
1.	Imperceptible	45.9	100.00	54.7	100.00
2.	Trace	53.2	—	44.4	—
3.	Moderate	0.9	—	—	—
4.	Pronounced	—	—	0.9	–

3.13 FOREHEAD HEIGHT

Bathudi and Sounti of both sexes are characterised by medium forehead heights but the Sounti females have more or less equal frequency of low and medium forehead height. High forehead heights have been observed only among the male individuals but the frequency is low. Table 3.12 presents the distribution of forehead height among the Bathudis and the Sountis.

Table 3.12

Forehead height among Buthudi and Sounti of both sexes

Sl. No.	Forehead height	Bathudi		Sounti	
		Males	Females	Males	Females
		N = 109	N = 110	N = 106	N = 105
		%	%	%	%
1.	High	0.9	—	1.9	—
2.	Medium	99.1	99.1	97.2	50.5
3.	Low	—	0.9	0.9	49.5

3.14 FOREHEAD SLOPE

Medium forehead slope has been found to occur in higher frequency in the present series. The Sounti males have greater frequency, almost double of medium slope of forehead as compared to the Sounti females. In contrast the Bathudi males have been found with less frequency of forehead slopes than its females. About five percent Bathudi and Sounti males have marked foreheads. Females of both populations have straight forehead slopes in fairly high frequency. Table 3.13 presents the distribution of forehead slope among the Bathudis and Sountis.

Table 3.13

Forehead slope among the Bathudi and Sounti of both sexes

Sl. No.	Forehead slope	Bathudi		Sounti	
		Males	Females	Males	Females
		N = 109	N = 110	N = 106	N = 105
		%	%	%	%
1.	Marked	4.6	—	4.7	—
2.	Medium	71.6	83.6	92.5	48.6
3.	Straight	23.8	16.4	2.8	51.4

3.15 NASION DEPRESSION

Medium followed by shallow Nasion depression has been found in higher frequency among the present series. Bathudi females and Sounti males have fairly greater frequency of medium Nasion depression than Bathudi males. The Sounti females have been found with double the frequency of shallow Nasion depression as compared to the medium nasion depression. Deep Nasion depression have preponderance among the Bathudi males. The Sountis of both sexes have fairly high occurrence of shallow Nasion depression as compared to the Bathudis. Table 3.14 presents the distribution of Nasion depression as compared to the Bathudis. Table 3.14 presents the distribution of Nasion depression among the Bathudis and the Sountis.

Table 3.14

Nasion depression among the Bathudi and Sounti of both sexes

Sl. No.	*Nasion depression*	*Bathudi*		*Sounti*	
		Male	*Female*	*Male*	*Female*
		N = 109	*N = 110*	*N = 106*	*N = 105*
		%	*%*	*%*	*%*
1.	Shallow	26.6	23.7	33.0	67.6
2.	Medium	46.8	74.5	66.1	32.4
3.	Deep	26.6	1.8	0.9	—

3.16 NASAL BRIDGE

Bathudi and Sounti of both sexes are characterised by concave followed by straight nasal bridges. Sountis have been found with greater occurrence of concave nasal bridges as compared to the Bathudis. It may also be pointed out that the females of both the populations are having higher frequencies of concave nasal bridges than their male counter parts. Frequency of straight nasal bridges are found in preponderance among the Bathudis of both the sexes than the Sountis. Similarly, the males of both the populations are reported with comparatively higher frequency of straight nasal bridges than their females. Low frequency of concave-convex nasal bridges have been observed among the Bathudi males (3.7%) and females (0.9%). Table 3.15 presents the distribution of nasal bridge among the Bathudis and the Sountis.

Table 3.15

Nasal bridges among the Bathudi and Sounti of both sexes

Sl. No.	Nasal bridge	Bathudi		Sounti	
		Males	Females	Males	Females
		N = 109	N = 110	N = 106	N = 105
		%	%	%	%
1.	Straight	31.2	22.7	17.0	13.3
2.	Concave	65.1	76.4	83.0	86.7
3.	Concave-convex	3.7	0.9	—	—

3.17 NASAL SEPTUM

Males and females of both the populations are found to have maximum occurrence of horizontal followed by upward nasal septums. Bathudi females and the Sountis of both sexes are having nearly equal frequencies of horizontal nasal septum. Among the Bathudi males, the frequency of horizontal nasal septum is less than half the frequencies as reported among other samples of the present study. Bathudis have less frequency of horizontal nasal septum than the Sountis. Similarly, the females of both the populations are observed with greater frequency of horizontal nasal septum as compared to their respective male populations. Bathudis have higher frequency of upward nasal septum than Sountis. Upward nasal septum occurs in higher frequency among the males of both populations than their females. Bathudi males only have down-ward nasal septum but its frequency is very low (7.3%). Table 3.16 presents the distribution of nasal septum among the Bathudis and the Sountis.

Table 3.16

Nasal septum among the Bathudi and Sounti of both sexes

Sl. No.	Nasal septum	Bathudi		Sounti	
		Males	Females	Males	Females
		N = 109	N = 110	N = 106	N = 105
		%	%	%	%
1.	Horizontal	57.8	93.6	94.3	99.1
2.	Upwards	34.9	6.4	5.7	0.9
3.	Down-ward	7.3	—	—	—

3.18 LIP THICKNESS

Medium lip thickness has preponderance among the Bathudi and Sounti of both sexes except Sounti males among whom thick lips have been observed in higher frequencies. Females of both the populations have larger frequencies of medium lip thickness as compared to their males. Bathudi males have nearly double the frequency of medium lip thickness as compared to the Sounti males. However, the Bathudi females have comparatively less occurrence of medium lip thickness than the Sounti females. Thin lips have been found in higher frequency among the Bathudi (21.8%) and Sounti (7.6%) females. Occurrence of thick lips among the Sounti males (69.8%) is much more than among the Bathudi males (40.4%). It may also be observed that Bathudis of both sexes have higher frequency of thin lips, while the Sounti males and females are observed with preponderance of thick lips. Table 3.17 presents the distribution of lip thickness among the Bathudis and the Sountis.

Table 3.17

Lip thickness among the Bathudi and Sounti of both sexes

Sl. No.	*Lip thickness*	*Bathudi*		*Sounti*	
		Males	*Females*	*Males*	*Females*
		N = 109	*N = 110*	*N = 106*	*N = 105*
		%	%	%	%
1.	Thin	7.3	21.8	1.9	7.6
2.	Medium	52.3	63.6	28.3	75.2
3.	Thick	40.4	14.6	69.8	17.2

3.19 CHIN

Bathudi and Sounti males and females have been characterised by round shape followed by oval shape of chin. Round chin shape is more common among the Sountis as compared to the Bathudis. Bathudi males have less frequency of round chin as compared to the Bathudi females. In contrast, the Sounti males have been found with relatively higher occurrence of round chin than the Sounti females. Oval chin has its preponderance among the Bathudis than Sountis. Oval chin is reported to be in greater frequency among the females of both populations than their males. Square chin occurs in low frequency among the Bathudi (9.2%) and Sounti (5.7%) males. Receding projection of chin has been observed among the males only, but its frequency is low (about 2%). Receding chin has not been observed among the Sounti females. Table 3.18 presents the distribution of chin among the Bathudis and the Sountis.

Table 3.18

Chin among the Bathudi and Sounti of both sexes

Sl. No.	Chin	Bathudi		Sounti	
		Males	Females	Males	Females
		N = 109	N = 110	N = 106	N = 105
		%	%	%	%
1.	Receding	1.8	0.9	1.9	—
2.	Oval	33.0	37.3	22.6	37.1
3.	Round	56.0	60.9	69.8	62.9
4.	Square	9.2	0.9	5.7	—

3.20 PROGNATHISM

Slight prognathism has been found among the males and females of both populations. Sountis have relatively higher frequency of slight alveolar prognathism as compared to the Bathudis. Slight alveolar prognathism is more frequent among the females as compared to the males. Prognathism has not been observed among 4.6% of males and 7.3% females of the Bathudis. Facial prognathism has not been found among the Sountis but about six percent of Bathudi males and one percent females have facial prognathism. Table 3.19 presents the distribution of prognathism among the Bathudis and Sountis.

Table 3.19

Prognathism among the Bathudi and Sounti of both sexes

Sl. No.	Prognathism	Bathudi		Sounti	
		Male	Female	Male	Female
		N = 109	N = 110	N = 106	N = 105
		%	%	%	%
1.	Alveolar-slight	87.2	91.8	94.3	99.1
2.	Alveolar-medium	1.8	—	5.7	0.9
3.	Facial-slight	3.7	0.9	—	—

(Contd.)

(Contd.)

4.	Facial-medium	2.7	—	—	—
5.	Absent	4.6	7.3	—	—

3.21 INCISOR FOLD

Incisor fold has not been found in the present series.

3.22 BOLD MUSCULATURE

Males and females are actively engaged in the manual labour and most of them work in their own agricultural field, some of them also work as labourers for other cultivators. This may possibly be the reason for the occurrence of Athletic body musculature in greater frequency among the present series. Asthetic body musculature has also been reported among the Sounti males (0.9%) and females (31.4%) only.

B. *Behavioural and morphological genetic characters:*

The results of morphological and genetical investigations of the Bathudi and the Sounti tribes have been reported by the author elsewhere [Singh, 1989].

3.23 HAND CLASPING

Lutz (1908), Downey (1926), Freire-Maia *et. al.* (1960), Freire-Maia and Almeida (1966), Chakraworty (1973) has discussed about importance and inheritance of hand clasping. R type has preponderance among the males as compared to the females. Bathudi males and females have been found with higher frequency of R types than the Sounti males and females. Table 3.20 presents the distribution of R type of hand clasping among the Bathudis and Sountis.

Table 3.20

Frequency distribution of R type of Handclasping among the Bathudi and Sounti of both sexes

Sl. No.	*Populations*	*Sex*	*Sample size*	*No.*	*Percentage*
1.	Bathudi	Male	109	69	63.30
2.	Bathudi	Female	110	58	52.73
3.	Sounti	Male	106	63	59.43
4.	Sounti	Female	105	54	51.43

3.24 HANDEDNESS

Rife (1940), Annet (1964 and 1973) discussed about the inheritance of handedness. Right handedness has been mostly found among the males and females of present series. Table 3.21 presents the distribution of R type of the handedness among the Bathudis and the Sountis.

Table 3.21

Frequency distribution of R type of handedness among the Bathudi and Sounti of both sexes

Sl. No.	*Populations*	*Sex*	*Sample size*	*No.*	*Percentage*
1.	Bathudi	Male	109	109	100.00
2.	Bathudi	Female	110	108	99.08
3.	Sounti	Male	106	105	99.06
4.	Sounti	Female	105	105	100.00

3.25 ARM FOLDING

Freira-Maia and Almeida (1966) discussed the phenomenon of arm folding. R type of arm folding has preponderance among the females as compared to the males. Bathudi males and females have been found with higher frequency of R type than the Sounti males and females. Table 3.22 presents the distribution of R type of arm folding among the Bathudis and the Sountis.

Table 3.22

Frequency distribution of R type of arm folding among the Bathudi and Sounti of both sexes

Sl. No.	*Populations*	*Sex*	*Sample size*	*No.*	*Percentage*
1.	Bathudi	Male	109	48	44.04
2.	Bathudi	Female	110	54	49.54
3.	Sounti	Male	106	45	42.54
4.	Sounti	Female	105	51	48.57

3.26 TONGUE ROLLING

Tongue rolling is a dominant trait (Sturtvant 1940, Beckman and Book 1960, Winchester 1966). Frequency of individuals who can roll the tongue has been found to be highest among the Sounti males and females as compared to the Bathudi males and females. Males of both the populations have greater frequency of rolling of tongue than their respective females. Table 3.23 presents the distribution of tongue rolling among the Bathudis and the Sountis.

Table 3.23

Frequency distribution of tongue rolling among the Bathudi and Sounti of both sexes

Sl. No.	*Populations*	*Sex*	*Sample size*	*No.*	*Percentage*
1.	Bathudi	Male	109	78	71.56
2.	Bathudi	Female	110	73	66.36
3.	Sounti	Male	106	82	77.36..
4.	Sounti	Female	105	79	75.24

3.27 TONGUE FOLDING

Inheritance of tongue folding has been discussed by Liu and Hsu (1949) and Winchester (1966). Frequency of tongue folders has been observed to be low. Bathudis have greater frequency of tongue folders than the Sountis. Males of both populations have been found with preponderance of tongue folding than their respective females. Table 3.24 presents the distribution of tongue folding among the Bathudis and Sountis.

Table 3.24

Frequency distribution of tongue folding among the Bathudi and Sounti of both sexes

Sl. No.	*Populations*	*Sex*	*Sample size*	*No.*	*Percentage*
1.	Bathudi	Male	109	16	14.68
2.	Bathudi	Female	110	11	10.00

(Contd.)

(Contd.)

3.	Sounti	Male	106	9	8.49
4.	Sounti	Female	105	5	4.76

3.28 OCCIPITAL HAIR WHORL

Bernstein (1925) and, Beckman and Book (1959) have discussed about the inheritance of occipital hair whorls. Single occipital hair whorl characterises the present series, but the frequency of single clockwise hair whorl has been found in higher frequency than single anti-clockwise hair whorl among the Bathudi and Sounti of both sexes. Bathudi and Sounti males have less frequency of double occipital whorls as compared to their females. Table 3.25 presents the distribution of occipital hair whorls among the Bathudis and the Sountis.

Table 3.25

Percentage frequency distribution of occipital hair whorls among the Bathudi and Sounti of both sexes

Sl. No.	*Populations*		*Single whorl*			*Double whorl*			
		Sex	*N*	+	—	+	− −	−+	− −
1.	Bathudi	Male	109	69.72	25.69	0.92	1.83	0.92	0.92
2.	Bathudi	Female	110	70.00	22.73	1.82	2.73	1.82	0.90
3.	Sounti	Male	106	70.75	23.58	2.83	0.94	1.89	—
4.	Sounti	Female	105	73.33	19.05	1.91	2.86	0.95	1.90

3.29 EAR LOBE ATTACHMENT

Hilden (1922), Quelprud (1934), Weiner (1937) and Gates (1952) discussed about the inheritance of Ear lobe attachment. Sounti males and females have been found with higher occurrence of completely attached ear lobes as compared to the Bathudi males and females. Most of the Bathudi and Sounti males and females are characterised by completely free ear lobes. Table 3.26 presents the distribution of ear lobe attachment among the Bathudis and the Sountis.

Table 3.26

Percentage frequency distribution of Ear lobe attachment among the Bathudi and Sounti of both sexes

Sl. No.	*Populations*	*Sex*	*Sample size*	*Completely attached*	*Inter mediate*	*Completely free*
1.	Bathudi	Male	109	11.93	19.26	68.81
2.	Bathudi	Female	110	12.73	23.64	63.63
3.	Sounti	Male	106	33.02	16.98	50.00
4.	Sounti	Female	105	21.90	13.33	64.76

3.30 DIGITAL FORMULAE

Kloepfer (1946), Phelps (1952), Winchester (1966) and Bansal (1966) explained about the inheritance of digital formulae. Digital formulas 2 < 4 followed by 2 = 4 and 2 > 4 is more common in the present series. If the pooled frequency of both the hands for digital formulae is considered, it is found that formulae 2 < 4 is more predominent among the Sountis as compared to the Bathudis and the females of both populations have been found with higher frequencies than the males. Formulae 2 = 4 is observed to be more frequent among the males than females of both populations. Formulae 2 > 4 occur in low frequency and it ranges from 7.62% (Sounti females) to 12.27% (Sounti males). Distribution of digital formulae among the Bathudis and Sountis is presented in table 3.27.

Table 3.27

Percentage frequency of Bimanual and combined (Right + Left) Occurrence of digital formulae among the Bathudi and Sounti of both sexes

Sl. No.	*Popul- ation*	*Sex*	*Sample size*	*Side*	*No.*	*2<4*	*2=4*	*2>4*
1.	Bathudi	Male	109	R	108	63.89	23.15	12.96
				L	109	72.48	20.18	7.34
				R+L	217	68.20	21.66	10.14

(Contd.)

(Contd.)

2.	Bathudi	Female	110	R	109	72.48	15.59	11.93
				L	110	81.82	6.36	11.82
				R+L	219	77.17	10.96	11.87
3.	Sounti	Male	106	R	106	68.87	17.92	13.21
				L	106	71.70	16.98	11.32
				R+L	212	70.28	17.45	12.27
4.	Sounti	Female	105	R	105	90.48	0.95	8.57
				L	105	89.52	3.81	6.67
				R+L	210	90.00	2.38	7.62

3.31 MID PHALANGEAL HAIR

Danforth (1921), Bernstein and Burk (1942) and Bernstein (1949) discussed about the genetics of middle phalangeal hair. Handlens was used to examine the middle phalangeal hairs on both the hands but this incidence has not been found in the present series.

3.32 DARWIN'S TUBERCLE

Quelprud (1934) ascertained the inheritance of Darwins tubercle. It is found that the Bathudi and Sounti of both sexes do not have Darwin's tubercle in the present sample.

3.33 CLEFT CHIN

According to Winchester (1966) cleft chin is inherited as a dominent characters. This trait has not been observed in the present sample.

4

ANTHROPOMETRIC CHARACTERS

HISTORICAL BACKGROUND

Anthropometric investigations were started in India in 1868. Various authors such as Drake-Brackman (1896), Thurston (1909), Risley (1915), Eickstedt (1939), Guha (1935), Chakladra (1936), Chatterjee (1948), Mazumdar (1949), Karve and Dandekar (1951), Roy-Choudhury (1952) and many others have used anthropometry for various purposes in the Indian context. Risley (1891) was the pioneer to undertake anthropometric measurements among some of the populations from Orissa. This was followed by the anthropometric studies on individual population groups by Eickstedt (1930), Guha (1935), Basu (1929), Roy (1935), Ray (1949), Ray (1958) and Roychoudhuri (1952). The most important contribution in the field of anthropometry specially in Orissa has been made by Karve (1954). Das *et. al.* (1968), Banerjee (1975), Sharma (1979) and Deka (1980) also made their contribution in the field of anthropometric investigations for various tribal populations of Orissa. In the present chapter the various anthropometric characters of the Bathudi and Sounti of both sexes and some of the indices derived from them have been analysed and interpreted in terms of their respective variation. The author has reported the results of Anthropometric characters among the Bathudis and Sountis elsewhere [Singh, 1986]. Singh *et. al.* (1968) is consulted for the classifications of various metric characters.

4.1 STATUS

According to Martin's classification (1928) most of the Bathudi and Sounti males and females have preponderance of short stature followed by below medium stature. Above medium and tall statures have low frequency among these people. The Bathudi males and females are comparatively taller then the Sounti males and females in their mean value by about two centimeters. The Bathudi males and females differ in their mean value by about ten centimeters, while the Sounti males and females are found to vary on an average by about eleven centimeters. The Bathudi and Sounti females mean value constitute 93.48 per cent and 92.96 per cent of the Bathudi and Sounti male mean value, respectively. The population and sex variations for stature have been found to differ significantly.

Table 4.1

Mean and other statistical constants of stature (in mms) among the Bathudi and Sounti of both sexes

Population	*Sex*	*N*	*Range*	*Mean*	+- *S.E*	*S.D*	+- *S.E.*	*C.V*	+- *S.E.*
Bathudi	Male	109	1466–1734	1597.33	5.77	60.26	4.08	3.77	0.26
Sounti	Male	106	1471–1712	1578.84	5.14	52.90	3.63	3.35	0.23
Bathudi	Female	110	1365–1611	1493.25	5.12	53.71	3.62	3.60	0.24
Sounti	Female	105	1352–1595	1467.68	4.65	47.66	3.29	3.25	0.22

Table 4.2

Classification of Stature (in mm) of the Bathudi and Sounti of both sexes

Class	*Sex*	*Range*	*Bathudi %*	*Sounti %*
Very short	Male	1300–1499	7.34	8.49
	Female	1210–1399	5.45	8.57
Short	Male	1500–1599	43.12	54.72
	Female	1400–1489	40.91	59.05
Below Medium	Male	1600–1639	24.77	27.36
	Female	1490–1529	30.00	23.81
Medium	Male	1640–1669	17.43	7.55
	Female	1530–1559	11.82	6.67
Above medium	Male	1670–1699	3.67	0.94
	Female	1560–1589	9.09	0.95
Tall	Male	1700–1799	3.67	0.94
	Female	1590–1679	2.73	0.95

N = Bathudi male = 109; Sounti male = 106; Bathudi female = 110, and Sounti female = 105.

4.2 SITTING HEIGHT

Trends observed in the distribution of stature are also reflected in the distribution of sitting height. Bathudis have higher mean value than of the Sountis. The variations in the mean value of the Bathudi males and females, the Sounti males and females for the sitting height is 6 centimeters and 5 centimeters respectively. The Bathudi and Sounti males, Bathudi and Sounti females have been found to differ for mean value of sitting height by about 3 centimeters and over 2 centimeters respectively. When the mean value of sitting height between the males and females are compared it is observed that the Bathudi and Sounti females constitute 92.33 per cent and 93.94 per cent of the Bathudi and Sounti male means, respectively. Both the populations and sexes have been found to differ significantly for their mean value of sitting height.

Table 4.3

Mean and other statistical constants of Sitting height (mm) among the Bathudi and Sounti of both sexes

Population	*Sex*	*N*	*Range*	*Mean*	*+- S.E*	*S.D*	*+- S.E.*	*C.V*	*+- S.E.*
Bathudi	Male	109	748–871	812.41	2.71	28.31	1.92	3.48	0.24
Sounti	Male	106	693–888	783.62	3.87	39.87	2.74	5.09	0.35
Bathudi	Female	110	678–827	750.13	2.47	25.91	1.75	3.45	0.23
Sounti	Female	105	663–794	736.17	2.58	26.42	1.82	3.59	0.25

Table 4.4

Mean and other Statistical constants of Relative sitting height index of the Bathudi and Sounti of both sexes

Population	*Sex*	*N*	*Range*	*Mean*	*+- S.E*	*S.D*	*+- S.E.*	*C.V*	*+- S.E.*
Bathudi	Male	109	47.67–54.64	50.88	0.13	1.34	0.09	2.63	0.18
Sounti	Male	106	32.62–54.25	49.65	0.23	2.32	0.16	4.67	0.32
Bathudi	Female	110	45.94–53.65	50.25	0.15	1.60	0.11	3.18	0.21
Sounti	Female	105	45.40–53.55	50.17	0.14	1.47	0.10	2.94	0.20

4.3 FOOT LENGTH

The mean value of Bathudi males and Sounti males have been found to differ over 6 millimeters, while the Bathudi and Sounti females do not have such variation in their mean value for foot length. The males have higher mean value by about 2 centimeters than that of the females of both the populations. The Bathudi and Sounti females constitute 90.90% and 83.50% of their respective male mean value of foot length. Except the Bathudi and Sounti females, the differences between both the populations and sexes are found to be statistically significant.

Table 4.5

Means and other statistical constants of foot length (in mm) among the Bathudi and Sounti of both the sexes

Population	*Sex*	*N*	*Range*	*Mean*	*+- S.E*	*S.D*	*+- S.E.*	*C.V*	*+- S.E.*
Bathudi	Male	109	203–274	238.21	1.07	11.21	0.76	4.71	0.32
Sounti	Male	106	201–261	231.46	1.13	1.59	0.80	5.01	0.34
Bathudi	Female	110	187–242	216.54	1.04	10.94	0.74	5.05	0.34
Sounti	Female	105	194–238	216.42	0.83	8.51	0.59	3.93	0.27

4.4 FOOT BREADTH

The mean value of foot breadth has been found to vary by about 2 millimeters among the Bathudi and Sounti males, and Bathudi and Sounti females. The Bathudi males have higher value of mean for foot breadth than that of the Sounti males. The Sounti females have been found to have broader foot than the Bathudi females. The Bathudi females constitute 84.63 per cent of the Bathudi males mean value, while the Sounti females constitute 88.60 per cent of the Sounti male mean value. The Bathudi and Sounti males and females thus show significant population differences.

Table 4.6

Mean and other Statistical constants of foot breadth (in mm) of the Bathudi and Sounti of both sexes

Population	*Sex*	*N*	*Range*	*Mean*	*+- S.E*	*S.D*	*+- S.E.*	*C.V*	*+- S.E.*
Bathudi	Male	109	74–108	90.50	0.56	5.85	0.40	6.47	0.44
Sounti	Male	106	67–109	88.75	0.75	7.69	0.53	8.66	0.59
Bathudi	Female	110	58–95	76.59	0.72	7.54	0.51	9.84	0.66
Sounti	Female	105	62–92	78.63	0.60	6.12	0.42	7.78	0.54

4.5 CHEST GIRTH

Male individuals of both the populations have been measured for chest girth, Mean value of the Sounti chest girth exceed by about 7 millimeters than that of the Bathudi. Greater intra-group variations have been found among the male of the Bathudi as compared to that of the Sounti males. Inspite of these differences, the Bathudi males and Sounti males are homogenous in respect of chest girth.

Table 4.7

Mean and other statistical constants of chest girth (in mm) among the Bathudi and Sounti males

Population	*Sex*	*N*	*Range*	*Mean*	*+- S.E*	*S.D*	*+- S.E.*	*C.V*	*+- S.E.*
Bathudi	Male	109	645–894	770.49	3.98	41.59	2.82	5.40	0.37
Sounti	Male	106	687–878	777.30	3.47	35.76	2.46	4.60	0.32

4.6 WEIGHT

Sounti males and females have been found with higher mean value of weight as compared to the Bathudi males and females. The differences are of about one kilogram each. The male individuals have greater mean value of their weight than the females of both the populations. The differences in the male and female series is about 6 kilograms. There is no significant population difference but the sex difference among both the population are found to be significant.

Table 4.8

Mean and other statistical constants of weight (kgms) among the Bathudi and Sounti of both sexes

Population	*Sex*	*N*	*Range (Kgms)*	*Mean*	*+- S.E*	*S.D*	*+- S.E.*	*C.V*	*+- S.E.*
Bathudi	Male	109	38–60	45.89	0.50	5.21	0.35	11.35	0.77
Sounti	Male	106	35–60	46.96	0.52	5.39	0.37	11.48	0.79
Bathudi	Female	110	30–64	39.86	0.53	5.61	0.38	14.07	0.95
Sounti	Female	105	27–53	40.25	0.50	5.13	0.35	12.74	0.88

HEAD AND FACE MEASUREMENTS AND SOME OF THEIR INDICES

4.7 HEAD LENGTH

Bathudis have higher mean value of head length as compared to the Sountis. This difference in the mean is slightly over 3 millimeters. The males and females of the Bathudi and Sounti differ over 8 millimeters each for the means of head length. The Bathudi and Sounti of both sexes, according to Lebzelter and Saller's classification (Saller 1930) can be put under the category of long heads. The Bathudi and Sounti female mean value constitute 95.43 per cent and 95.38 per cent of the Bathudi and Sounti male mean value respectively. The Bathudi and Sounti are found to differ significantly both sex-wise and population-wise for the head length.

Table 4.9

Mean and other statistical constants of head length (in mm) among the Bathudi and Sounti of both sexes

Population	*Sex*	*N*	*Range*	*Mean*	*+- S.E*	*S.D*	*+- S.E.*	*C.V*	*+- S.E.*
Bathudi	Male	109	176–201	188.32	0.56	5.81	0.39	3.08	0.21
Sounti	Male	106	157–197	185.08	0.62	6.40	0.44	3.46	0.24
Bathudi	Female	110	159–197	179.72	0.62	6.54	0.44	3.64	0.25
Sounti	Female	105	159–194	176.53	0.60	6.17	0.43	3.49	0.24

4.8 HEAD BREADTH

Bathudis have broader heads than that of the Sountis. Mean value of the Bathudi and Sounti males differ over 1 millimeter, while the Bathudi and Sounti females have these variations over 3 millimeters. The males and females of the Bathudi and Sounti exceed in their mean value of head breadth over 4 millimeters and 6 millimeters respectively. Both the sexes of Bathudi and Sounti, according to Lebzelter and Saller's classification (Saller, 1930), belong to narrow category of head breadth. Bathudi and Sounti female mean value constitute 97.11 percent and 95.78 per cent of the male means, respectively. Bathudis have been found with more intra-group variations as compared to the Sountis. There are significant sex and population differences among the Bathudi and Sounti.

Table 4.10

Mean and other statistical constants of head breadth (in mm) among Bathudi and Sounti of both sexes

Population	*Sex*	*N*	*Range*	*Mean*	*+- S.E*	*S.D*	*+- S.E.*	*C.V*	*+- S.E.*
Bathudi	Male	109	131–158	138.95	0.50	5.23	0.35	3.76	0.25
Sounti	Male	106	121–148	137.12	0.50	5.12	0.35	3.73	0.26
Bathudi	Female	110	122–146	134.94	0.52	5.41	0.36	4.01	0.27
Sounti	Female	105	123–145	131.34	0.44	4.52	0.31	3.44	0.24

4.9 CEPHALIC INDEX

As the females have relatively higher head breadth when compared to their head length then the males among the Bathudi and Sounti tribes, the mean value of cephalic index has been found to be greater among the females than that of the males of both the populations. According to Saller's classification (1930) the Bathudi and Sounti males and females have been characterised by dolichocephalic heads followed by mesocephalic heads. Sountis have higher frequency of dolichocephalic heads than the Bathudis. Bathudi males are found to have greater occurrence of dolichocephalic heads than their females. However, the Sounti males have less frequency of dolichocephalic heads as compared to the Sounti females. Brachycephalic heads have been reported, though its frequency is low among the Bathudi males ((5.50%) and Sounti males (3.77%), Sounti females are devoid of brachycephalic head, while only 1.82 per cent Bathudi females are characterised by them. Sounti males and Bathudi females have been found with greater mean value of Cephalic index as compared to the Bathudi males and Sounti females, respectively.

Table 4.11

Mean and other statistical constants of cephalic index among the Bathudi and Sounti of both sexes

Population	*Sex*	*N*	*Range*	*Mean*	*+- S.E*	*S.D*	*+- S.E.*	*C.V*	*+- S.E.*
Bathudi	Male	109	65.83–88.27	73.86	0.36	3.80	0.26	5.14	0.35
Sounti	Male	106	64.36–92.36	74.18	0.38	3.87	0.27	5.22	0.36
Bathudi	Female	110	68.39–84.28	75.14	0.30	3.19	0.22	4.25	0.29
Sounti	Female	105	68.25–86.50	74.47	0.32	3.28	0.38	4.40	0.30

Table 4.12

Classification of Cephalic index of the Bathudi and Sounti males and females

Class	*Sex*	*Range*	*Bathudi %*	*Sounti %*
Hyperdolichocephalic	Male	x–70.9	21.10	16.04
	Female	x–71.9	20.00	22.86
Dolichocephalic	Male	71.0–75.9	56.88	58.49
	Female	72.0–76.9	50.00	60.00
Mesocephalic	Male	76.0–80.9	16.51	21.70
	Female	77.0–81.9	28.18	15.24
Brachycephalic	Male	81.0–85.4	3.67	1.89
	Female	82.0–86.4	1.82	—
Hyperbrachycephalic	Male	85.5–90.9	1.83	1.88
	Female	86.5–91.9	—	—

4.10 HEAD CIRCUMFERENCE

The Bathudi and Sounti males, the Bathudi and Sounti females have been found to vary in means for head circumference over 6 millimeters and 7 millimeters respectively. The Bathudi males and females, Sounti males and females vary in means over 9 millimeters and 11 millimeters, respectively. The mean value of head circumference among the Bathudi and Sounti females is 98.24 per cent and 97.76 per cent of the mean value of their respective males. These differences have been found to be statistically significant for both the sexes and populations.

Table 4.13

Mean and other statistical constants of head circumsference (in mm) among the Bathudi and Sounti of both sexes

Population	*Sex*	*N*	*Range*	*Mean*	*+- S.E*	*S.D*	*+- S.E.*	*C.V*	*+- S.E.*
Bathudi	Male	109	498–598	532.73	1.43	14.96	1.01	2.81	0.19
Sounti	Male	106	497–561	527.73	1.34	13.81	0.95	2.62	0.18
Bathudi	Female	110	479–564	523.33	1.35	14.16	0.95	2.71	0.18
Sounti	Female	105	478–556	515.89	1.85	18.92	1.31	3.67	0.25

4.11 AURICULAR HEIGHT

The male and female series of the Bathudi and Sounti tribes have been found to differ in mean value for auricular height over 1 millimeter. But the Bathudi and Sounti, when compared according to their sexes, it is observed that their mean value differ over 6 millimeters for each population. Sountis have been found to show greater intragroup variability than the Bathudi. Mean value of the Bathudis and Sounti females are 95.14 per cent and 94.98 per cent of the Bathudi and Sounti male mean value, respectively. Males and females of both the populations differ significantly for the auricular height. There is no significant population difference among the Bathudi and Sounti for this character.

Table 4.14

Mean and other statistical constants of Auricular height (in mm) among the Bathudi and Sounti of both sexes

Population	*Sex*	*N*	*Range*	*Mean*	*+- S.E*	*S.D*	*+- S.E.*	*C.V*	*+- S.E.*
Bathudi	Male	109	109–133	120.32	0.49	5.09	0.34	4.23	0.29
Sounti	Male	106	107–131	119.11	0.51	5.30	0.36	4.45	0.31
Bathudi	Female	110	104–131	114.47	0.44	4.57	0.31	3.99	0.27
Sounti	Female	105	99–127	113.13	0.45	4.64	0.32	4.10	0.28

4.12 LENGTH HEIGHT INDEX

The Sountis have more mean value of length height index by about one unit than the Bathudi male and female series. The Bathudi males and Sounti males have slightly more mean value than the Bathudi females and Sounti females, respectively. According to Saller's classification (1930), both the populations have the maximum frequency of Hypsicephal category. Males have been found to show more intra group variations for this index as compared to the females of both the populations.

Table 4.15

Mean and other statistical constants of length height index among the Bathudi and Sounti of both sexes

Population	*Sex*	*N*	*Range*	*Mean*	*+- S.E*	*S.D*	*+- S.E.*	*C.V*	*+- S.E.*
Bathudi	Male	109	57.07–71.51	63.93	0.27	2.86	0.19	4.47	0.30
Sounti	Male	106	57.22–77.71	64.39	0.32	3.31	0.23	5.14	0.35
Bathudi	Female	110	57.22–71.70	63.74	0.25	2.65	0.18	4.15	0.28
Sounti	Female	105	57.38–72.39	64.13	0.27	2.77	0.19	4.32	0.30

4.13 BREADTH HEIGHT INDEX

The Bathudis have less mean value for Breadth height index than the Sountis. Similar trend was also observed in case of length height index between these populations. The Bathudi and Sounti of male series have been found with higher mean value for breadth height index than the Bathudi and Sounti of female series, respectively. Similarly, the male series have more intra group variations as compared to the female series for this index.

Table 4.16

Mean and other statistical constants of breadth- height index among the Bathudi and Sounti of both sexes

Population	*Sex*	*N*	*Range*	*Mean*	*+- S.E*	*S.D*	*+- S.E.*	*C.V*	*+- S.E.*
Bathudi	Male	109	76.97–96.38	86.68	0.41	4.23	0.29	4.88	0.33
Sounti	Male	106	76.98–97.60	86.95	0.42	4.30	0.30	4.94	0.34
Bathudi	Female	110	74.65–95.16	84.92	0.36	3.76	0.25	4.42	0.30
Sounti	Female	105	74.48–93.70	86.20	0.38	3.85	0.27	4.46	0.31

4.14 MINIMUM FRONTAL BREADTH

Sounti males and Bathudi females have been found with higher mean value of minimum frontal breadth than the Bathudi males and Sounti females, respectively. The males have broader foreheads than the females. Among Bathudis and Sountis the six variations for this character in their mean value is over 2 millimeters and 3 millimeters, respectively. The mean value of the Bathudi and Sounti

Table 4.17

Mean and other statistical constants of Minimum frontal breadth (in mm) among the Bathudi and Sounti of both sexes

Population	*Sex*	*N*	*Range*	*Mean*	*+- S.E*	*S.D*	*S.E.*	*C.V*	*+- S.E.*
Bathudi	Male	109	92–112	103.42	0.36	3.78	0.26	3.65	0.25
Sounti	Male	106	95–116	103.68	0.40	4.13	0.28	3.98	0.27
Bathudi	Female	110	92–113	101.37	0.38	4.01	0.27	3.96	0.27
Sounti	Female	105	92–112	100.26	0.36	3.67	0.25	3.66	0.25

females constitute 98.02 per cent and 96.70 per cent of the Bathudi and Sounti male mean values, respectively. Bathudi and Sounti males and females have significant differences for the minimum frontal breadth both sex-wise and population-wise except the Bathudi and Sounti female series.

4.15 BIZYGOMATIC BREADTH

The male series and female series of Bathudi and Sounti have been found to vary in respect of mean values for Bizygomatic breadth over 1 millimeter and 2 millimeters, respectively. The males have more mean value than the females as observed in case of other characters. The sex variations among the Bathudi and Sounti are over 5 millimeters and 7 millimeters, respectively. According to Lebzelter and Saller's classification (Saller, 1930), males and females of the Bathudi and Sounti would belong to narrow and very narrow categories, respectively, for this measurement. The Bathudi and Sounti female mean value constitute 95.60 per cent and 94.49 per cent of their respective male mean value. Except the male series the differences between both the sexes, and female series of the Bathudi and Sounti are observed to be significant.

Table 4.18

Mean and other statistical constants of Bizygomatic breadth (in mm) among the Bathudi and Sounti of both sexes

Population	*Sex*	*N*	*Range*	*Mean*	*+- S.E*	*S.D*	*+- S.E.*	*C.V*	*+- S.E.*
Bathudi	Male	109	119–143	132.48	0.43	4.53	0.31	3.42	0.23
Sounti	Male	106	120–144	131.30	0.45	4.63	0.32	3.53	0.24
Bathudi	Female	110	116–138	126.65	0.51	5.39	0.36	4.25	0.29
Sounti	Female	105	112–132	124.06	0.41	4.19	0.29	3.38	0.23

4.16 BIGONIAL BREADTH

Bathudis have greater mean value than the Sountis. Among the male and female series the differences are of about one millimeter. While both sexes among the Bathudi and Sounti have variation over 4 millimeters. Bathudis have greater intra group variability as compared to the Sountis for the Bigonial breadth. The Bathudi and Sounti mean value constitute 95.38 percent and 95.14 per cent of the Bathudi and Sounti male mean value. There are no significant differences between the male and female series of the Bathudi and Sounti. But the males and females of both populations show significant sex differences.

Table 4.19

Mean and other statistical constants of Bigonial breadth (in mm) among the Bathudi and Sounti of both sexes

Population	*Sex*	*N*	*Range*	*Mean*	*+- S.E*	*S.D*	*+- S.E.*	*C.V*	*+- S.E.*
Bathudi	Male	109	91–118	101.65	0.47	4.93	0.33	4.85	0.33
Sounti	Male	106	91–115	100.93	0.46	4.72	0.32	4.68	0.32
Bathudi	Female	110	88–111	96.95	0.46	4.80	0.32	4.95	0.33
Sounti	Female	105	96–109	96.02	0.45	4.59	0.32	4.78	0.33

4.17 TOTAL FACIAL HEIGHT

The male series and female series have been found to show differences in mean value for total facial height of about 1 millimeter and 3 millimeters, respectively. The sex variations of both these populations have been observed to be over 8 millimeters and 11 millimeters among the Bathudis and Sountis, respectively. There are significant population and sex differences for total facial

Table 4.20

Mean and other statistical constants of Total facial height (in mm) among the Bathudi and Sounti of both sexes

Population	*Sex*	*N*	*Range*	*Mean*	*+- S.E*	*S.D*	*+- S.E.*	*C.V*	*+- S.E.*
Bathudi	Male	109	94–127	107.71	0.58	6.04	0.41	5.61	0.38
Sounti	Male	106	94–122	107.14	0.58	6.01	0.41	5.61	0.39
Bathudi	Female	110	85–116	98.91	0.60	6.26	0.42	6.33	0.43
Sounti	Female	105	81–107	95.86	0.58	5.90	0.41	6.15	0.42

height except the Bathudi males and Sounti males. The Bathudi and Sounti female mean value of total facial height constitute 91.83 per cent and 89.47 per cent of the Bathudi and Sounti male mean value respectively.

4.18 TOTAL FACIAL INDEX

Sounti males and Bathudi females have greater mean value for total facial index than the Bathudi males and Sounti females respectively. The mean value place the Bathudi males and Sounti of both sexes under Euryprosopic class of Martin and Saller's classification (Saller 1930). Bathudi females have higher frequency of long faces than the Bathudi males. But among the Sountis the males have been found with more long faces than their females.

Table 4.21

Mean and other statistical constants of Total facial index among the Bathudi and Sounti of both sexes

Population	*Sex*	*N*	*Range*	*Mean*	*+- S.E*	*S.D*	*+- S.E.*	*C.V*	*+- S.E.*
Bathudi	Male	109	71.22–96.21	81.36	0.46	4.77	0.32	5.87	0.40
Sounti	Male	106	69.63–96.06	81.68	0.49	5.05	0.35	6.18	0.42
Bathudi	Female	110	66.41–94.17	78.20	0.53	5.58	0.38	7.14	0.48
Sounti	Female	105	64.29–91.45	77.34	0.50	5.09	0.35	6.58	0.45

Table 4.22

Classification of Total facial index among the Bathudi and Sounti of both sexes

Class	*Sex*	*Range*	*Bathudi %*	*Sounti %*
Hyperprosopic	Male	x–78.9	32.12	34.91
	Female	x–76.9	41.82	48.57
Euryprosopic	Male	79.0–83.9	37.61	35.85
	Female	77.0–80.9	30.91	29.52
Mesoprosopic	Male	84.0–87.9	23.85	18.87
	Female	81.0–84.9	17.27	15.24

(Contd.)

(Contd.)

Leptoprosopic	Male	88.0–92.9	5.50	8.49
	Female	85.0–89.9	6.36	5.72
Hyperleptoprosopic	Male	93.0–x	0.92	1.88
	Female	90.0–x	3.64	0.95

N=BM=109, SM=106, BF=110, SF=105.

4.19 UPPER FACIAL HEIGHT

The Bathudi have longer upper faces as compared to the Sountis. These differences are over 2 millimeters among both the males and females. The males of both populations have longer upper faces than that of the females. The variations among the Bathudi and Sounti have been found in their mean value over 3 millimeters each. Accordingly the Bathudi and Sounti female means of upper facial height constitute 94.78 per cent and 94.27 per cent of the Bathudi and Sounti and Sounti male means respectively. There are significant differences for the upper facial height of both the populations and sexes.

Table 4.23

Mean and other statistical constants for Upper facial height (in mm) among the Bathudi and Sounti of both sexes

Population	*Sex*	*N*	*Range*	*Mean*	*+- S.E*	*S.D*	*+- S.E.*	*C.V*	*+- S.E.*
Bathudi	Male	109	53–77	64.04	0.43	4.49	0.30	7.01	0.47
Sounti	Male	106	52–70	61.45	0.42	4.31	0.30	7.01	0.48
Bathudi	Female	110	51–73	60.70	0.43	4.47	0.30	7.37	0.50
Sounti	Female	105	49–67	57.93	0.39	4.02	0.28	6.93	0.48

4.20 UPPER FACIAL INDEX

Sounti males and females have been characterised by the higher frequency of short and wider upper faces as compared to the Bathudi males and females. While the females of both the populations have preponderance of short and wider faces as compared to the males, the mean value of male series and female series of both the populations differ by a unit, while males and females of the Bathudi and Sounti population have variations in their mean value over one unit for the upper facial index. According to Martin and Saller's classification (Saller, 1930), the Bathudi and Sounti of both the sexes have been found to be characterised by Euryen faces except the Bathudi males, who have higher frequency of Mesen faces. Bathudi males and females have greater frequency of lepten type of upper faces as compared to the Sounti males and females. Frequency of lepten upper faces has been found to be greater among the females as compared to the males of both the groups.

Table 4.24

Mean and other statistical constants for Upper facial index among the Bathudi and Sounti of both sexes

Population	*Sex*	*N*	*Range*	*Mean*	*+- S.E*	*S.D*	*+- S.E.*	*C.V*	*+- S.E.*
Bathudi	Male	109	40.00–58.33	48.36	0.32	3.38	0.23	7.00	0.47
Sounti	Male	106	39.10–57.94	46.85	0.34	3.49	0.24	7.45	0.51
Bathudi	Female	110	39.84–62.14	48.00	0.39	4.09	0.28	8.52	0.57
Sounti	Female	105	39.06–54.87	46.73	0.33	3.35	0.23	7.16	0.49

Table 4.25

Classification of Upper facial index among the Bathudi and Sounti of both sexes

Sl. No.	*Class*	*Range*	*Males*		*Females*	
			Bathudi N=109 %	*Sounti N = 110 %*	*Bathudi N= 110*	*Sounti N = 105 %*
1.	Hypereuryen	x–42.9	4.59	15.10	8.18	10.48
2.	Euryen	43.0–47.9	39.45	45.28	45.45	51.43
3.	Mesen	48.0–52.9	45.87	35.85	34.54	33.33
4.	Lepten	53.0–56.9	9.17	2.83	9.10	4.76
5.	Hyperlepten	57.0–x	0.92	0.94	2.73	—

4.21 NASAL HEIGHT

The Bathudis have longer noses as compared to the Sountis. The male series and female series of both the populations have been found to differ over 2 millimeters in their mean value. The males have longer noses than the females. The Bathudi and Sounti of both the sexes show variations over 3 millimeters in their mean value for nasal length. The Bathudi and Sounti female mean value constitute 93.44 per cent and 90.69 per cent of their male mean value, respectively. There are significant differences in the nasal height among the Bathudi and Sounti of both sexes.

Table 4.26

Mean and other statistical constants of Nasal height (in mm) among the Bathudi and Sounti of both sexes

Population	*Sex*	*N*	*Range*	*Mean*	*+- S.E*	*S.D*	*+- S.E.*	*C.V*	*+- S.E.*
Bathudi	Male	109	39–53	46.33	0.31	3.19	0.22	6.89	0.47
Sounti	Male	106	35–54	44.21	0.35	3.61	0.25	8.17	0.54
Bathudi	Female	110	38–54	43–37	0.27	2.80	0.19	6.44	0.43
Sounti	Female	105	34–48	41–08	0.29	3.01	0.21	7.33	0.51

4.22 NASAL BREADTH

The variation for nasal breadth are small as this is a small measurement. Sounti males have been found with broader noses than the Bathudi males. Similarly, the Bathudi females are characterised by the higher frequency of broad noses as compared to the Sounti females. The difference in the mean value of nasal breadth in the male series and female series is less than a millimeter. According to Schlaginhaufen's classification of nasal breadth, the males and females have been found with higher frequency of 'above medium' and 'medium' categories, respectively. The mean value of the Bathudi and Sounti females constitute 93.44 per cent and 90.69 per cent of their male mean value, respectively. The Bathudi males and females as well as the Sounti males and females show variations in their mean value of nasal breadth over 2 millimeters and 3 millimeters, respectively. There are no significant population differences but the sex differences for the nasal breadth are found to be significant for both the populations.

Table 4.27

Mean and other statistical constants of Nasal breadth (in mm) among the Bathudi and Sounti of both sexes

Population	*Sex*	*N*	*Range*	*Mean*	*+- S.E*	*S.D*	*+- S.E.*	*C.V*	*+- S.E.*
Bathudi	Male	109	31–44	36.87	0.27	2.80	0.19	7.59	0.51
Sounti	Male	106	31–43	37–38	0.28	2.86	0.20	7.64	0.52
Bathudi	Female	110	28–43	34.45	0.27	2.86	0.19	8.31	0.56
Sounti	Female	105	27–41	33.90	0.24	2.48	0.17	7.31	0.56

4.23 NASAL INDEX

The Bathudis have sharp noses as compared to the Sountis, who have broader noses. The females have been found with sharper noses than the males. The differences among the male series and female series for mean value is over 3 and 5 units respectively. The mean value of Bathudi males and females show differences for less than a unit, while as the Sounti males and females have differences over 2 units. According to Martin and Saller's

Table 4.28

Mean and other statistical constants of Nasal Index among the Bathudi and Sounti of both sexes

Population	*Sex*	*N*	*Range*	*Mean*	*+- S.E*	*S.D*	*+- S.E.*	*C.V*	*+- S.E.*
Bathudi	Male	109	63.46–97.73	79.89	0.71	7.38	0.50	9.24	0.63
Sounti	Male	106	63.46–110.53	85.11	0.92	9.51	0.65	11.17	0.77
Bathudi	Female	110	59.57–102.56	79.75	0.78	8.16	0.55	10.24	0.69
Sounti	Female	105	67.39–105.56	82.89	0.77	7.92	0.55	9.55	0.66

classification (1930), Bathudi males and females as well as the Sounti females have preponderance of Mesorrhine followed by Platyrrhine nose types. But the Sounti males are characterised by Platyrrhine followed by Mesorrhine noses. Leptorrhine noses are found in low frequency among the Sountis as compared to the Bathudi.

Table 4.29

Classification of Nasal index among the Bathudi and Sounti of both sexes

Sl. No.	*Class*	*Range*	*Males*		*Females*	
			Bathudi N=109 %	*Sounti N = 110 %*	*Bathudi N= 110 %*	*Sounti N = 105 %*
1.	Leptorrhine	55.0–69.9	10.09	5.66	10.00	5.71
2.	Mesorrhine	70.0–84.9	61.47	43.40	62.73	59.05
3.	Platyrrhine	85.0–99.9	28.44	45.28	26.36	30.48
4.	Hyper platyrrhine	100.0–x	—	5.66	0.91	4.76

4.24 NASAL DEPTH

It is the smallest of all the measurements and the extent of variation in the present series has been found to be still smaller. Bathudis have more mean value than the Sountis. Similarly, the males of both the populations are characterised by greater mean value as compared to the females. The differences in the male series is less than one millimeter but among the female series the variations are more than a millimeter. The Bathudi males and females,

Table 4.30

Mean and other statistical constants of Nasal depth (in mm) among the Bathudi and Sounti of both sexes

Population	*Sex*	*N*	*Range*	*Mean*	*+- S.E*	*S.D*	*+- S.E.*	*C.V*	*+- S.E.*
Bathudi	Male	109	13–25	17.79	0.21	2.23	0.15	12.55	0.85
Sounti	Male	106	13–22	17.29	0.18	1.86	0.30	10.77	0.74
Bathudi	Female	110	12–20	16.85	0.15	1.53	0.10	9.07	0.61
Sounti	Female	105	11–22	15.40	0.21	2.11	0.15	13.75	0.95

the Sounti males and females have greater mean differences by about a millimeter and 2 millimeters, respectively. The mean value of Bathudi and Sounti females constitute 94.72 per cent and 89.07 per cent of their male mean value respectively. Bathudi and Sounti of both sexes differ significantly except the males series of these two populations.

5

FINGER AND PALM DERMATOGLYPHIC CHARACTERS

DERMATOGLYPHICS RESEARCHES IN INDIA

Biswas (1936, 1968), Sarkar (1954), Mavalwala (1963), Sharma (1964), Das (1959), Mukherjee (1962, 1963, 1965, 1975), Mukherjee and Chakraborty (1964), Chakraborty and Mukherjee (1961, 1962, 1964), Sreevastava and Shukla (1966), Dutta and Gupta (1967), Sharma (1968 and 1970), Mukherjee *et. al.* (1980), Malhotra (1980) and many others contributed for the dermatoglyphics research in India. To what extent such characters can throw light to our assessment of the relative positions of the Bathudi and Sounti in the ethnic milieu of the region, finger and palmar dermatoglyphic characters of the two tribes are discussed here. The results of finger and palmar dermatoglyphics among the Bathudis and Sountis have been reported elsewhere by the author [Singh, 1984].

QUALITATIVE CHARACTERS

5.1 FINGER PATTERNS

The finger print patterns have been identified as whorls, ulnar loops, radial loops, tented arches and plain arches following the method of Galton (1892), Mukherjee (1967), and Penrose (1968).

5.1.1 Sex and Population Differences

Bathudi and Sounti of both sexes are characterised by the highest frequency of loops followed by whorls and arches. Whorl/loop index shows maximum value among the Bathudi males and females. The Sounti females have minimum value of whorl/loop index. The Bathudi males and females have been found with highest frequency of whorls, while the Sounti males and females have preponderance of loops. Arch/whorl index has highest frequency among the females as compared to the males, while the Sounti have its greater value than the Bathudis. The females are characterised by the higher frequency of ulnar loops and arches and lower frequency of whorls and radial loops.

Table 5.1

Percentage frequency of pattern types and indices among the Bathudi and Sounti for both sexes

Pattern type	*Percentage frequency of patterns*			
	Males		*Females*	
	Bathudi N=1095*	*Sounti* N=1076**	*Bathudi* N=1086**	*Sounti* N=1060
Whorls	48.58	40.99	43.46	40.19
Ulnar loops	47.12	54.92	51.84	55.28
Radial loops	1.83	1.21	0.92	0.94
Total loops	48.95	56.13	52.76	56.22
Tented arches	0.64	0.37	0.28	0.28
Plain arches	1.83	2.51	3.50	3.31
Total arches	2.47	2.88	3.78	3.59

Indices	*Males*		*Females*	
	Bathudi N′ = 110	*Sounti* N′ = 108	*Bathudi* N′ = 109	*Sounti* N′ = 106
Pattern intensity index	14.68	13.85	13.97	13.69
Furuhata index (W/L x 100)	99.25	73.01	82.37	71.48
Dankmeijer index (A/W x 100)	5.07	7.03	8.69	8.92

N = Number of fingers, N′ = Number of individuals.

* Less five fingers.

** Less four fingers.

5.1.2 Bimanual Differences

Whorls occur more frequently on the right hands of males and left hands of the females. Contrary to this, loops have been found to be predominant on left hands of males and the right hands of the females. Radial loops and arches have preponderance on the left hands.

Table 5.2

Bimanual and sex differences in the percentage frequency of pattern types of the Bathudi and Sounti

Pattern Type	*Side*	*Males*		*Females*	
		Bathudi %	*Sounti* %	*Bathudi* %	*Sounti* %
Whorls	Right	50.36	41.63	40.77	37.93
	Left	46.80	40.33	46.14	42.45
Ulnar loops	Right	46.71	55.20	56.09	59.43
	Left	47.53	54.64	47.61	51.13
Radial loops	Right	0.73	0.74	0.55	0.56
	Left	2.92	1.67	1.28	1.32
Total loops	Right	47.44	55.95	56.64	59.99
	Left	50.45	56.32	48.89	52.45
Tented arches	Right	0.55	0.19	—	0.19
	Left	0.73	0.55	0.56	0.38
Plain arches	Right	1.64	2.23	2.59	1.89
	Left	2.01	2.79	4.41	4.72
Total arches	Right	2.19	2.42	2.59	2.08
	Left	2.75	3.35	4.97	5.10

5.1.3 Digital Differences

Whorls are frequently found on digit IV and I. While ulnar loops have preponderance on digit III among the males and digit V of the females of both populations, radial loops and arches are reported mostly on the II digit in the present series.

Table 5.3

Percentage frequency of patterns on different digits of the Bathudi males and females

Pattern types		*Percentage frequency on digits*				
	Sex	*I*	*II*	*III*	*IV*	*V*
Whorls	Male	60.00	45.91	32.73	66.51	37.79
	Female	52.75	45.11	33.48	60.55	25.34
Ulnar loops	Male	35.45	39.55	66.36	33.02	61.29
	Female	43.58	45.11	62.38	36.24	71.89
Radial loops	Male	0.91	7.27	0.45	—	0.46
	Female	0.46	3.72	—	0.46	—
Total loops	Male	36.36	46.82	66.81	33.02	61.75
	Female	44.04	48.84	62.38	36.70	71.89
Plain arches	Male	3.64	4.09	0.46	—	0.46
	Female	3.21	5.11	4.13	2.75	2.59
Tented arches	Male	—	3.18	—	0.46	—
	Female	—	0.93	—	—	0.46
Total arches	Male	3.64	7.27	0.46	0.46	0.46
	Female	3.21	6.04	4.13	2.75	2.76

Table 5.4

Percentage frequency of patterns on different digits of the Sounti males and females

Pattern types	*Sex*	*Percentage frequency on digits* I	II	III	IV	V
Whorls	Male	45.37	39.53	27.11	61.11	31.45
	Female	44.34	41.04	26.41	63.21	25.94
Ulnar loops	Male	50.93	49.30	69.44	37.50	67.61
	Female	49.53	48.58	70.76	34.90	72.64
Radial loops	Male	0.46	5.12	—	0.46	—
	Female	0.47	4.72	—	0.47	—
Total loops	Male	51.39	54.42	69.44	37.96	67.61
	Female	50.00	52.36	70.76	35.37	72.64
Plain arches	Male	3.24	5.58	1.85	0.93	0.94
	Female	5.66	6.13	2.83	0.95	0.95
Tented arches	Male	—	0.46	1.39	—	—
	Female	—	0.47	—	0.47	0.47
Total arches	Male	3.24	6.05	3.24	0.93	0.94
	Female	5.66	6.60	2.83	1.42	1.42

5.2 MONOMORPHIC HANDS

Whorls are reported to be most frequency on right hands, while ulnar loops have preponderance on the left hands. Males have higher frequency of whorls but the females are found to have more occurrence of ulnar loops. The Bathudi females are characterised by the maximum frequency of monomorphic hands

(25.68%) followed by the Bathudi males (26.46%). Low frequency of monomorphic hands are found among the Sounti females (21.70%). No significant difference has been found for monomorphic hands between the right and left hands, between males and females, and between Bathudis and Sountis.

5.3 SYMMETRICAL PATTERNS ON ALL HOMOLOGOUS FINGERS

Bathudi females (31.19%) followed by Sounti males (29.63%) have the highest frequency of hands with symmetrical patterns on all homologous fingers. Lowest frequency of symmetrical patterns on all the homologous fingers has been observed among the Sounti females (18.87%).

Table 5.5

Frequency of individuals with symmetrical patterns on all homologous fingers of the Bathudi and Sounti of both sexes

Frequency of individuals with symmetrical pattern			
Male		*Females*	
Bathudi	*Sounti*	*Bathudi*	*Sounti*
N = 110	N = 108	N = 109	N = 106
28 (25.45)	32 (29.63)	34 (31.19)	20 (18.87)

Figures in brackets are percentages.

5.4 QUALITATIVE TRAITS ON PALM

5.4.1 Bimanual Differences

Hypothenar, II and III interdigital patterns have higher frequency on the right hand, while the thenar/Ist and IVth interdigital patterns have preponderance on the left hands of the males. II and III interdigital patterns are more frequent on the right hand, and Hypothenar, I and IV, interdigital patterns occur in higher frequency on left hands of the females.

Table 5.6

Percentage frequency of pattern on right, left and both hands of males of the Bathudi and Sounti

Palmar area	*Population*	*Percentage frequency of patterns*			
		Right hand	*Left hand*	*Right hand*	*Left hand*
Hypothenar	Bathudi	25.45	21.82	47.27	23.64
	Sounti	25.93	20.37	46.30	23.15
1st Interdigital	Bathudi	3.66	18.18	21.82	10.91
	Sounti	1.85	6.48	8.33	4.17
IInd Interdigital	Bathudi	4.55	0.91	5.46	2.73
	Sounti	8.34	6.48	14.82	7.41
IIIrd Interdigital	Bathudi	60.91	42.73	103.64	51.82
	Sounti	36.11	24.07	60.18	30.09
IV Interndigital	Bathudi	42.73	55.46	98.19	49.09
	Sounti	62.96	72.22	135.18	67.59

N = Bathudi = 110.
N = Sounti = 108.

5.4.2 Sex and Population Differences

The Bathudi females have greater frequency of Hypothenar, I and III interdigital patterns, while the Sounti females are characterised by the abundance of II and IV interdigital pattern on the palm. But the Bathudi males has been found with higher frequency of I, II and III interdigital pattern than Sounti males. Bathudi males and females are characterised by the higher frequency of Hypothenar, I and IV interdigital patterns, when compared to the Sounti males and females.

Table 5.7

Percentage frequency of pattern on right, left and both hands of females of the Bathudi and Sounti

Palmar area	*Population*	*Percentage frequency of patterns*			
		Right hand	*Left hand*	*Right hand*	*Left hand*
Hypothenar	Bathudi	24.77	28.44	53.21	26.60
	Sounti	20.75	27.35	48.10	24.05

(Contd.)

(Contd.)

1st Interdigital	Bathudi	0.92	4.59	5.51	2.75
	Sounti	—	2.83	2.83	1.41
IInd Interdigital	Bathudi	1.83	0.92	2.75	1.37
	Sounti	3.77	0.94	4.71	2.35
IIIrd Interdigital	Bathudi	50.45	35.77	86.22	43.11
	Sounti	42.45	21.69	64.14	32.07
IV Interdigital	Bathudi	53.21	57.79	111.00	55.50
	Sounti	66.98	75.47	142.46	71.23

N = Bathudi = 109.
N = Sounti = 106.

5.5 AXIAL TRIRADII 't'

5.5.1 Bimanual Differences

Right and left hands are characterised by the highest frequency of axial triradius 't' among the Bathudi and Sounti of both sexes followed by the preponderance of axial triradius t. But the right and left hands do not show significant differences for the distribution of axial tripadii t.

5.5.2 Sex and population differences

Bathudi and Sounti males and females have preponderance of axial triradii t' followed by axial triradii t. Sounti males and females have been found with the highest frequency of axial triradius t'. Similarly, Bathudi and Sounti males have more frequency of axial triradius t as compared to the Bathudi and Sounti females. Axial triradii tt"t" and tt't' have been observed among the Sounti females only. Axial triradii t show significant differences for their distribution between both the sexes and populations.

Table 5.8

Percentage frequency of axial triradii 't' on the right and left hands among the Bathudi and Sounti of both sexes

Sl. No.	*Axial triradii*	*Sex*	*Bathudi*			*Sounti*		
			Right	*Left*	*Right + Left*	*Right*	*Left*	*Right + Left*
1.	t	M	37.27	33.63	35.45	39.81	36.11	37.96
		F	37.61	32.11	34.86	39.25	24.53	26.89

(Contd.)

(Contd.)

2.	t′	M	44.55	46.36	45.46	50.00	52.78	51.39
		F	45.87	46.79	46.33	52.83	56.60	54.71
3.	tt′	M	6.36	10.00	8.18	6.48	5.56	6.02
		F	10.09	11.01	10.55	11.32	9.43	10.37
4.	tt′	M	—	1.82	0.91	0.93	1.85	1.39
		F	2.75	—	1.38	0.94	-	0.48
5.	t′t′	M	4.55	2.73	3.64	—	0.92	0.46
		F	0.92	1.83	1.38	—	0.95	0.48
6.	tt″	M	1.82	2.73	2.27	—	0.93	0.46
		F	0.92	3.67	2.29	0.94	3.77	2.35
7.	t′t″	M	5.45	2.73	4.09	2.78	1.85	2.39
		F	1.84	4.59	3.21	4.72	2.83	3.77
8.	tt″t″	M	—	—	—	—	—	—
		F	—	—	—	—	0.95	0.48
9.	tt′t″	M	—	—	—	—	—	—
		F	—	—	—	—	0.94	0.47

N = Bathudi Male = 111　　Sounti Male = 108
Bathudi Female = 109　　Sounti Female = 106

5.6 MAIN LINE B ENDING

Bimanual differences

Right hand is found to have largest frequency of main line B ending at position 7, while on the left hands it terminates most frequently at position 5′ or 5″, with a single exception of the Sounti males. The bilaterial variations in the present series are not found to be significant.

Sex and Population differences

Main line B termination has preponderance at position 7 among the males and females of both the populations. The males are characterised by the highest frequency of main line B ending at position 7 and 5″, while the females have been found with B line ending at position 7 and 5″ The Bathudi and Sounti show significant differences for the termination of main line B for both the sexes and populations.

Table 5.9

Percentage frequency of main line B ending on the right and left hands among the Bathudi and Sounti of both the sexes

B line ending	*Sex*	*Bathudi*			*Sounti*		
		Right hand	*Left hand*	*Right + left hands*	*Right hand*	*Left hand*	*Right + left hands*
3	M	—	0.91	0.45	—	—	—
	F	—	0.92	0.46	—	1.89	0.94
5′	M	12.73	14.54	13.64	24.07	25.93	25.00
	F	23.85	30.27	27.06	37.73	38.68	38.21
5″	M	23.64	32.73	28.18	25.93	24.07	25.00
	F	20.18	18.35	19.27	15.74	21.70	18.87
6	M	8.18	19.09	13.64	3.70	3.70	3.70
	F	5.51	13.76	9.63	—	4.71	2.36
7	M	48.18	31.82	40.00	43.52	44.45	43.98
	F	49.54	36.70	43.12	44.34	33.02	38.68
8	M	5.45	—	2.73	2.78	1.85	2.32
	F	—	—	—	1.89	—	0.94
9	M	1.82	0.91	1.36	—	—	—
	F	0.92	—	0.46	—	—	—

N = Bathudi Male = 110 Bathudi Female = 109
Sounti Male = 108 Sounti Female = 106

5.7 ENDING OF C LINE TYPE

Bimanual differences

Right hand has the preponderance of radial ending of C line, while left hand has been found with higher frequency of ulnar followed by proximal and absent types of C line endings among the present series, with a single exception of the Bathudi females among whom radial and ulnar ending of C lines occur in higher frequency on the right hand and the proximal and absent endings. are more frequent on the left hands. Significant Bimanual difference has been found in the present series except the Bathudi females.

Sex and Population differences

Bathudi males and females have been observed with more frequent radial C line endings, while the Sounti males and females have abundances of ulnar C line endings. Radial C line endings are found more frequently among the males and ulnar C line endings are observed more among the females. Bathudi and Sounti are homogenous for the distribution of C line endings of both the sexes but differ significantly for its distribution in respect of both the population.

Table 5.10

Percentage frequency distribution of ending of C line type on right and left hands among the Bathudi and Sounti of both the sexes

C line ending	*Sex*	*Bathudi*			*Sounti*		
		Right hand	*Left hand*	*Right + left hands*	*Right hand*	*Left hand*	*Right + left hands*
Radial	M	60.91	42.73	51.82	40.74	23.15	31.94
	F	49.54	34.86	42.20	42.45	19.81	31.13
Ulnar	M	29.09	40.00	34.54	44.44	49.07	46.76
	F	35.78	44.04	39.91	52.83	56.60	54.72
Proximal	M	7.27	11.82	9.55	7.41	16.67	12.04
	F	5.51	11.01	8.26	2.83	9.44	6.13
Absent	M	2.73	5.45	4.09	7.41	11.11	9.26
	F	9.17	10.09	9.63	1.89	14.15	8.02

Number of Undividuals = Bathudi Male = 110 Bathudi Female = 109.
Sounti Male = 108 Sounti Female = 106.

5.8 MAIN LINE D ENDING

Right hand is characterised by the highest frequency of D line ending at position 11, while the left hand has preponderance of D line ending at position 10, followed by 11, 9, 8 and 7. D line ending is absent on the left hand of Sounti females, among about one per cent individuals. There are no significant bimanual differences for D line ending. Bathudi and Sounti females have higher frequency of D line ending at position 11 and 7. But the Bathudi and Sounti males have frequent D line ending at position 10, 9 and 8. Among Bathudi males and females D line ending have been observed with more occurrence at position 11, 10 and 8, and at position 9 and 7 among the Sounti males and females. Bathudi males and females differ significantly for the distribution of D line ending both sex-wise and population wise.

Table 5.11

Percentage frequency distribution of main line D endings on right and left hands of the Bathudi and Sounti males and females

D line ending	*Sex*	*Bathudi*			*Sounti*		
		Right hand	*Left hand*	*Right + left hands*	*Right hand*	*Left hand*	*Right + left hands*
11	M	53.64	23.64	38.64	36.11	26.85	31.38
	F	46.79	33.03	39.91	40.57	32.07	36.32
10	M	10.90	28.18	19.54	11.11	11.11	11.11
	F	8.26	13.76	11.01	2.83	5.66	4.24
9	M	13.64	20.00	16.82	21.30	25.00	23.15
	F	12.84	12.84	12.85	16.04	16.04	16.04
8	M	2.73	3.64	3.18	1.85	2.78	2.32
	F	2.75	0.92	1.83	—	—	—
7	M	19.09	24.54	21.82	29.63	33.33	31.48
	F	29.36	39.45	34.40	40.56	46.23	43.40
Absent	M	—	—	—	—	0.93	0.46
	F	—	—	—	—	—	—

Table 5.12

Mean and other statistical constants of ridge counts on both the hands and sexes of the Bathudi

Digit	Sex	Right hand				Left hand				Right + Left hand			
		Mean	*± S.E.*	*S.D. ±*	*S.E.*	*Mean*	*± S.E.*	*S.D. ±*	*S.E.*	*Mean*	*± S.E.*	*S.D. ±*	*S.E.*
I	M	18.08	0.62	6.51	0.44	15.95	0.54	5.71	0.38	17.02	0.42	6.20	0.30
	F	15.80	0.55	5.75	0.39	13.98	0.46	4.77	0.32	14.89	0.36	5.35	0.26
II	M	11.47	0.56	5.85	0.39	10.84	0.56	5.86	0.40	11.15	0.39	5.85	0.28
	F	12.01[2]	0.46	4.73	0.32	10.39	0.57[1]	5.88	0.40	11.20[3]	0.37	5.39	0.26
III	M	12.90	0.46	4.88	0.33	13.16	0.43	4.54	0.31	13.03	0.32	4.70	0.22
	F	12.86	0.45	4.66	0.32	12.34	0.49	5.51	0.37	12.60	0.33	4.89	0.23
IV	M	15.15[2]	0.46	4.79	0.32	14.94	0.44	4.62	0.31	15.04[1]	0.32	4.69	0.22
	F	15.04	0.51	5.31	0.36	13.78	0.53	4.80	0.32	14.41	0.37	5.44	0.26
V	M	13.02[1]	0.39	4.04	0.27	12.63[2]	0.37	3.88	0.26	12.82[3]	0.27	3.95	0.19
	F	12.31[1]	0.47	4.84	0.33	11.97	0.46	5.37	0.16	12.41[1]	0.33	4.81	0.23
Total	M	14.12	0.25	5.75	0.17	13.51	0.23	5.28	0.16	13.82	0.17	5.52	0.12
	F	13.61	0.23	5.29	0.16	12.50	0.16	5.36	0.11	13.05	0.16	5.36	0.11

N = Bathudi males = 110 individuals ; Bathudi females = 109 individuals

1 = One finger less ; 2 = Two fingers less ; 3 = Three fingers less.

Table 5.13

Mean and other statistical constants of ridge counts on both the hands and sexes of the Sounti

Digit	Sex	Right hand				Left hand				Right + Left hand			
		Mean	*± S.E.*	*S.D. ±*	*S.E.*	*Mean*	*± S.E.*	*S.D. ±*	*S.E.*	*Mean*	*± S.E.*	*S.D. ±*	*S.E.*
I	M	16.58	0.62	6.41	0.44	14.19	0.56	5.81	0.40	15.39	0.42	6.22	0.30
	F	15.22	0.62	6.41	0.44	13.30	0.59	6.09	0.42	14.26	0.43	6.31	0.31
II	M	11.04[1]	0.51	5.24	0.36	10.64	0.49	5.07	0.35	10.84[1]	0.35	5.15	0.25
	F	10.59	0.48	4.98	0.34	10.70	0.49	5.01	0.34	10.65	0.34	4.98	0.24
III	M	12.76	0.44	4.56	0.31	12.44	0.48	4.99	0.34	12.60	0.32	4.77	0.23
	F	12.36	0.42	4.28	0.29	12.25	0.48	4.93	0.34	12.31	0.32	4.61	0.22
IV	M	14.39	0.44	4.56	0.31	13.58	0.45	4.65	0.32	13.99	0.31	4.61	0.22
	F	14.25	0.44	4.55	0.31	14.00	0.44	4.54	0.31	14.13	0.31	4.54	0.22
V	M	12.80[1]	0.44	4.59	0.31	12.08[1]	0.42	4.39	0.30	12.44[2]	0.31	4.49	0.22
	F	12.34	0.38	3.95	0.27	11.10	0.41	4.26	0.29	11.72	0.28	4.15	0.20
Total	M	13.52	0.23	5.43	0.17	12.59	0.22	5.14	0.16	13.05	0.16	5.31	0.11
	F	12.95	0.22	5.15	0.16	12.87	0.22	5.14	0.16	12.61	0.16	5.16	0.11

N = Sounti male = 108 ; Sounti females = 106
1 = One finger less ; 2 = Two fingers less.

QUANTITATIVE CHARACTERS ON FINGERS

5.9 FINGER RIDGE COUNTS

Digital Difference

Digit I, IV, III, V and II of both hands, sexes, and populations of the present study can be arranged in decreasing orders of their means for ridge counts.

5.9.2 Bimanual Differences

Right hands of both sexes and populations have preponderence of mean ridge counts on all the digits as compared to the left hands, except the III digits of the Bathudi males and II digit of Sounti females.

5.9.3 Sex and Population Differences

The Bathudi males have higher mean value of ridge counts on all the digits as compared to the Bathudi females, except the II digit. Similarly the Sounti females have been found with lower mean value of ridge counts as compared to the Sounti males on all the digits except IV digit. The males of both the populations have been characterised by higher mean value of ridge counts on all the digits as compared to their females. The Bathudi males and females, Bathudi males and Sounti males differ significantly. While the Sounti males and females and Sounti and Bathudi females do not differ significantly for the finger ridge counts.

5.10 TOTAL FINGER RIDGE COUNTS

The values of the total finger ridge count have been found in the present series which ranges from 0 to 219. The Bathudi males and females are characterised by the higher mean values of total finger ridge count as compared to the Sounti males and females. The males of the Bathudi and Sounti tribes have greater means for it, than the females of those two populations. Each distribution of the total finger ridge counts is characterised by the presence of several peaks. The Bathudi females and Sounti males have greater intra group variability as compared to the Sounti females, who show minimum variability. The variations between both the sexes and populations do not differ significantly. Distribution of male and female series of total finger ridge count are presented in Fig. 5.1 and 5.2.

5.11 TOTAL NUMBER OF TRIRADII ON FINGERS

The total number of triradii per individual vary from 3 to 20 in the present series. Bathudi males and Bathudi females have higher mean value then the Sounti males and females. The Sounti females have the least mean value for it. Higher mean value has been observed among the males than females of both the populations. Several peaks, as observed in case of total finger ridge counts, are also present. The Bathudi and Sounti show homogeneity for the distribution of total number of triradii on finger, both sex-wise and populationwise. Distribution of total number of finger triradii among both the sexes of Bathudi and Sounti are shown in Fig. 5.3 to 5.4.

QUANTITATIVE TRAITS ON PALM

5.12 TRIRADII ON PALM

Most of the individuals have more than ten number of palmar triradii in the present series. The mean value of triradii on palm has been found to be highest among the Bathudi and Sounti males as compared to the females of these two populations. The Bathudi and Sounti females are closer in their distribution than the males of these two populations. The Bathudi males and females only differ significantly for the number of triradii on palm, while the Sounti males and females, Bathudi and Sounti males and Bathudi and Sounti females are found to be homogeneous. Distribution of palmar triradii is presented according to sexwise in Fig. 5.5 and 5.6 of the Bathudi and Sounti tribe.

5.13 a-b RIDGE COUNT

Right hands have slightly more mean value of a-b ridge counts then the left hands, except among the Bathudi females. The differences between the right and left hands in the distribution of a-b ridge count are not statistically significant. Mean value of a-b ridge count have been found to be maximum among the Sounti females followed by Bathudi males. The Sounti males have minimum mean of a-b ridge counts. Bathudi males and females have large intra-group variations for a-b ridge counts as compared to the Sounti males and females. Similarly, males have higher intra-group variability then the females. There are statistically significant differences for a-b ridge count for both the sexes and populations. The sexwise distribution of a-b ridge count among the Bathudi and Sounti is shown in fig. 5.7 and 5.8.

5.14 MAIN LINE INDEX

In the present series main line index ranges from 8 to 24 and the mean value of right hand for main line index have been observed to be higher. Except the Bathudi females, right hand has greater intra-group variations. Among males the mean value have been found to be higher. Similarly, Bathudis of both sexes have preponderance of mean value of main line index then the Sountis. There are no significant sex variations but the population differences are significant. Distribution of main line index is presented according to both the sexes in figure 5.9 and 5.10.

6

GENETIC VARIATIONS

6.1 Classification of human population is mostly made on the basis of skin, hair and eye colour, stature and shape of head. It is well known that with one or two possible exceptions such characters are not inherited according to any simple rule and geneticists have shown that in case of certain these characters, the qualitative expression of any one of them is controlled by a number of independent gene. Further, most of the measurable features of human beings bear the mark not only of heredity but in varying degree of environment and specially of the state of nutrition during early life. But in case of blood factors we are dealing with unitary and obviously discontinuous characters which are determined at conception and remain fixed for life, that is to say, with separate effects of individual genes which are sharply differentiated from one another and which are therefore less subject to presonal errors of observation than are many of the characters hitherto used. It appears likely that natural selection due to the external environment is slight for most of the blood factors (though certain combination of blood groups are known to be intrinsically unstable) (Mourant, 1976).

6.2 SEROLOGICAL RESEARCH IN INDIA

Blood group studies in India were primarily aimed at taxonomic and geographical classification of its people. Regional differences in genetic characters within same endogamous groups have been observed by Sarkar (1954, 1959), Mukherjee and Chakravarti (1964) and Basu (1969). Das *et. al.* (1966) and Ahmad (1975) investigated 7 tribal populations of Koraput for Serogenetical investigation, Kumar (1975) discussed the intra affiliations of the Munda populations of Bihar. Bhattacharyya (1954, 1957) Mitra (1936), and Chakraborty (1965) investigated the populations for serological study from North Eastern India. Tiwari (1952), Srivastava (1965) and Kumar (1968) studied some populations of Uttar Pradesh, and many others studies have been conducted to know the genetic composition of various Indian populations.

6.3 The Bathudi and Sounti unrelated males and females were the subjects for blood samples discussed in this study. The samples were collected from different villages of Karanjia sub- division of Mayurbhanj district (Table 6.1). Test were performed strictly according to Standard procedures (Weiner, 1943, Race and Sanger, 1954). Positive and negative controls were included in each series of tests. Weak positive and negatives were tested again as and when felt necessary.

Table 6.1

Places of investigations for serological study among the Bathudis and Sountis

Sl. No.	*Population*	*Sample*	*Tehsil*	*Villages*			
1.	Bathudi	219	Karanjia	1.	Ankura	2.	Bisipur
				3.	Batpalsa	4.	Beuria
				5.	Barandiha,	6.	Kalakad
				7.	Kenjra	8.	Nihangandi
				9.	Patbil	10.	Padampur
				11.	Rasamtla	12.	Tato
2.	Sounti	220	Karanjia	1.	Baliposi	2.	Chamakpur
				3.	Digdhar	4.	Guhaldiha
				5.	Bandifuta	6.	Khamdiha
				7.	Khuntaposi	8.	Mituani
					and		
				9.	Nihangondi		

6.4 The percentage frequencies of ABO blood groups with subtypes of A blood group among the Bathudis and Sountis are shown in Table 6.2.

Table 6.2

Phenotypic frequencies of ABO blood groups among the Bathudis and Sountis

Population		*N*	*Blood groups*					
			O	A_1	A_2	*B*	A_1B	A_2B
Bathudis	f	219	37	59	0	86	32	5
	%		16.9	26.9	0.0	39.3	14.6	2.3
Sounti	f	220	33	56	3	83	36	9
	%		15.0	25.5	1.4	37.7	16.4	4.1

Bathudis : The male and female data of the Bathudis has been pooled as there are no statistically significant differences. The pooled data show the highest frequency of B (39.3%) followed by A_1 (26.9%) and O (16.9%) blood groups among the Bathudi.

Sountis : The male and female data of the Sountis is pooled for A_1A_2 BO blood groups as there are no statistically significant sex differences. The Sountis are characterised by the highest frequency B (37.7%) followed by A_1 (25.5%) and O (15.0%) blood groups A_2 occurs in low frequency (1.4%).

6.5 GOODNESS OF FIT TEST

X^2 test has been performed to see the Goodness of fit among the present sample.

The pooled male and female samples of the Bathudi and Sounti for ABO blood groups were subjected to Goodness of fit test. X^2 value for Sountis at 1 degree of freedom is 2.342 at probability level $0.20 > P > 0.10$. While among the Bathudis the X^2 value at 1 degree of freedom is 0.011 at probability level $0.95 > P > 0.90$. Both the Bathudi and Sounti samples of present data indicate a satisfactory agreement with the known mode of inheritance. A_1 and A_2, A_1 B and A_2B have been merged for Chi square test. Results of Goodness of fit are presented in table 6.5.

Table 6.3

Goodness of fit test among the Bathudis and Sountis

Sl. No.	Population	N	d.f.	X2 value	Probability level
1.	Bathudis	219	1	0.011	0.95>P>0.90
2.	Sountis	220	1	2.342	0.20>P>0.10

A_1A_2 and A_1 B and A_2 B have been merged for Chi square test.

The gene frequencies P_1, P_2, q and r have been estimated by the maximum likelihood method as suggested by Bhale (1970) and presented in Table 6.4.

Table 6.4

Gene frequencies of A_1A_2 BO blood groups among the Bathudis and Sountis

Population	N	P_1	± S.e	P_2	± S.e	q	± S.e	r	± S.e
Bathudis	219	0.2362	0.01510	0.0151	0.00470	0.3382	0.01770	0.4105	0.01932
Sountis	220	0.2366	0.01662	0.0363	0.00713	0.3508	0.01810	0.3763	0.01974

From the pooled male and female gene frequencies of the Bathudi and Sounti tribes it may be observed that increase of gene frequency r among the Bathudi (0.0342) is at the cost of q (0.0126), P_2 (0.0212) and P_1 (0.0004) gene among the Sounti.

6.7 HOMOGENEITY TEST FOR INTER POPULATION DIFFERENCES

Bathudi and Sounti tribes are found to have maximum frequency of B blood group, B blood group frequency among the Bathudi and Sounti being 39.3% and 37.7% respectively. Next in order is A_1 blood group having more or less equal frequencies among both the populations. A_2 has not been observed among the Bathudi but Sounti have 1.4% A_2 frequency. According to Mourant *et. al.* (1958) this is an indication of the presence of the Caucasoid element in the population but at the same time the allele responsible for A_2 is rare among the tribal populations of India (Mourant, 1954). O blood group occurs in slightly higher frequency among the Bathudi (16.9%) than Sounti (15.0%). It may be further observed that the Bathudi have higher frequency of B, A_1 and O blood groups, while Sounti have been observed with greater frequency of A_2, A_1B and A_2B blood groups.

The order of phenotype frequencies of the Bathudi and Sounti is B > A > O. Homogeneity test have been performed to ascertain whether the variations between the phenotypic frequencies of both the population are statistically significant. Chi square value 0.542 at 3 degree of freedom indicates ($0.95 > P > 0.90$) that there are no significant variations for the ABO blood groups of the Bathudi and Sounti tribes. The results of A_1A_2BO blood groups of the Bathudi and Sounti have already been reported elsewhere by the author [Singh, 1989].

6.8 COLOUR BLINDNESS

The incidence of colour-blindness among the Bathudis and Sountis have already been reported elsewhere by the author [Singh, 1987].

A sample of unrelated male students from various schools of Karanjia sub-division was collected for colour blindness with the help of Ishihara chart. 154 Bathudi and 114 Sounti males were tested for colour blindness. Incidence of colour blindness among the Bathudi and Sounti is presented in Table 6.5.

Table 6.5

Incidence of colour blindness among the Bathudi and Sounti males of Mayurbhanj district

Population	*Number tested*	*Protan*		*Deutan*		*Percentage of colour blindness*
		Strong %	*Mild %*	*Strong %*	*Mild %*	
Bathudi	154	0.65	—	1.30	0.65	2.60
Sounti	114	0.88	—	3.51	—	4.39

The proportion of deutan (green) to protans (red) colour blinds among Bathudi is 3:1 and 4:1 among the Sounti. The Sounti have higher incidence (4.39%) of colour blind as compared to the Bathudi (2.60%). No significant difference between the Bathudi and Sounti for colour blindness have been observed by the X^2 value 0.212 at 1 d.f. (probability level $0.70 > P > 0.50$).

7

GROUP CHARACTERS

In the present chapter an attempt has been made to highlight group characteristics of the present series of data gathered from the Bathudi and Sounti of both the sexes. Chatterjee (1929) was among the first to make observations about the physical characteristics of the Bathudis while describing their marriage ceremonies. According to him "Physically, they are long headed, of medium stature of stout build, deep brown colour and medium nose which is slightly depressed at the root and of stiff hair and brown eyes". After that no major systematic attempt was made to study the somatoscopic observations of the Bathudis. As there are sex variations for the various Morphological and genetical parameters, the males and females of both the populations will be treated separately for highlighting the group characteristics.

7.1 BATHUDI MALES

(*a*) *Anthroposcopic observations*

Most of the Bathudi males work as labourers. Few have their own agricultural fields. Sometimes they engage themselves as labourers in the fields of others. This phenomenon is likely to have its reflections upon their Anthroposcopic characteristics. About 30 per cent of the males are light brown in skin complexion, while rest of them are brown to dark brown in skin colour. They have black, straight or low wavy head hairs with medium texture of thick quantity. Beard and moustach are mostly scanty. Eyes are black in colour. The Mongoloid type of eye fold is absent and when present only its traces have been found. Eyes are mostly straight with yellow sclera and medium eye brow thickness. Traces of supra orbital ridges have been observed. Forehead has medium height and slope. Face has concave nose with medium nasal depression and horizontal or upward nasal septum. Lips are mostly medium or thick. Face has slight alveolar prognathism. Body musculature is mostly athletic. The joint percentage frequencies of Skin colour, Hair colour and Eye colour (Fig. 7.1), chin, pip thickness and nasal depression (Fig. 7.2) & eye brows, beared & moustaches (Fig.7.3) further support and strengthens these observations.

(*b*) *Anthropometric measurements*

Bathudi males are characterised by short stature with mean value 1597 milimeters. Values of sitting height and the relative sitting height of the Bathudi males are more than that of the Sounti males. Similarity, the foot length and breadth of the Bathudi have also shown higher values than that of the Sounti males. Weight and Chest circumsference of the Bathudi males are comparatively less than that of the Sounti males in the mean values. Head length and head breadth mean values have been observed greater among the Bathudi males than among the Sounti males resulting in long and narrow dolichocephalic heads. Head circumsference and auricular height of the Bathudi have also greater mean value in the series than of the Sounti. Face has more or less similar mean value of minimum forehead breadth. Bizygomatic breadth of the Bathudi indicate narrow faces. Total facial height and upper facial height and their respective indices also shows that the Bathudis have short and relatively wider faces. Mean nasal breadth is 36.87 milimeters and is less than that of the Sounti males. The Bathudi males have relatively longer noses which has resulted in comparatively low nasal index. Most of them have mesorrhine nose with greater value of mean nasal depth. Noses of the Bathudi males are comparative sharper. About 10 per cent of the individuals have leptorrhine nose.

(*c*) *Finger and Palmar dermatoglyphics*

Bathudi males are characterised by 48.95 per cent loops, 48.58 per cent whorls, and 2.47 per cent arches on fingers. The Pattern intensity index, Furuhata index and Dankmeijer index are worked out to be 14.68, 99.25 and 5.07 respectively. When the patterns are analysed according to their bimanual distribution among them, it is observed that whorls occur more frequently on the right hand, while the loops and arches have preponderance on left hands. Similarly, when the digitwise distribution of patterns is analysed it is found that digit IV and I have the highest frequency of whorls; total loops is the characteristic feature of III and V digits ; radial loops and arches are mostly found on II digit. Finger ridge counts just like the pattern types occur in higher frequency on the right

Table 7.1

Joint Percentage frequencies of skin, Hair and Eye colours among Bathudi & Sounti & both Sexes

Skin Colour	Hair Colour	Eye colour: Black				Dark Brown				Brown				Light Brown				Total			
		BM	BF	SM	SF	BM	BF	SM	SF	BM	BF	SM	SF	BM	BF	SM	SF	BM	BF	SM	SF
Blackish Brown	BL	0.92	0.91	1.89	—	10.09	9.09	23.58	7.62	4.59	—	4.71	0.95	0.92	—	—	—	16.51	10.00	30.18	8.57
	DB	—	—	1.89	—	4.59	1.82	3.77	1.90	3.67	0.91	—	0.96	—	—	—	—	8.26	2.73	5.66	2.36
	RB	—	—	—	—	0.92	—	—	—	—	—	—	—	1.83	—	—	—	2.75	—	—	—
Dark Redish Brown	BL	—	—	—	—	7.32	0.91	1.89	2.86	1.83	—	—	—	1.83	—	—	—	11.01	0.91	1.89	2.86
	DB	—	—	—	—	3.67	—	—	0.96	1.83	—	—	0.95	0.92	—	—	—	6.42	—	—	1.91
	RB	—	—	—	—	0.92	—	—	—	—	—	—	—	—	—	—	—	0.92	—	—	—
Reddish Brown	BL	1.83	—	—	—	3.67	5.45	7.55	18.09	—	2.72	3.77	14.29	0.92	—	—	—	6.42	8.18	11.32	32.38
	DB	—	—	—	—	0.92	—	2.83	2.86	—	—	—	1.90	3.67	—	—	—	4.59	—	2.83	4.76
	RB	—	—	—	—	—	—	—	—	—	—	—	—	—	—	—	—	—	—	—	—
Brown	BL	1.83	—	—	—	4.59	31.81	21.70	14.29	0.92	11.81	2.83	14.28	0.92	1.82	0.94	—	8.26	45.45	25.48	28.57
	DB	—	1.82	—	—	4.59	2.73	8.49	7.62	0.92	2.73	2.83	2.86	0.92	1.82	—	—	6.42	7.28	11.32	10.48
	RB	—	—	—	—	—	—	—	—	—	—	—	—	—	—	—	—	—	—	—	—
Light Brown	BL	—	—	—	—	8.26	11.82	2.83	1.90	2.75	0.91	1.89	3.81	3.67	1.82	—	—	14.68	14.54	4.72	5.71
	DB	0.92	—	—	—	2.75	2.73	4.72	1.90	4.59	2.73	1.89	—	4.59	1.82	—	—	12.84	9.09	6.60	1.90
	RB	—	—	—	—	—	—	—	—	—	—	—	—	—	—	—	—	—	—	—	—
Olive Yellow	BL	—	—	—	—	—	—	—	—	—	—	—	—	—	—	—	—	—	—	—	—
	DB	—	—	—	—	—	—	—	—	—	—	—	—	0.92	—	—	—	0.92	—	—	—
	RB	—	—	—	—	—	—	—	—	—	—	—	—	—	—	—	—	—	—	—	—
Yellowish	BL	—	—	—	—	—	—	—	—	—	—	—	—	—	—	—	—	—	—	—	—
	DB	—	—	—	—	—	—	—	—	—	1.82	—	—	—	—	—	—	—	1.32	—	—
	RB	—	—	—	—	—	—	—	—	—	—	—	—	—	—	—	—	—	—	—	—
Total	BL	4.58	0.91	1.89	—	33.94	59.09	57.54	44.76	10.09	17.27	13.21	33.33	8.27	3.64	0.94	—	56.89	80.91	73.58	78.09
	DB	0.92	3.64	1.89	—	16.51	7.27	19.81	15.24	11.01	6.36	4.72	6.67	11.01	1.82	—	—	39.94	19.09	26.42	21.91
	RB	—	—	—	—	1.83	—	—	—	—	—	—	—	1.83	—	—	—	3.67	—	—	—
Total		5.50	4.55	3.78	—	52.29	66.36	77.36	60.00	21.10	23.63	17.92	40.00	21.10	5.46	0.94	—	100.00	100.00	100.00	100.00

BM = Bathudi male; SM = Sounti male; BL = Black; DB = Dark Brown; RB = Reddish Brown;
BF = Bathudi Female; SF = Sounti Female;

Table 7.2

Joint percentage frequencies of Chin, Lip thickness and Nasal depression among Bathudi and Sounti of both Sexes

		Nasal Depression															
	Lip Thickness	Shallow				Medium				Deep				Total			
Chin		BM	BF	SM	SF	BM	BF	SM	SF	BM	BF	SM	SF	BM	BF	SM	SF
Receeding	Thin	0.92	—	—	—	—	—	—	—	—	—	—	—	0.92	—	—	—
	Medium	—	0.91	—	—	—	—	—	—	—	—	—	—	—	0.91	—	—
	Thick	—	—	—	—	0.92	—	1.89	—	0.92	—	—	—	1.84	—	1.89	—
	Total	0.92	0.91	—	—	0.92	—	1.89	—	0.92	—	—	—	2.76	0.91	1.89	—
Oval	Thin	—	6.36	—	2.86	2.75	6.37	0.94	1.90	—	—	—	—	2.75	12.73	0.94	4.76
	Medium	5.51	1.82	1.89	12.38	10.09	10.91	5.66	14.29	3.67	—	—	—	19.27	12.73	7.55	26.67
	Thick	1.83	0.91	8.49	0.95	5.51	5.45	4.72	3.81	3.67	0.91	—	—	11.01	7.27	12.20	4.76
	Total	7.34	9.09	10.37	16.19	8.35	22.73	11.32	20.00	7.34	0.91	—	—	33.03	32.73	21.69	36.19
Round	Thin	0.92	1.82	—	2.86	0.92	6.36	0.94	—	0.92	—	—	—	2.75	8.18	0.94	2.86
	Medium	9.34	10.91	5.66	38.09	11.00	38.18	12.26	10.48	10.09	—	—	—	28.44	49.29	17.92	48.57
	Thick	4.59	1.82	14.15	8.57	13.26	5.45	36.80	3.81	5.50	0.91	0.94	—	23.85	18.18	51.89	12.38
	Total	12.84	14.54	19.81	49.52	25.68	50.00	50.00	14.29	16.51	0.91	0.94	—	55.04	65.45	70.76	63.81
Square	Thin	0.92	—	—	—	—	—	—	—	—	—	—	—	0.92	—	—	—
	Medium	2.75	—	0.94	—	—	—	1.89	—	1.83	—	—	—	4.58	—	2.83	—
	Thick	1.83	—	1.89	—	1.83	0.91	0.94	—	—	—	—	—	3.67	0.91	2.83	—
	Total	5.51	—	2.83	—	1.83	0.91	2.83	—	1.83	—	—	—	9.17	0.91	5.66	—
Total	Thin	2.75	8.18	—	5.71	3.67	12.73	1.89	1.90	0.92	—	—	—	7.34	20.91	1.89	7.62
	Medium	15.60	13.63	8.49	50.48	21.11	49.09	19.81	24.76	15.60	—	—	—	52.29	62.73	28.30	75.24
	Thick	8.26	2.73	24.53	9.52	22.01	11.82	44.34	7.63	10.07	1.82	0.94	—	40.37	16.36	69.81	17.14
	Total	26.61	24.54	33.02	65.71	46.79	73.64	66.04	34.29	26.60	1.82	0.94	—	100.00	100.00	100.00	100.00

BM = Bathudi male, BF = Bathudi female, SM = Sounti male SF = Sounti female

Table 7.3

Joint percentage frequencies of Eye brows, Beard and Moustaches among the Bathudi and Sounto Males

Eye Brows	*Beard and Moustache*									
	Scanty		*Medium*		*Thick*		*Absent*		*Total*	
	BM	*SM*	*BM*	*SM*	*BM*	*SM*	*BM*	*SM*	*BM*	*SM*
Thin	36.70	67.93	5.50	5.66	—	—	1.83	—	44.04	73.59
Medium	42.20	19.81	9.17	6.60	0.92	—	2.75	—	55.04	26.41
Thick	0.92	—	—	—	—	—	—	—	0.92	—
Total	79.82	87.74	14.67	12.26	0.92	—	4.58	—	100.00	100.00

BM = Bathudi male, BF = Bathudi female, SM = Sounti male, SF = Sounti female.

hand as compared to the corresponding digits of the left hand except digit III. Digit I, IV, VII, V and II of both the hands can be arranged in decreasing order of their mean value of ridge counts. 26.36 per cent right hands and 24.54 per cent left hands have monomorphic pattern on its digits. 25.45 per cent Bathudi male individuals have symmetrical pattern on all the fingers on both the hands. On palmar area B line endings has been found more frequently at position 7 on right hands and at 7 or 5" on left hands. The Bathudi males are found to have the highest frequency of radial and ulnar endings of C line on right and left hands respectively. Proximal and absent types of main line C ending also occur frequently on left hands. Radial (51.82%) followed by Ulnar (34.54%) type of C line have preponderance among the Bathudi males. Main line D endings occur more frequent at position 11 on right had at position 10 or 11 on left hands. When right and left hands are considered together for the main line D ending, it is found that termination at position 11 and 7 are most frequent. Mean value of total finger ridge counts have been found to be the highest among the Bathudi male in the present series. Similarly, the number of triradii shows its mean value as 14.68. Mean value of triradii on palm (10.75), a-b ridge counts (72.55) and main line index (17.14) among the Bathudi males have been observed to be greater than the Sounti males. The right hands have equal or more means than the left hands for the number of triradii on palm, a-b ridge counts and main line index among the Bathudi males. Except the main line C type there is no significant bilateral difference for the qualitative character among the Bathudi males. Similarly for 'a-b' ridge count and triradii on palm, there are no bilateral significant variations. The pattern on right and left hands are found to differ significantly for I and III inter digital areas only.

(*d*) *A_1 A_2 Bo blood groups and Colour Vision deficiency*

Blood groups B and A has preponderance among the Bathudis. Incidence of colourblindness is low (2.6%) among the Bathudi males.

7.2 BATHUDI FEMALE

(*a*) *Anthroposcopic Observations*

Bathudi females assist their husbands in the out door field activities. Some of them work in their own fields and the rest of them are employed by the other local agriculturists as daily labourers. Apart from working in the fields sometimes as and when the chances are remote of their employment, they go to the nearly forest for the collection of forest products and wood. Complexion of the Bathudi females is mostly Brown (52.70%) or light brown (25.5%), still 20% of the Bathudi females are characterised by dark skin complexion. But as compared to their male counter parts they are of lighter in skin colour. Head hairs are mostly black (80.9%), straight (91.8%) with medium texture (67.3%), but higher frequency of fine (14.5%) hairs than that of their males, which are thick (72.7%) or medium (27.3%) in quantity. Eyes have been found with preponderance of dark brown (65.4%) or brown (24.6%) complexion, straight eyes with thin (60.0%) or medium (40.0%) eye brows. Epicanthus fold is absent. Supraorbital ridges are mostly imperceptible. Forehead is mostly with medium height and slope. Over 16 per cent (16.4%) of the Bathudi females have been found with straight forehead. Noses are mostly concave with medium (74.5%) or shallow (23.7%) nasal depression. Nasal septum is mostly horizontal. Face is round (56.0%) or oval (37.3%) with slight alveolar prognathism and medium (63.6%) or thin lips (21.8%). Among 14.6 per cent of the Bathudi females thick lips have been observed. Most of the females have proportionate body without fat and perhaps due to the physical labour, they have a athletic body musculature.

(*b*) *Anthropometric measurements*

Stature ranges among the Bathudi females from 1365-1611 millimeter with 1493 millimeters as the mean value. Most Bathudi females have short (40.91%) or below medium (30.0%) stature. The frequency of tall stature is low (2.73%). The heads are narrow in length and breadth, with higher mean cephalic index than the males. Higher cephalic index is due to more head breadth than head length among the Bathudi females. Dolichocephalic and Hyperdolichocephalic heads characterise 50 per cent and 20 per cent individuals respectively, Brachycephalic heads occur in low frequency (1.82%). Bizygomatic breadth indicates narrow faces. Total facial index and upper facial index indicate short and wider faces among the Bathudi females. Hypereuryprosopic (41.82%) followed by euryprosopic (30.91%) faces are more common. Leptoprosopic (6.36%) and Hyperleptoprosopic (3.64%) faces are more common. Leptoprosopic (6.36%) and Hyperleptoprosopic (3.64%) faces are more frequent among the females than males of the Bathudi. Euryen (45.45%) or Mesen (34.54%) upper facial indices have preponderance among the Bathudi females. Nasal length and nasal breadth means are lower than the Bathudi males but the nasal index means are closer to each other. Mesorrhine (62.73%) followed by platyrrhine (26.36%) nose are found in higher frequency. Leptorrhine (10.00%) noses occur in lower frequency.

(*c*) *Finger and Palmar dermatoglyphics*

Finger and palmar dermatoglyphic data among the Bathudi females are characterised as follows :

Loops (52.76%) have preponderance followed by whorls (43.46%) and arches (3.78%). Pattern intensity, Furuhata and Dankmeijer indices among the Bathudi females are 13.97, 82.37 and 8.69 respectively. Whorls have been found more frequently on left hand, while the ulnar loops occur more on right hands. Radial loops and plain arches show preferences for left hand. The trend shown by total loops is similar to that of ulnar loops. When the patterns are studied on the digits, it is found that among Bathudi females whorls are having the highest frequency on digits IV

(60.55%) and I (52.75%), Ulnar loops and total loops are characteristics of V and III digits. Radial loops and arches occur in more intensity on digit II. As observed in case of various pattern on the fingers the mean value of ridge count among the Bathudi females has been found higher on the right hand on all the corresponding digits of left hand. The mean ridge count is maximum on digit I and digits IV, III, V and II can be arranged in decreasing order of their mean ridge counts. About 26 (25.68%) per cent individual have monomorphic pattern on right and left hands with 31.19% individual having symmetrical pattern on both hands. Main line endings is most frequently found at position 11 on right and left hands. Radial (49.54%) ending of main line C type occurs in greater frequency on right hands, while Ulnar (44.04%) proximal (11.01%) and Absent (10.09%) types have their preponderance on left hands. Bathudi females are characterised by Radial (42.20%) endings of C line type followed by ulnar type (39.91%). The B line endings are more frequent on Right hand (49.54%) at position 7 and on left hand at position 7(36.70%) and 5(30.27%). About 43 per cent and 27 per cent B line endings are observed at position 7 and 5′. Axial triradii t′ has been found in higher frequency among the Bathudi females. When the bimanual variations are considered, left hand has the highest frequency of axial triradius t′ (46.79%) and right hand has more frequency of t triradius on right hand (37.61%) as compared to the left hand (32.11%). II, III interdigital patterns have been found in higher frequency on right hands while on Hypothenar, thenar/1st and IV interdigital pattern are having their greater frequency on left hands. Highest frequency of palmar patterns have been present on IV inter digital followed by III interdigital and hypothener areas. The mean value of Total finger ridge count (131.31), triradii on fingers (13.97), triradii on palm (10.28), 'a-b' ridge counts (68.96) and Main line index (16.52) have been observed among the Bathudi females.

There are statistically significant differences between the right and left hands for Bathudi females for patterns on fingers, and patterns on palmar areas at Thenar/I interdigital and III interdigital patterns. The Bimanual difference are not significant for monomorphic patterns, ending of main line D and B and ending of C type, axial triradii, patterns on Hypothenar, II interdigital and IV interdigital palmar areas, 'a-b' ridge counts and triradii on palm.

7.3 SOUNTI MALES

(*a*) *Anthroposcopic Observations*

Sounti males are mostly characterised by Brown (36.8%) and blackish brown (39.8%) skin complexion. Little over 11 per cent individuals are light brown in skin colour. Head hair are predominantly Black (73.6%) or dark brown (26.4%), straight (65.1%) followed by low wavy (34.0%) with medium (89.6%) or coarse (10.4%) texture with mostly thick (52.8%) or medium quantity. Beard and moustaches have scanty growth (87.7%). Eyes are characterised with dark brown (77.4%) or brown colour. (17.9%). Epicanthus fold is mostly absent (97.2%) and only traces have been observed among 2.8 per cent individuals. The straight eye slits have been observed in most of the individuals of present samples. Sclera of eye is yellow (56.6%) or Clear (26.4%) and sometimes dull (17.0%). Eye brows are thin (71.7%) or medium (26.4%) Supra orgital ridges are imperceptible (54.7%) and when present have only the traces (44.4%). Pronounced supra-orbital ridges are found in low frequency (0.9%). Medium height and slope of forehead have been found among the Sounti males. Nose has a medium (66.1%) or shallow (33.0%) depression, with Concave (83.0%) or straight nasal bridge (17.0%) and horizontal or upward nasal septum. Most of the individuals have thick (69.8%) or medium (28.3%) lips. Face is supported by a round (69.8%) or oval chin (22.6%) and slight alveolar prograthism. Body is mostly athletic.

(*b*) *Anthropometric measurements*

Sounti males has 1578 millimeters mean stature with 1471 - 1712 millimeters of range. Mean value of stature put the Sounti males in short category. Most of the Sounti males are characterised by short (54.72%) or below medium (27.36%) stature. Sounti males have more mean value of chest girth and weight as compared to the Bathudi males. The head length and head breadth fall in the narrow categories. Mean value of cephalic index is 74.18 and it fails in the dolichocephalic class. Most of the Sounti males have preponderance of dolichocephalic heads (58.49%) or mesocephalic heads (21.70%). Brachycephalic heads occur in very low frequency (3.77%). Bizygomatic breadth of the Sounti males has mean value of 131.30 millimeters and it indicates that it belongs to the narrow category of lebzelter and Saller's classification. Total facial index has the highest frequency of Euryprosopic (35.85%) or Hypereuryprosopic faces, while the upper facial index has been found with preponderance of Euryen (45.28%) followed by Mesen (35.85%) faces. Mean values of nasal length is less and the mean of nasal breadth is more among the Sounti males than the corresponding values of Bathudi male, resulting in the higher mean value of nasal index. Mean value of nasal index indicates Platyrrhine type of nose. Sounti male have preponderance of platyrrhine and mesorrhine nose types. Leptorrhine noses have low frequency (5.66%).

(c) *Finger and Palmar dermatoglyphics*

Sounti males are characterised by the highest frequency of loops (56.13%) followed by whorls (40.99%) and arches (2.88%) on the fingers. The various indices derived from the different pattern are, pattern intensity (13.85), Furahata index (73.01) and Dankmeijer index (7.03). Whorls and ulnar loops occur more frequently on right hand fingers. The finger patterns of total loops, radial loops and arches occur in greater frequency on the left hand. Finger patterns on the various digits show that whorls are characteristic of digits IV and I, while the ulnar loops have been found more frequently on digit III and V, similar is the position in connection with the total loops. Radial loops and arches are greatly found on digit II. Mean value of finger ridge counts have greater values on right hand for all the digits. The digits I, IV, V, III and II can be arranged in decreasing order of mean ridge counts. Over 24 per cent hands have monomorphic patterns on the fingers and 29.63 per cent individuals have symmetrical pattern on both hand of their fingers. D line ending is not frequent on right hands at position 11 and at position 7 on left hands. Sounti males have main line D endings frequently at position 7(31.48%) followed by 11(31.88%). Ending of main line c type is mostly found to be ulnar or radial. Radial C type endings occur in large frequency on right hand, ulnar C type has its preponderance on left hand. Similarly, proximal and absent C types also occur more on left hands. B line ending has its preponderance at position 7 on the right and left hands of the Sounti males. Axial triradii t' and t occur more frequently on the right and left hands. Sounti males are characterised by axial triradii at t' (51.39%) followed by t (37.96%). Pattern on palm among the Sounti males shows that right hand has preponderance of pattern on Hypothenar, II and III inter digital areas, similarly, the left hand have been found with greater frequency of pattern at 1st interdigital and IV interdigital areas. The highest frequency of patterns occur on IV interdigital, followed by III interdigital and hypothenar area. Mean value of right hands are more for main line index and 'a-b' ridge counts, while for triradii on palm left hand has more mean value. The various quantitative characters on finger and palm have the following mean value for Sounti males : Total finger ridge count (130.77), triradii on finger (13.85), triradii on palm (10.52), 'a-b' ridge count (68.69) main line index (15.81).

Though, there are variations for different characters of finger palm between right and left hands. The differences have been found to be statistically significant for bimanual variation for ending C line type and interdigital patterns only.

(*d*) *A_1 A_2 BO Blood groups and incidence of Colour Vision deficiency*

Sountis have been characterised by the highest frequency of B blood groups followed by A blood groups. A_2 occurs in low frequency. Indicence of colour blindness is 4.39%.

7.4 SOUNTI FEMALE

(*a*) *Anthroposcopic Observations*

Skin colour of the Sounti females is mostly brown (39.1%) followed by reddish brown (37.1) and blackish brown (11.4%). Light brown skin complexion has been found in low frequency (7.6%). Head hairs are characterised by black (78.1%) or dark brown (21.9%) colour, straight (85.7%) followed by low wavy form and mostly medium (61.9%) or fine (20.0%) texture but thick (52.4%) or medium quantity of head hairs. They have dark brown (60.0%) eyes without epicanthus fold and straight eye slits. Sclera is mostly clear (36.2%) or yellow (32.4%). All the individuals have been found with imperceptible supra-orbital ridges and mostly thin eye brows, the frequency of medium eye brows is low (5.7%). Forehead is supported by medium or low height and medium or straight slope. Nose is characterised by concave bridge, shallow depression and mostly horizontal septum. Medium (75.2%) or thick (17.2%) lips are relatively more common. Chin is mostly round (62.9%) or oval (37.1%), face has slight alveolar prognathism. Most of the Sounti do not possess their own land or have any other source of income. Those Sounti people who have their own land is not enough to fullfil their needs. Most of the males and females have to work in the fields of local cultivators. Sounti females have proportionate and athletic body. About 31.4 per cent female also have asthetic body.

(*b*) *Anthropometric measurements*

Stature of Sounti females ranges from 1352-1598 millimeters with mean value of 1467 millimeters which indicates short stature. Most of the Sounti females are of a short (59.05%) or below medium (23.81%) stature. Head length and head breadth of the Sounti females belong to long and narrow classes respectively. Mean cephalic index of the Sounti females is 74.47 and belong to dolichocephalic category. Most of them belong to dolichocephalic (60.00%) or mesocephalic (15.24%) categories. Mean value of minimum frontal breadth is minimum in the present series. Bizygomatic breadth according to Lebzelter and Saller's classification (Saller, 1930) is narrow. Bigonial breadth mean is the smallest in the present series. The upper and total facial indices indicate short and wider faces. Hyper Euryprosopic and Euryprosopic occur among about 69 per cent individuals. Similarily, Euryen and mesen faces have preponderance among 51.43 per cent and 33.33 per cent individuals respectively. The nasal length is shorter and the nasal breadth is broader than the Bathudi females resulting in higher mean nasal index among the Sounti females. Mesorrhine (59.05%) or platyrrhine (30.48%) nose types have been found in higher frequency. Frequency of leptorrhine nose types is low (5.71%). Mean nasal depth is the lowest among the Sounti females in the present series.

(*c*) *Finger and Palmar dermatoglyphics*

Sounti females have preponderence of loops (56.22%) or whorls (40.19%) on the finger balls. Arches occur in low frequency (3.59%). Various indices worked out are Pattern intensity index (13.69%), Furuhata index (71.48), and Dankmeijer index (8.92). Whorls, radial loops and arches occur more frequently on the left fingers but ulnar loops and the total loops have preponderance on the right hand finger balls. IV and I digits have been characterised by the highest occurrence of ulnar loops and the total loops. II digit has relatively greater intensity of radial loops and arches. The digits I, IV, III, V and II among the Sounti females can be arranged in the decreasing order of mean finger ridge counts. Except II digit all the digits have been found with greater mean value for finger ridge counts on the right hand. Monomorphic patterns on finger balls have been found among 21.7 per cent individuals, while the 18.87 per cent individuals have symmetrical patterns on all the homologous fingers. Main line D ending occurs frequently at position 7 (43.40%) or 11 (36.32%). When the D line ending is examined at right hand and left hand it is found to be more frequent at 11 or 7 position (40.57% each) and 7(46.23%) or 11(32.07%) respectively. Main line ending C type is found to be ulnar (54.72%) or Radial (31.13%). Radial type has greater intensity on right hand and the ulnar on the left hands. Proximal and absent C line types are found frequently on the left hands. Main line B endings are frequent at 7(38.68%) or 5′(38.21%) followed by 5" (18.87%). Right hands have preponderance of D line ending at 5(5′ + 5" about 53 per cent) or 7 (44.34 per cent), while on the left hand it terminates at 5′ and 5" (about 60%) or 7(33.02%). Axial triradius has greater occurrence on palm at t′ (54.71%) or t(26.89%), t has been observed more frequently on the right hand and t′ on the left hands. Patterns on right hands occur frequently on II interdigital and III interdigital areas, while on the left hands patterns have been found frequently on Hypothenar, thenar/I interdigital and IV interdigital areas. The highest patterns are observed on palmar areas at IV interdigital followed by III interdigital and Hypothenar. Though there are variations between the right and left hands for various dermatoglyphic characters on fingers and palms among the Sounti female but these differences are statistically significant for patterns on finger, C line type and patterns on III interdigital palmar area only. While the monomorphic and symmetrical patterns on fingers, main endings D and B, axial triradii t, Hypothenar, I interdigital, II and IV interdigital are bimanually homogenous. Through a-b ridge counts, triradii on palm, main line index have more mean values on right hands. But there are no statistically significant bimanual differences for a-b ridge counts, triradii on palmar region and main line index. The various quantitative characters of the Sounti females with their respective mean values are as follows. Total finger ridge count (126.03), triradii on finger (13.69%) triradii on palm (10.43%), a-b ridge counts (72.89) and main line index (15.29).

8

POPULATION AND SEX VARIATIONS

A. POPULATION VARIATIONS

8.1 MALE SERIES

(a) Anthroposcopic Observations

Bathudi and Sounti males are characterised by dark shades of skin colour. Blackish brown skin colour has been observed among 25.7 per cent Bathudi and 35.8 per cent Sounti males, Reddish brown colour of the skin occurs in less frequency among the Bathudi (11.0%) and Sounti males (14.2%). Brown skin colour has a preponderance among the Sounti males (36.8%) over the Bathudi males (14.7%). Light brown complexion mostly characterises the Bathudi males (29.4%) as compared to the Sounti males (11.3%). Hair is characterised by black (56.9%) or dark brown (39.4%) colour among the Bathudi males, while the Sounti males have preponderance of black (73.6%) followed by dark brown (26.4%) hair. Hair form is mostly straight or low wavy, with medium texture. Coarse hair have been found in higher frequency among the Bathudi (20.2%) than that of the Sounti (10.4%). Bathudi have preponderance of thick (68.8%) hair on the head as compared to the Sounti (52.8%). Beard and moustaches are scanty. Eyes are found with dark brown or brown colour. Epicanthic fold is mostly absent and its traces have been observed among Bathudi (5.5%) and (2.8). Eyes are straight. Yellow sclere occurs more frequently among the Sounti (56.6%) than Bathudi (43.1%). Bathudi has mostly medium (55.0%) or thin (44.0%) eye brows. Thin eye brows have been found to occur in preponderance among the Sounti. Supra orbital ridges are either imperceptible or only its traces are present. Forehead has medium height and slope. Straight forehead slope has been observed in higher frequency among the Bathudi (23.8%) than among the Sounti. Nose has a concave nasal bridge. Straight nasal bridge has been found in higher frequency among the Bathudi (31.2%) than among the Sounti (17.0%). Nasal depression is mostly medium or shallow. Nasal septum is either horizontal or upward. Medium lips are the characteristics of Bathudi, while thick lips have been mostly found among the Sounti. Face is supported by a found or oval chin and slight alveolar prognathism. Incisor fold is absent in the present sample. The body masculature is Athletic.

(b) Morpho-genetic traits

R type of handedness, hand clasping is predominant. 44.04 per cent and 42.45 per cent of arm folding respectively has been found among the Bathudi and Sounti respectively. Male of Bathudi (71.56%) and Sounti (77.36%) are mostly tongue rollers. The frequency of tongue folders is high among the Bathudi (14.68%) than among the Sounti (8.49%). About 70 per cent individuals of both the populations have single clockwise occipital hair whorls. Completely free ear lobe is most common among the males of both the populations. About 12 per cent Bathudi and 33 per cent Sounti individuals have attached ear lobes. About 68 per cent Bathudi and Sounti males have 2 < 4 digital formula. Cleft chin, Darwin's tubercle and middle phalangeal hairs in the prevent samples have not been observed.

(c) Anthropometric measurements

Stature of the Bathudi and Sounti males ranges from 1466- 1734 millimeters and 1471-1712 millimeters respectively. Mean value of stature of the Bathudi males is 1597.33 millimeters while that of Sounti males it is 1578.84 millimeters. Most of the Bathudi and Sounti males are short or below medium in stature. Very short and tall individuals occur in lower frequencies. Sitting height, foot lengths and breadths and relative sitting height index have more means among the Bathudi than Sounti of male series. Mean of chest girth and weight have greater values among the Sounti as compared to the Bathudi males. Short stature, broad chest and more body weight of the Sounti give them stout appearance in comparison to the Bathudi. Mean value of head length among Bathudi (188 millimeters) and Sounti (185 millimeters) indicate about their long categories. Similarly head breadth of the Bathudi and Sounti males belong to narrow category according to their mean values. Cephalic indices characterise these 2 populations as long headed people. Mesocephalic head forms occur in slightly higher frequency among the Sounti (21.70%) than Bathudi (16.51%) males. About 5.0% Bathudi and 4.0% Sounti have brachycephalic head forms. Bathudi have greater mean value of Head circumference and Auricular heights than Sounti males. But mean of length height index has greater mean value among the Sounti (64.39) as compared to the Bathudi (63.93). Means of length height belong to Hypsicephal category. Minimum frontal breadth, Bizygomatic breadth and Bigonial breadth have higher mean values among the Bathudi males as compared to the Sounti males. Total facial height and the total facial index has categorised most of the Bathudi and Sounti males with short and wider faces with jutting check bones. Higher mean value of upper facial height of Bathudi males has resulted in their greater mean for upper facial index as compared to the Sounti males. Bathudi males has preponderance of Mesen and the Sounti males have been found with higher frequency of Euryen upper faces. Lepten types of upper faces are more frequent among the Bathudi than the Sounti males. Bathudi males have greater nasal length and less nasal breadth resulting in lower mean value of nasal index as compared to Sounti males. Over 61 per cent (61.47%) nose types are mesorrhine and 28.44% are platyrrhine among the Bathudi, while 45.28% and 43.40% Sounti are characterised by platyrrhine and mesorrhine noses respectively. Nose depth has been found with more mean value among Bathudi males as compared to the Sounti males.

(d) Finger and Palmar dermatoglyphics

The finger and palmar dermatoglyphics for the sake of comparison between the groups of Bathudi and Sounti has been treated separately digitwise, handwise, sexwise and populationwise because the patterns and other dermatoglyphic characters follow a particular trend in their occurrence:

1. Digital variations

(a) Pattern types :

Bathudi and Sounti males have the highest frequency of whorls on IV and I digits; ulnar loops and total loops have their preponderance on III digit. Radial loops and arches have been found more frequently on II digit. Bathudi has higher occurrences of whorls, Radial loops and arches, while the Sounti has preponderance of ulnar loops on its digits.

(b) Ridge count on the finger :

Mean finger ridge counts on the digits I, IV, III, V and II can be arranged in decreasing orders among the Bathudi males and Sounti males. Mean ridge count have greater value among the Bathudi males on all the homologous fingers than Sounti.

2. *Bimanual variations*

(a) Pattern types and ridges counts on finger :

Left and Right hands of the Bathudi males has preponderance of whorls, radial loops, while the left and right hands of the Sounti males are characterised by ulnar loops, total loops and arches. Similarly except III digit of the Bathudi, all the digits of right hands of both populations are found with higher mean than their corresponding digits on the left hands.

(b) Monomorphic patterns :

Whorls have been found in higher frequency on right and left hands as monomorphic patterns among Bathudi males. While the loops as monomorphic patterns on right and left hands have preponderance among the Sounti males.

(c) Symmetrical patterns on all homologous fingers :

Sounti males (29.63%) are found with higher frequency of symmetrical patterns on all homologous fingers as compared to the Bathudi males (25.45%).

(d) Main line D endings :

Termination of main line D is most predominant at position 11 on right hands of both populations. But on the left hands it is found to be more common at position 10 or 7 among the Bathudi males, while the Sounti males have main line D ending frequently at 7 or 11 followed by 9. When both the right and left hands are considered together D line ending has been found to be more common at position 11 or 7.

(e) Main line B endings :

Main line B ending is common at position 7 among the Bathudi and Sounti males. Right and left hands of the Bathudi males have been found with preponderance of main line B ending at position 7 or 5″, while the Sounti males are characterised by main line B ending on right and left hands at position 7 followed by 5′ and 5″.

(f) Ending of C line type :

Right hands and left hands of Bathudi males have preponderance of Radial followed by proximal C type. Right and left hands are characterised by the higher frequency of ulnar types among the Sounti males. When both the hands are considered together, Bathudi males have higher frequency of Radial followed by ulnar C line type, while the Sounti males are characterised by the highest frequency of ulnar followed by Radial ending of C line type.

(g) Main line index, a-b ridge count and triradii on palm :

Mean value of main line index, a-b ridge count and triradii on palm has been observed more among the Bathudi males on the right hand and left hands as compared to the corresponding right and left hands of the Sounti males. Right hand has more mean than that of the left hand for all the above three characters among both the males populations.

(h) Patterns on Palmar area :

Among both populations patterns are frequently found on Hypothenar, II interdigital and III interdigital areas of right palms, and thenar/I interdigital and IV interdigital palmar areas of left hand. Bathudi males have preponderance of palmar pattern on III interdigital followed by IV interdigital and Hypothenar areas on Right and left hands. But Sounti males on right and left palm has more occurrence of patterns on IV interdigital followed by III interdigital and Hypothenar palmar area.

(i) Axial triradius :

Axial triradii t′ or t occur frequently among the males of Bathudi and Sounti. Axial triradii t has been found frequently on the right hand and t′ on left hand.

3. Population variation

Whorls have been found in higher frequency among the Bathudi males (48.58%), while Sounti males are characterised by the preponderance of radial loops, total loops, and arches. Sounti males has higher value of Dankmeijer index and the Bathudi males have more values of pattern intensity index and Furuhata index. Frequencies of whorls and loops are more closer among the Bathudi males. Bathudi males have higher frequency of monomorphic hands, while the Sounti males have greater frequency of symmetrical patterns on homologous fingers. D and B main line endings are mostly found to be 11, 7, 5′ or 7, 5″. 11, 7 are more common among the Bathudi males, while 7, 5′ and 7, 5″ are more frequently observed among the Sounti males. C line type is mostly Radial or Ulnar among the Bathudi males and Ulnar or Radial among the Sounti males. Axial triradii, t′ is most common among the individual of both populations. Palmar patterns are found in greater intensity on III and IV interdigital areas of the Bathudi males and IV interdigital and III interdigital areas of Sounti males. Means of total finger ridge count, triradii on palm, a-b ridge count and main line index show higher value among the males of Bathudi as compared to the Sounti.

8.2 FEMALE SERIES

(a) *Anthroposcopic Observations*

Bathudi females have preponderance of Brown (52.7%) or light brown (25.5%) skin colour. Sounti females have comparatively darker skin complexion with reddish brown (37.1%) or brown (39.1%) skin colour. Hair are characterised by black or dark brown colour, straight medium or fine forms. Hairs on head mostly have thick or medium growth. Eyes are mostly dark brown or brown, straight and without epicanthic fold. Most of the Bathudi females have clear or dull sclera, while the Sounti females are characterised by clear (36.2%) followed by yellow (32.4%) or dull (31.4%) sclera. Sounti females have been found with higher frequency (94.3%) of thin eye-brows as compared to the Bathudi (60.0%), with imperceptible supra-orbital ridges among both population. Forehead is mostly with medium height and slope among the Bathudi female. Sounti females have been observed with medium or low forehead height with medium or straight slope. Bathudi females have concave noses with medium nasal depression. But the Sounti females have greater occurrence of concave noses with shallow nasal depression. Nasal septum is mostly horizontal. Lips are mostly medium, but Bathudi females have preponderance of thin lips (21.8%). Greater frequency of found or oval chin has been observed among both populations. Body musculature is mostly athletic.

(b) *Morpho-genetic traits*

Most of the Bathudi and Sounti female are found with Right type of hand clasping and handedness. R type of arm folding has been observed among 49.54 per cent Bathudi and 48.57 per cent Sounti females. Tongue rollers are more frequent among the females of Sounti (75.24%) than among the Bathudi (66.36%). Tongue folding has been reported in low frequency among the Sounti (4.76%) when compared with the Bathudi (10.0%). Occipital hair whorls have preponderance of single clockwise or single anticlockwise. Ear lobe is mostly free but completely attached ear lobe occur in greater frequency among the Sounti (21.90%) than Bathudi (12.73%). Digital formulae 2 < 4 is more common among the Sounti than among the Bathudi. Midphalangeal hair, Darwin's tubercle and cleft chin as observed in the male series are also absent among the female series.

(c) Anthropometic measurements

Range of stature is 1368-1611 millimeters and 1352-1598 millimeters among the Bathudi and Sounti females respectively. Mean value of Stature are 1493 millimeters and 1467 millimeters among the Bathudi and Sounti females respectively. As observed in case of male series, Bathudi females have more mean stature than the Sounti females. Short stature is more predominant among the Sounti (59.05%) than among the Bathudi females (40.91%). Bathudi females are found with higher frequency of below medium, medium, above medium and tall stature than its corresponding frequences of the Sounti females. Relative sitting height index and the sitting height have been observed to be higher among the Bathudi than the Sounti. Mean foot length is slightly more among the Bathudi females but foot breadth mean is greater among the Sounti females. This has resulted in more broader feet of Sounti. The Sounti have more mean weight in the male series, Sounti females also have higher weight than the Bathudi. Heads are long and narrow among most of the females of Bathudi and Sounti. Dolichocephalic heads are not observed among the Sounti, while about 2% of Bathudi females have been found with Brachycephlic heads. Head circumference and Auricular height have more mean value among the Bathudi females. Bathudi and Sounti females have Hypsicephal and Metriocephal or Acrocephal length height and Breadth height indices respectively. Mean value of Bizygomatic breadth belongs to very narrow category. Total facial length and upper facial length mean value indicate longer faces among the Bathudi than Sounti. Most of the Bathudi and Sounti mean values have preponderance of hypereuryprosopic faces but its frequency is greater among the Sounti female. Bathudi have greater occurrence of mesoprosopic, leptoprosopic and hyperleptoprosopic faces than the Sounti. Upper facial index is characterised by Euryen or Mesen faces. Euryen faces are common among the Sounti, while Mesen and Lepten are frequent among the Bathudi females. Bathudi have more long nose with greater nasal depth. Nasal index among the famales of Bathudi and Sounti is mostly mesorrhine. Platyrhine nose forms occur frequently among the Sounti females.

(d) Finger and Palmar dermatoglyphics

(i) Digital finger pattern and ridge count variations. Whorls on fingers have been found frequently on digits IV or I, Ulnar loops on V or III digits. The radial loops and arches are mostly found on II digit. The mean value of finger ridge count on I,IV,III,V and II digits can be arranged in decreasing order.

(ii) Bimanual variations. Whorls, radial loops and arches have been observed in higher frequency on the left hands, while the ulnar loops and total loops have preponderance on right hands. Except II digits of Sounti females, the right hands have more mean ridge value than the corresponding fingers on the left hand. Monomorphic patterns have preponderance on the right hand than left hands. Bathudi females are characterised by higher occurrence of monomorphic patterns on fingers of right and left hands as compared to the corresponding hands of the Sounti females. Main line D and B endings are most common as 11, 7, or 7, 5′ on right hand; and 11, 7 among the Bathudi left hands and 7, 5′ Sounti left hands. Sounti and Bathudi females right hands have the preponderance of radial C line type and the left hands are frequent with ulnar, proximal and absent C line type. Axial triradii t′ and t is most common, t′ has been found frequently on left hand and t on right hands. Right hands of females have preponderance of palmar patterns on II interdigital and III interdigital areas. The left hands of females are characterised by higher frequency of patterns on the Hypothenar, I interdigital and IV interdigital areas.

Sounti females have greater mean values on right hands for main line index, a-b ridge count and triradii on palm. Bathudi females have greater mean value on left hands for triradii on palm a-b ridge count but right hands have more mean value for main line index.

(iii) Population variations. Arches and whorls are observed in higher frequency among the Bathudi females. Loops including ulnar and radial are predominant among the Sounti females. Pattern intersity index, Furuhate index is more frequent among the Bathudi females. Dankemijer index has more value among the Sounti females. Monomorphic patterns and symmetrical patterns on the finger ball are predominant among the Bathudi females. Main line D ending 11 is more common among the Bathudi females and while as D ending at 7 has preponderance among the Sounti females. B line ending has been found to be mostly at 7 among the Bathudi females and 7 or 5′ among the Sounti females. C line type has been characterised as radial and ulnar among most of the Bathudi and Sounti females respectively. Axial triradius t′ is most common in the female series. Maximum patterns on palmar areas are on IV interdigital followed by III interdigital and Hypothenar areas least patterns on I and II interditial areas. Bathudi females have more palmar pattern as compared to the Sounti females on Hypothenar, I interdigital and III interdigital. The Sounti females have preponderance of pattern on palmar areas at II interdigital and IV interdigital.

Mean values of Bathudi females are greater for total finger ridge counts, triradii on finger and main line index, while the Sounti females has more mean value for triradii on palm and a-b ridge counts.

B. SEX VARIATION

8.3 BATHUDI MALES AND FEMALES

(a) Anthroposcopic Observations :

Bathudi males have higher frequency of dark shades, while the Bathudi females are mostly brown or light brown in skin complexion. Black hair colour have preponderance among the females but males have a higher frequency of dark brown hair colour. Straight hair are observed more among the Bathudi females as compared to the Bathudi males. Males of Bathudi have higher frequency of low wavy hair. Hair texture is mostly medium. Fine head hair are reported in abundance among the Bathudi females.

Head hairs are mostly thick. Eyes are mostly dark brown or brown among both sexes but light brown eyes are found in greater frequency among the Bathudi males. Epicanthic fold among Bathudi males and females are mostly absent, but its traces are present more among the males. Eyes are straight, Sclera is generally yellow or dull among the Bathudi males and clear or dull among the Bathudi females. Eye brows are medium or thin with traces or imperceptible supra-orbital ridges among the Bathudi males. Females of Bathudi have thin or medium eye-brows with mostly imperceptible supra-orbital ridges. Foreheads have medium height and medium or straight slope among both sexes. Nose has a concave or straight nasal bridge with medium or shallow nasion depression. Deep nasion depression has frequently been found among the Bathudi males. Horizontal nasal septum is common. About Seven percent (7.3%) Bathudi males have downward nasal septum. Thick lips have preponderance among the Bathudi males, while the Bathudi females have higher occurrence of thin lips. Most of the Bathudi males and females have medium lip thickness. Round or oval chin has preponderance, oval chin is frequently found among the Bathudi females, and square chin has higher frequency among the Bathudi males. Slight alveolar prognathism is present among the Bathudi males and females. Body musculature is mostly athletic.

(*b*) *Morpho-genetic traits* :

R-type of handclasping is more common among the Bathudi males, while R type of arm folding is more frequent among the Bathudi females. Most of the Bathudi females and all the Bathudi males are Right-handed. Bathudi males (71.56%) and females (66.36%) are mostly Tongue rollers, incidence of tongue folding has been observed to be low but slightly higher among the Bathudi males (14.68%) than among the Bathudi females (10.0%). Bathudi males and females are characterised by the preponderance of single clockwise and single anticlockwise occipital hair whorl. Double occipital hair whorls have more frequency among the Bathudi female. Completely free ear lobes are more frequent among the Bathudi males and females. Attached ear lobes have slightly higher frequency among the Bathudi female. Digital formulae 2 < 4 characterise most individuals, 2 = 4 digital formulae is frequent among the Bathudi males. 2 > 4 has slightly higher incidence among the

Bathudi females. Midphalangeal hair, Darwin's tubercle and cleft chin has not been observed in the present sample of the Bathudi.

(c) Anthropometric characters

Stature of the Bathudi males range from 1466-1734 millimeters with its mean value as 1597 millimeters put them under the short class. Similarily, the Bathudi females have stature which is mostly short with mean value of 1493 millimeters and ranges from 1368-1611 millimeters. Bathudi females are shorter than the Bathudi males in their mean values over 10 centimeters. Bathudi males and females have long and narrow heads with preponderance of dolichocephalic heads. Mesocephalic head forms are more frequent among the Bathudi females. Brachycephalic heads are found in low frequency among the Bathudi males (5.5%) and females (1.82%). Females have preponderance of Hypsicephalic and Metriocephalic heads, while as among the males acrocephalic heads are most common. Bizygomatic breadth of Bathudi females are very narrow and that of Bathudi males as narrow. Euryprosopic faces and Hypereuryprosopic faces are frequently found among the Bathudi males and females. Long faces occur frequently among the Bathudi males and females (10.0%) than Bathudi males (5.42%). Upper facial index indicate higher occurrence of Euryen faces among Bathudi females and mesen faces among the Bathudi males. Lepten and Hyperlepten face types have been found in higher frequency among the Bathudi females than males. Bathudi males and females are mostly characterised by mesorrhine, and platyrrhine nose types. Leptorrhine nose types occur in low frequency (10.0%) among both the Bathudi males and females. Female mean divided by male mean and multiplied by hundred for all the anthropometric characters show that Bathudi males have greater mean value for all the 17 measurements than that of Bathudi females.

Mean value of Bathudi males and females show maximum variations for foot breadth, weight and foot length, while they are relatively closer in respect of head circumference, minium frontal breadth, head breadth, bizygomatic breadth, head length, bigonial breadth and auricular height. Moderate sex variations are observed for stature and sitting height. Females have been found to be relatively closer for head breadth as compared to the head length. Sex variations are found to be greater for nasal height, Nasal length, Nasal depth, Upper facial length and total facial length.

(d) Finger and Palmar dermatoglyphics

Finger pattern types and ridge counts:

(i) Digital variations

Whorls are found frequently on IV and I digits of both sexes, ulnar loops and total loops on digit III of Bathudi males and digit V of Bathudi females. Radial loops and arches on II digit of Bathudi males and females. Ridge count on finger I, IV, III, V and II can be arranged in decreasing order of both sexes. Males of Bathudi have greater mean value of ridge count on all the digits than the Bathudi females except II digit.

(ii) Bimanual Variations

Whorls have been found frequently on right hand of Bathudi males and left hands of Bathudi females. Ulnar loops and total loops have preponderance on left hands of Bathudi males and right hands of Bathudi females. Radial loops and arches are common on left hands of both sexes. Finger ridge counts have been characterised by higher frequencies on right hands among the Bathudi males and females except III digit of Bathudi males. Monomorphic pattern occur in greater frequency on right hand among both sexes. Main line D ending 11 is most common on the right hand of both sexes, left hand has preponderance of D line ending 10 followed by 7 and 11 among the Bathudi males, and 7 followed by 11 of the Bathudi female. B line ending 7 is more common on right hand of both sexes and 7 or 5″ on the left hand of Bathudi males and females. Radial C line type is characteristic of right hand and ulnar, proximal and absent types have been found to be predominant on left hands of both sexes. Axial triradii t is more common on the right hand and t′ and t″ on the left hands of both sexes. Patterns on palmar areas of Bathudi males are frequent on the Hypothenar, II interdigital, III interdigital of right hand and I interdigital and IV interdigital of left hand. Contrary to this, Bathudi females have preponderance of patterns on right hands at II interdigital, III interdigital palmar area and on the left hands at Hypothenar, I interdigital and IV interdigital areas. Main line index, 'a-b' ridge count and triradii on palm has greater mean value for right hands among the Bathudi males and left hands among the Bathudi females except main line index. Right and left hands of Bathudi males have greater mean value than Bathudi females for main line index, 'a-b' ridge count and triradii on palm.

(iii) Sex variations

Whorls and radial loops are predominant amòng Bathudi males. Ulnar loops, total loops and arches are common among the Bathudi females. Pattern intensity and Furuhata indices have high value among the Bathudi males and Dankmeijer index is found to be frequent among the Bathudi females. Monomorphic and symmetrical patterns have greater intensity among the Bathudi females. Main line D and B endings 11,7, or 7,5′ and 7,5″ are frequently observed among the both sexes of Bathudi. Radial or ulnar C line types are found in higher frequency among the Bathudi males and females. Radial C line types are frequent among the Bathudi males and Ulnar C line types have preponderance among the Bathudi female. Patterns on palmar area have been found to be most frequent among the Bathudi males on III interdigital, Hypothenar, I interdigital and II interdigital areas. Females have the highest frequency of patterns on IV interdigital followed by III interdigital Hypothenear, I interdigital and II interdigital. When Bathudi males and females are compared males have been found with more occurrence of patterns on I,II and III interdigital palmar areas, while Bathudi female have preponderance of palmar pattern on Hypothenar and IV interdigital areas. Males of Bathudi have more means than their females for total finger ridge counts, triradii on fingers, triradii on palm, 'a-b' ridge count and main line index.

8.4 SOUNTI MALE AND FEMALES

(a) Anthroposcopic Observartions

Skin colour is mostly blackish brown (35.8%) or brown (36.8%) among the Sounti males and brown (39.1%) or reddish brown (37.1%) among the Sounti females. Dark shades of skin colour have been found in lower frequency among the females. Hairs are mostly black, straight or low wavy among the Sounti males with medium texture coarse and fine hairs have preponderance among the sounti females. Quantity of head hair is mostly thick or medium. Eyes are mostly dark brown but brown eyes have been observed in higher frequency among the Sounti females as compared to the Sounti males. Eye fold is usually absent but among 2.8% Sounti males only the traces has been found. Eyes are characterised by straight eye slits, yellow sclera among males and clear or yellow sclera among females. Thin eye brows have been found in greater frequency but medium eye brows are frequent among Bathudi males. Supra orbital ridges are imperceptible among all the females and males of Sounti (54.7%). Traces of Supra orbital ridges are reported among 44.4% males. Males have preponderance of medium height and slope of forehead. Females of Sounti are characterised by medium or low height and medium or straight slope. Nasion depression is mostly medium among Sounti males and shallow among Sounti females. Nose has concave bridge but straight nasal bridge has also been found in low frequency among both sexes. Nose has a horizontal septum. Lips are predominantly medium among Sounti females and thick among Sounti males. Thin lips have been found more commonly among females. Round chin supports the face of both males and females. Slight alveolar prognathism has been observed among both sexes. Athletic body is more frequent among both sexes, but Sounti females with asthetic body are also been found.

(b) Morpho-genetic traits

Most of the males and females of Sounti are right handed and R type of hand clasping is most predominant among them. Females of Sounti are characterised by high frequency of R type armfolding (48.57%) than males (42.45%). Males have preponderance of tongue rollers and folders than females. Occipital hair whorls are found to be single clockwise or single anticlockwise. Single clockwise occipital hair whorls are more common among the Sounti females and single anticlockwise has higher frequency among the Sounti males. Earlobe attachment has been observed among the Sountis. Completely free earlobes have been found in higher frequency among the Sounti females, while as the completely attached ear lobes have been found in more frequency among the Sounti males. Digital formulae $2 < 4$ occurs in higher frequency among females and $2 = 4$ and $2 > 4$ has high frequency among the Sounti males. Mid phalangeal hair, Darwin's tubercle and cleft chin has not been observed in the present sample of males and females of Sounti.

(c) Anthropometric measurements

Stature of males and females of Sounti tribe is characterised as Short or below medium. Females on an average are shorter than males over 11 centimeters. Head length indicates long heads.

Females have slightly more cephalic index than males. Dolichocephalic head forms are most common. But dolichocephalic and hyperdolichocephalic heads are frequent among the Sounti females as compared to the Sounti males, Mesocephalic head forms occur more frequently among the Sounti males than females. Brachycephalic heads are not found among the females but about 4.0% of Sounti males have broad heads. Length height and breadth height indices mostly belong to Hypsicephalic and Acrocephalic categories respectively. Sounti males have narrow and Sounti females mostly have very narrow Bizygomatic breadth but the cheek bones are well developed among both the sexes. Hypereuryprosopic faces are found in less frequency and Euryprosopic faces in higher frequency among the Sounti males as compared to the Sounti females. Euryen faces have greater occurrence among the Sounti females and mesen face types are found in preponderance among the Sounti males. Lepten faces occur in lower frequency but are more common among the Sounti females. Nose type mesorrhine has preponderance among the Sounti females. Males of Sounti have higher frequency of platyrrhine nose type. Leptorrhine noses are observed in low frequency among both sexes of the Sounti tribe.

Sex differences for the 17 measurement have been calculated by dividing the female mean value by male mean value and multiplying the quotient by hundred for each measurement. Male mean value is greater for all the measurements than female mean. Weight, foot breadth, total facial height, nasal depth, nasal breadth, nasal height, stature and foot length have greatest sex variations as observed in case of Bathudi. Similarly, Sounti females are more closer to the Sounti males in head breadth as compared to the head length. There are less sex variations for head circumference and minimum frontal breadth. Bizygomatic breadth, Bigonial breadth, Auricular height and upper facial height can be arranged in between the measurement having greater and lesser differences.

(d) Finger and Palmar dermatoglyphics

Finger pattern types and ridge counts

(i) Digital variations

Whorls have been found frequently on digits IV and I among both sexes of the Sounti. The ulnar loops and the total loops have preponderance of digit III and V among the Sounti males and sounti females respectively. Radial loops and arches are common on digit II among both sexes of Sounti. As the finger pattern types have particular trend of distribution on the various digits among the males and females of the Sounti. Similarly, the finger ball ridge counts can be arranged in descending order on digits I,IV, III, V and II among the males and females of the Sounti.

(ii) Bimanual variations

Whorls have preponderance on the right hands of Sounti males and left hands of females of Sounti. Ulnar loops among both sexes are observed in higher frequency on the right hands but the radial loops being most frequent on the left hands of both sexes have resulted in the greater frequency of total loops on left hand of males and right hands of females. The arches are also frequent on left hands of Sounti males and females. Right hands have higher mean value of finger ridge counts on all the digits among both sexes except II digit of the Sounti female.

Monomorphic patterns are found to be common on the left hands of Sounti males and right hands of Sounti females. Main line D endings 11 or 7, 9 are found in higher frequencies on the right hands of Sounti males and 11 and 7 D line endings have equal frequencies on the right hand of Sounti females, while on left hand maximum frequency of D line ending is 7 or 11 among Sounit males and females. Main line B ending 7 followed by 5″ and 5′ are frequent on the right hand of Sounti males and 7 or 5′ and 5″ of Sounti females. On the left hand B line ending 7 or 5″, 5′ is frequent among the Sounti males and 5′ or 7, 5″ among the Sounti females. Radial ending of C line type is frequent on the right hands, while ulnar, proximal and absent C line types are found to be in higher frequency on the left hands of both sexes. Axial triradii t, t″ is observed frequently on right hands and t′ has preponderance on the left hands of both sexes. Right hands have preponderance of pattern types on Hypothenar, II interdigital and III interdigital palmar areas and left hands are characterised by the higher frequency of pattern types on I interdigital and IV interdigital palmar areas of Sounti males. While among the Sounti females right hands are characterised by greater occurrence of patterns on II interdigital and III interdigital palmar areas, left hands have greater frequency of Hypothenar, I interdigital and IV interdigital palmar patterns.

Main line index, a-b ridge counts and triradii on palm have greater mean value on right hand for both sexes of the Sounti except for triradii on palm among the males of the Sounti tribe.

(iii) Sex variations

Whorls and radial loops are frequent among the males, while the ulnar loops, total loops and arches have preponderance among the females of Sounti tribe. Pattern intensity and Furuhata indices have greater value among the Sounti males but Dankmeijer index indicates higher frequency among the Sounti females. Except digit IV, males have more finger ridge count for all the digits than females. Males have been characterised by the higher frequency of monomorphic and symmetrical patterns on the fingers. Main line D ending 11, 7 is frequently observed among the males and females, while B line ending 7 followed by 5′ and 5″ have preponderance among both the sexes. Axial triradii t″ followed by t and t″, have preponderance among both sexes. Females have been found with higher frequency of axial triradii t′ and t″, while the Sounti males have greater occurrence of axial triradius t. Hypothenar, III interdigital and IV interdigital palmar areas have preponderance of patterns among the sounti females. I interdigital and II interdigital paterns on palmar areas are frequent among the Sounti males.

Total finger ridge counts, Triradii on finger, Triradii on palm, 'a-b' ridge count and main line index have been found with higher means among the Sounti males as compared to the Sounti females except 'a-b' ridge counts among the Sounti females.

8.5 TEST OF SIGNIFICANCE :

As the males and females differ at the chromosomal level, there are variations between the males and females for somotoscopic characters, Anthropometric measurements, finger and palm dermatoglyphics, ABO blood group and other traits. Now an attempt will be made to ascertain whether those differences, between the sexes and both populations for various characters are statistically significant.

(a) *Anthroposcopic observations*

Chi-square test has been performed for the various Anthroposcopic observations between both the populations and sexes of Bathudi and Sounti. The Anthroposcopic characters for which the differences between the Bathudi and Sounti for both the sexes and populations are significant at 1 per cent level are presented in table 8.1. As expected Bathudi and Sounti males have beard and moustaches and supra orbital ridges in preponderance, while among their female counterparts these characters are absent. Bathudi and Sounti males differ significantly for about 41 per cent of the Anthroposcopic characters, while the Bathudi and Sounti females are more homogeneous and differ signifincantly for about 23 per cent of the total Anthroposcopic observations only. The sex differences have been found to be significant for 35 percent and 40 percent Anthroposcopic characters among the Bathudi and Sounti tribes respectively (Table 8.2).

Table 8.1

Anthroposcopic characters for which differences between populations and sexes are significant for chi-square at 1 per cent level

Sl. No.	*Comparison between*	*Characters*
1.	Bathudi male x Sounti male	Skin colour, Hair texture, Eye colour, Eye brows, Nasion depression, Nasal bridge, Nasal septum, Forehead slope, Lip thickness.
2.	Bathudi female x Sounti female	Skin colour, Hair quantity, Eye brows, Nasion depression, Forehead scope
3.	Bathudi male x Bathudi females	Skin colour, Hair form, Hair colour, Eye colour, Sclere, Nasion depression, Nasal septum.
4.	Sounti male x Sounti female	Skin colour, Hair form, Hair texture, Sclera, Eye brow, Nasion depression, Forehead scope, Lip thickness.

Table 8.2

Percentage frequency of differences significant at 1 percent level between both populations and sexes for various observations

Sl. No.	*Comparison between*	*Total characters*	*Differences significant*	*Percentage*
1.	Bathudi male x Sounti male	22	9	40.91

(Contd.)

(Contd.)

2.	Bathudi female x Sounti female	22	5	22.73
3.	Bathudi male x Bathudi female	20	7	35.00
4.	Sounti male x Sounti female	20	8	40.00

(b) Behavioural and other morpho-genetic traits:

X^2 test for Handclasping, Handedness, Armfolding, Tongue rolling, Tongue folding, Earlobe attachment, Occipital hairwhorls, Digital formulae, Mid phalangeal hair, Darwins tubercle and cleft chin has been performed for both the populations and sexes. No bimanual significant difference for digital formulae have been found for both sexes and populations of the Bathudi and Sounti. Bathudi and Sounti males show significant difference for ear lobe attachment at 1 percent level of probability. Bathudi females and Sounti females differ significantly for Digital formulae at 1 percent level of probability. While Bathudi and Sounti show sex differences for digital formulae at 5 per cent and 1 percent level of probability. The population and sex differences for various morpho-genetic characters significant at 1 percent level of probabily are presented in Table 8.3.

Table 8.3

Population and sex differences for various morphogenetic characters significant at 1 per cent level of probability

Sl. No.	*Comparison between*	*Total characters*	*Differences significant*	*Percentage*
1.	Bathudi male x Sounti male	11	1	9.09
2.	Bathudi female x Sounit female	11	1	9.09
3.	Bathudi male x Bathudi female	11	—	—
4.	Sounti male x Sounti female	11	1	9.09

(c) *Anthropometric characters* :

The mean values for various anthropometric measurements among the Bathudi and Sounti of both sexes are presented in Table 8.4.

Bathudi males have more mean value for all the measurements than Sounti males except minimum frontal breadth, nasal breadth, weight and thoracic circumference, while the Bathudi females have more mean than Sounti females for all the measurements except foot breadth and weight. The Bathudi and Sounti males have higher mean value for all the corresponding measurements of their respective females. Various characters having significant differences for t-value at 5 percent and 1 percent level of probability for both populations and sexes are presented in Table 8.5.

Table 8.4

Mean values for various metric characters (in mm) among Bathudi and Sounti of both sexes

Sl. No.	*Characters*	*Males*		*Females*	
		Bathudi N = 109	*Sounti N = 106*	*Bathudi N = 110*	*Sounti N = 105*
1.	Stature	1597.3	1578.8	1493.2	1467.6
2.	Sitting height	812.4	783.6	750.1	736.1
3.	Head length	188.3	185.1	179.7	176.5
4.	Head breadth	138.9	137.1	134.9	131.3
5.	Minimum frontal breadth	103.4	103.7	101.4	100.3
6.	Bizygomatic breadth	132.5	131.3	126.6	124.1
7.	Bigonial breadth	101.6	100.9	96.9	96.0
8.	Total facial height	107.7	107.1	98.9	95.8
9.	Upper facial height	64.0	61.4	60.7	57.9
10.	Nasal height	46.3	44.2	43.4	41.0

(Contd.)

(Contd.)

11.	Nasal breadth	36.8	37.3	34.4	33.9
12.	Nasal depth	17.8	17.2	16.8	15.4
13.	Head circumference	532.7	527.7	523.3	515.8
14.	Auricular height	120.3	119.1	114.5	113.1
15.	Foot length	238.2	231.4	216.5	216.4
16.	Foot breadth	90.5	88.7	76.6	78.6
17.	Weight (Kgms)	45.9	46.9	39.9	40.2
18.	Thoracic circumference	770.5	777.3	—	—

N = Number of individuals.

Table 8.5

t-values for various anthropometric characters between Bathudi and Sounti of both sexes

Sl. No.	*Characters*	*Bathudi male x Sounti male*	*Bathudi female x Sounti female*	*Bathudi male x Bathudi female*	*Sounti male x Sounti female*
1.	Stature	2.38*	3.68**	13.49**	16.03**
2.	Sitting height	6.11**	3.91**	16.98**	10.18**
3.	Head length	3.88**	3.67**	10.28**	9.87**
4.	Head breadth	2.95**	5.28**	5.57**	8.69**
5.	Minimum frontal breadth	0.48	2.11*	3.89**	6.35**
6.	Bizygomatic breadth	1.88	3.92**	8.66**	11.90**
7.	Total facial height	0.69	3.67**	10.58**	13.75**
8.	Upper facial height	4.31**	4.77**	5.50**	6.13**
9.	Nasal height	4.56**	5.77**	7.30**	6.83**
10.	Nasal breadth	1.32	1.50	6.32**	9.43**

(Contd.)

(Contd.)

11.	Nasal depth	1.78	5.78**	3.64**	6.90**
12.	Bigonial breadth	1.09	1.45	7.14**	7.65**
13.	Head circumference	2.54*	3.27**	4.77**	5.19**
14.	Auricular height	1.70	2.13*	8.95**	8.71**
15.	Foot length	4.34**	0.08	14.47**	10.73**
16.	Foot breadth	1.88	2.17*	15.24**	10.57**
17.	Body weight (Kg.)	1.48	0.53	8.24**	9.26**
18.	Thoracic circumference	1.28	—	—	—
		d.f. = 213	d.f = 213	d.f = 217	d.f = 209

* Significant at 5% level of probability.

** Significant at 1% level of probability.

The percentage number of significant differences of t value at 1 percent level for anthropometric characters for the Bathudi and Sounti of both sexes are shown in table 8.6. As proposed by Das *et. al.* (1968) "We may reasonably consider a t-value as significant for our present studies when the probability level is as low as 1 percent instead of the usual 5 percent level". The males of both populations differ for 33.33 per cent characters, while the female of these two tribal populations differ for 58.8 per cent characters. Das *et. al.* (1968) have shown among the similar study among the five tribal populations from Koraput that "the tribal groups more distrinctly differentiated in their female populations than in the males. There are a large number of significant 't' in women".

Table 8.6

Number of differences significant at 1 percent level for metric characters among the Bathudi and Sounti of both sexes

Sl. No.	*Comparison between*	*Total characters*	*Differences significant*	*Percentage*
1.	Bathudi male x Sounti male	18	6	33.33
2.	Bathudi female x Sounti female	17	10	58.82

(Contd.)

(Contd.)

3.	Bathudi male x Bathudi female	17	17	100.00
4.	Sounti male x Sounti female	17	17	100.00

The results of analysis of variance expressed in terms of the well known variance ratio 'F' definitely point out that the tribal sample means of the anthropometric characters are significantly heterogeneous in most of the characters. The male group show 6 F-values significant at 1 percent level and 2 F- values significant at 5 per cent level out of 18 F-values calculated. But in case of Female group 10 F-values out of 17 F- values calculated differ significantly at 1 per cent level and 5 percent level respectively. As observed in case of t-values, F- values have been found with the similar observations, the females are significantly heterogeneous in more number of characters than the males. The female populations show the inter tribal discrimination more conspiciously than their male counter parts. The results of F-values are presented in Table 8.7.

Table 8.7

F-values for various Anthropometric measurements among Bathudi and Sounti of both sexes

Sl. No.	*Characters*	*Bathudi male x Sounti male*	*Bathudi female x Sounti female*
1.	Stature	5.70*	13.58**
2.	Sitting height	37.43**	15.28**
3.	Head length	15.18**	13.47**
4.	Head breadth	6.73**	27.81**
5.	Minimum frontal breadth	0.22	4.51*
6.	Bizygomatic breadth	3.53	15.37**
7.	Total facial height	0.47	13.50**
8.	Upper facial height	18.54**	22.70**

(Contd.)

(Contd.)

9.	Nasal height	20.88**	33.61**
10.	Nasal breadth	1.71	2.33
11.	Nasal depth	3.12	33.22**
12.	Bigonial breadth	1.18	2.12
13.	Head circumference	6.49*	10.72**
14.	Auricular height	2.90	4.54*
15.	Foot length	18.83**	0.008
16.	Foot breadth	3.50	4.70*
17.	Weight	2.20	0.27
18.	Thoracic circumference	1.65	—

* Significant at 5% level of probability.

** Significant at 1% level of probability.

Sex differences in the metric characters have been calculated by dividing the female mean value by male value and multiplying the ratio by hundred for each character of both the populations. The ratio of 17 characters for both the populations is presented in table 8.8. The females mean value is less than the male mean for each character among the Bathudi and Sounti tribes. When the table 8.8 is more closely examined we find that the females are more close to the males for the cranial vault measurements as compared to the face and other body measurements. Weight and foot breadth have been found with greatest sex differences. The females are closer to the males in head breadth as compared to the head length. Head circumference, Minimum frontal breadth and Head breadth have slight sex variations. The difference for face and nose measurements are more marked. Stature and sitting height have comparatively more moderate sex differences. The trends of sex variations as observed in case of Bathudi and Sounti are comparable with the similar study conducted among the Nicobarese (Ganguly, 1976).

Table 8.8

Female mean/male mean x 100 ratios among Bathudi and Sounti tribes

Sl. No.	*Characters*	*Bathudi*	*Sounti*
1.	Stature	93.48	92.96
2.	Sitting height	92.33	93.94
3.	Head length	95.43	95.38
4.	Head breadth	97.11	95.78
5.	Minimum frontal breadth	98.02	96.70
6.	Bizygomatic breadth	95.60	94.49
7.	Total facial height	91.83	89.47
8.	Upper facial height	94.78	94.27
9.	Nasal height	93.61	92.27
10.	Nasal breadth	93.44	90.69
11.	Nasal depth	94.72	89.07
12.	Bigonial breadth	95.38	95.14
13.	Head circumference	98.24	97.76
14.	Auricular height	95.14	94.98
15.	Foot length	90.90	93.50
16.	Foot breadth	84.63	88.60
17.	Weight	86.86	85.71

Intergroup variations

The use of standard deviations for comparing male and female variabilities is not satisfactory because females in general have smaller body dimensions than males and therefore, tend to have smaller standard deviation unless variability among them is markedly higher. The coefficient of variation seems to be a more useful constant in this respect (Ganguly, 1976). The co-efficient of variation for various Anthropometric measurements among the Bathudi males and females are shown in table 8.9.

Table 8.9

Co-efficient of variation for various Anthropometric measurements among Bathudi and Sounti of both sexes

Sl. No.	*Characters*	*Males*		*Females*	
		Bathudi *N = 109*	*Sounti* *N = 106*	*Bathudi* *N = 110*	*Sounti* *N = 105*
1.	Stature	3.77	3.35	3.60	3.25
2.	Sitting height	3.48	5.09	3.45	4.59
3.	Head length	3.08	3.46	3.64	3.49
4.	Head breadth	3.76	3.73	4.01	3.44
5.	Minimum frontal breadth	3.65	3.98	3.96	3.66
6.	Bizygomatic breadth	3.42	3.53	4.25	3.38
7.	Bigonial breadth	4.58	4.68	4.95	4.78
8.	Total facial height	5.61	5.61	6.33	6.15
9.	Upper facial height	7.01	7.01	7.37	6.93
10.	Nasal height	6.89	8.17	6.44	7.33
11.	Nasal breadth	7.59	7.64	8.31	7.31
12.	Nasal depth	12.55	10.77	9.07	13.73
13.	Head circumference	2.81	2.62	2.71	3.67
14.	Auricular height	4.23	4.45	3.99	4.10
15.	Foot length	4.71	5.01	5.05	3.93
16.	Foot breadth	6.47	8.66	9.84	7.78
17.	Weight (Kgms)	11.35	11.48	14.07	12.74
18.	Thoracic circumference	5.40	4.60	—	—

"The characters with pronounced skeletal reference points are the most stable. They become less stable if the reference point has to be located under some fat. Also, characters involving the nasion as a reference point show relatively more variability than the other. In other words the differences in the relative variability of the characters thus appears to be due: 1. association of the characters with morphological factors such as fat deposition, and 2. factors in the method of measurements such as difficulty in locating the reference points, variations in pressure excerted etc". (Malhotra *et. al.* 1981). S.R.Das *et. al.* (1968) made the following observation, while discussing the high value of co- efficient of variation among 5 tribal population of Koraput, "the high value of C.V. for some characters such as morph upper face height, nasal height, nasal breadth and most remarkably for body weight and nasal depth are due chiefly to the wide margins of the errors of measurements rather than to biological variations in these characters. Experienced anthropologists will certainly realise this point. Clothing could be responsible to some extent in causing the high variations in the body weight besides the other uncertain factors (food, drink, excretion, etc.). The innate difficulty in locating and marking the nasal in the living may most probably be the important disturbing factor in the morph. face height and nasal height measurements. Easy pliability and movement of the alae seem to be the cause of high C.V. in the nasal breadth. Nasal depth measurements has the largest C.V. of all, ranging from 14.5 to 16.6 which is attributable to the great difficulty in accurately setting the calliper relative to the pronasale, sub nasale and the Frankfurt plane and partly also to the softness of tissues at the land mark involved. All conclusions based on these, measurements and their variance should be carefully taken into consideration in the above mentioned experimental errors. Unawareness of this fact may lead the statisticians and the anthropologists to wrong inferences about inter tribal relationship or distance".

Indices

Median values of 13 indices among the Bathudi and Sounti of both sexes are presented in Table 8.10.

Table 8.10

Median values of indices among Bathudi and Sounti of both sexes

Sl. No.	Index	Male		Female	
		Bathudi	Sounti	Bathudi	Sounti
1.	Ponderal	0.22	0.23	0.23	0.23
2.	Relative sitting height	50.93	49.88	50.35	50.11
3.	Cephalic	73.39	74.05	74.83	74.42
4.	Length height	64.03	64.46	63.73	64.31
5.	Breadth height	86.85	87.00	84.82	86.77
6.	Morpho facial	81.31	81.80	77.54	77.63
7.	Upper facial	48.50	46.67	47.71	46.20
8.	Fronto-parietal	74.46	75.36	75.38	76.46
9.	Fronto-Zygomatic	78.17	79.22	80.00	80.46
10.	Transverse cephalofacial	95.36	95.31	94.03	94.81
11.	Zygomandibular	76.65	77.00	76.48	77.38
12.	Nasal	79.10	84.84	80.44	82.09
13.	Foot	37.84	38.21	36.06	36.55
		N = 109	N = 106	N = 110	N = 105

(d) Finger and Palmar dermatoglyphics

The pattern types on different digits and hands have been found to occur not in a haphazard manner but in some order as discussed earlier. To ascertain whether these variations are statistically significant or not, X^2 test and t-test have been calculated for the qualitative and quantitative characters respectively. The observations of pattern types and ridge counts on fingers of the present study are in agreement with the earlier observations of Dankmeijer (1938), Cummins and Midlo (1943), Holt (1968) and many others.

(i) Bimanual variations:

As observed in case of digits, the pattern type and the ridge counts on the right and left hands follow a particular trend (Table 8.11). Out of various qualitative finger and palmar characters such as Finger patern type, monomorphic patterns, axial triradius t, B line and D line ending and C line type, pattern on palmar areas Hypothenar, I, II, III and IV interdigital, Bathudi males differ significantly for C line type, I interdigital and III interdigital patterns on palm; Sounti males have been found with significant differences for C line type and I interdigital palmar patterns. Bathudi females are observed with significant bimanual differences for Finger pattern type, I interdigital and III interdigital palmar patterns, while the Sounit females donot have significant difference except for finger pattern types, C line type and pattern on III interdigital palmar areas. Out of 4 quantitative dermatoglyphics characters mean values of ridge counts per hand, triradii on palm, a-b ridge count and main line index none of the Bathudi and Sounti males and females have been found with significant differences, though the mean values follow a particular trend and in most of the case right hands have greater mean values than that of the left hands. This is in agreement with the similar observations of Cummins and Midlo ((1943), Holt (1954) for finger pattern types; Holt (1949), for ridge counts on finger; Cummins *et. al.* (1931), Leche (1933), Fang (1950), Seth (1963), Pons (1964), Das Sharma (1966), Holt (1968), for a-b ridge counts; Cummins and Midlo (1943), Sharma (1957), Pons (1959), Holt (1968) for palmar main line index; Ghosh (1981) for the variability of palmar triradii. Sounti males (18.18%) have least bimanual differences, while Bathudi male, Sounti and Bathudi females have variation for 27.22 per cent characters for each populations (Table 8.12).

(ii) Sex variations

Though the males and females have variations as observed in case of two hands and different digits for various finger and palmar dermatoglyphic characters, but out of 12 qualitative and 5 quantitative dermatoglyphic characters, Bathudi males and females differ significantly for finger pattern types, B and D line endings, Interdigital palmar area of left hand. The Sounti show sex difference for axial triradius t, D and B line endings, and II interdigital palmar area. Out of the 5 quantitative dermatoglyphics characters the sex differences have been found to be significant for triradii on palm among the Bathudi, 'a-b' ridge count among the Bathudi and

Sounti. While for the total finger ridge counts, triradii on fingers and main line index, both the populations show homogeneity for both the sexes. Bathudi and Sounti show significant sex variation for 28.57 percent qualitative characters each. While for quantitative characters Bathudi and Sounti have significant sex variations for 40 percent and 20 percent characters respectively (Table 8.13, 8.14, 8.15 and 8.17). While for the total finger ridge counts, triradii on fingers and main line index, both the populations show homogeneity for both the sexes. Bathudi and Sounti show significant sex variation for 28.57 percent qualitative characterrs each. While for quantitative characters Bathudi and Sounti have significant sex variations for 40 per cent and 20 percent characters respectively (Table 8.13, 8.14, 8.15 and 8.17).

(iii) Population variations

Out of the various qualitative finger and palmar dermatoglyphics characters such as Finger pattern types, monomorphic patterns, symmetrical patterns on homologous fingers, axial triradius, ending of D and B lines, C line type, patterns on palmar area Hypothenar, I interdigital, II interdigital, III interdigital and IV interdigital, Bathudi and Sounti males have been found with statistically significant differences for pattern types on fingers, axial triradii, B and D endings and C line type, pattern on palmar area I interdigital, II interdigital, III and IV interdigital, while as the Bathudi and Sounti females show statistically significant differences for D and B line ending, C line ending, C line type, III interdigital palmar area for left hands IV inter digital palmar area. Out of five quantitative dermatoglyphic characters namely total finger ridge counts, triradii on fingers, triradii on palm, 'a-b' ridge counts and main line index; Bathudi and Sounti males, Bathudi and Sounti females show significant differences for a-b ridge counts and main line index. Bathudi and Sounti have been found to difference significantly for 64.28 percent characters and 42.86 percent characters of male series and female series respectively for qualitative characters. While for the quantitative dermatoglyphic configurations the male series and female series have significant difference for 40% characters each (Table 8.13, 8.14, 8.16 and 8.17).

Table 8.11

Chi-square values for bilateral asymmetry of qualitative finger and palmar dermatoglyphics characters among the Bathudi and Sounti of both sexes

Sl. No.	*Characters*	*d.f*	*Male*		*Females*	
			Bathudi	*Sounti*	*Bathudi*	*Sounti*
1.	Finger patterns	2	1.56	0.92	8.95*	10.77**
2.	Monomorphic patterns	1	1.78	0.10	1.02	0.16
3.	Axial triradii 't'	2	0.34	0.32	1.09	0.60
4.	B line ending	2	3.23	0.14	1.47	1.91
5.	C line type	2	7.53*	9.74**	4.97	22.19**
6.	D line ending	2	3.73	1.77	2.46	0.81
7.	Hypothenar pattern	1	0.40	0.93	0.37	1.26
8.	I interdigital pattern	1	10.52**	0.086*[1]	0.0181*[1]	0.1231[1]
9.	II "	1	0.106[1]	0.27	0.500[1]	0.179[1]
10.	III "	1	7.28**	3.71	4.78*	10.47**
11.	IV "	1	3.56	2.57	0.46	1.86

* Significant at 5% level of probability.
** Significant at 1% level of probability.
1 Exact probability calculated since the cell frequencies are less than 5.

Table 8.12

Proportion of significant differences at 5 percent and 1 percent level for qualitative Dermatoglyphic characters for bimanual variations among the Bathudi and Sounti of both sexes

Sl. No.	*Total characters*		*5%*	*1%*	*Total difference*	*Percentage Significant difference*
1.	Bathudi male	11	1	2	3	27.27
2.	Sounti male	11	1	1	2	18.18

(Contd.)

(Contd.)

3.	Bathudi female	11	3	—	3	27.27
4.	Sounti female	11	—	3	3	27.27

Table 8.13

Chi-square values for sex and population variations of various qualitative finger and palmar dermatoglyphic characters among the Bathudi and Sounti tribes

Sl. No.	*Characters*	*d.f*	*Bathudi male x Sounti male*	*Bathudi female x Sounti female*	*Bathudi male x Bathudi female*	*Sounti male x Sounit female*	*Side*
1.	Finger patterns	3	15.18**	2.61	11.81**	1.26	Right + left hand
2.	Monomorphic pattern	1	2.46	2.37	2.33	2.18	do
3.	Symmetrical patterns on fingers	1	0.42	4.34*	0.88	3.36	do
4.	Axial triradius	2	6.19*	3.17	0.03	8.69*	do
5.	B line endings	3	19.52**	14.18**	14.68**	10.27*	do
6.	D line endings	3	11.89*	9.13*	13.22**	15.91**	do
7.	C line type	2	17.93**	9.51**	4.25	4.43	do
8.	Hypothenar pattern	1	0.27[11]		0.51	0.04	do
9.	I interdigital pattern	1 1	0.15 6.87	0.50[1] 0.10[1]	0.18[1] 10.00**	0.25[1] 0.88	Right + left hand
10.	II interdigital pattern	1	4.05*	0.15	0.43	4.81*	Right + Left hand

(Contd.)

(Contd.)

11.	III interdigital pattern	1 1	13.41*** 8.51**	1.38 5.19	2.42 1.10	0.90 0.19	Right + left hand
12.	IV interdigital pattern	1	27.33***	11	1.80	0.50	Right + Left

* Significant at 5% level of probability.
** Significant at 1% level of probability.
*** Significant at 0.1% level of probability.

1 Exact probability calculated since the cell frequencies are less than 5.

11 Male and female data pooled as there are no significant sex variations for the purpose of calculation of group variations.

Table 8.14

Proportion of significant sex and population differences at 5 per cent and 1 percent level for qualitative dermatoglyphic characters among the Bathudi and Sounti

Comparison	*Total variables*	*Significant difference at 5%*	*1%*	*Total*	*Percentage Significant difference*
Sex variations					
Bathudi male x Bathudi female	14	—	4	4	28.57
Sounti male x Sounti female	14	3	1	4	28.57
Population variations					
Bathudi male x Sounti male	14	2	7	9	64.28
Bathudi female x Sounti female	14	3	3	6	42.86

Table 8.15

t value for sex differences for quantitative dermatoglyphic characters among the Bathudi and Sounti

Sl. No.	Variable	Population	d.f.	Mean difference	t value
1.	Total finger ridge count	Bathudi	210	6.52	1.20
		Sounit	209	4.74	0.90
2.	Triradii on finger	Bathudi	217	0.71	1.42
		Sounti	212	0.16	0.34
3.	Triradii on palm	Bathudi	217	0.47	3.50**
		Sounti	212	0.09	0.58
4.	a-b ridge	Bathudi	217	3.59	2.92**
		Sounti	212	4.20	3.55**
5.	Main line index	Bathudi	217	0.62	1.20
		Sounti	212	0.52	0.90

** Significant at 1% level of probability.

Table 8.16

t value for population variations for quantitative dermatoglyphic characters among the Bathudi and Sounti of male series and female series

Sl. No.	Variable	Series	d.f.	Mean difference	t value
1.	Total finger ridge count	Male	210	7.06	1.34
		Female	209	0.28	0.97
2.	Triradii on finger	Male	216	0.83	1.74
		Female	213	0.28	0.57
3.	Triradii on palm	Male	216	0.23	1.53
		Female	213	0.15	1.25
4.	a-b ridge count	Male	216	3.86	3.20**
		Female	213	3.93	3.26
5.	Main line index	Male	216	1.33	2.51**
		Female	213	1.23	2.19**

** Significant at 1% level of probability.

Table 8.17

Proportion of significant sex and population differences for qualitative dermatoglyphic characters among the Bathudi and Sounti tribes at 1% level

	Comparison	*Total variables*	*Significant differences*	*Percentage*
	Sex variations			
1.	Bathudi male x Bathudi female	5	2	40.00
2.	Sounti male x Sounti female	5	1	20.00
	Population variations			
1.	Bathudi male x Sounti male	5	2	40.00
2.	Bathudi female x Sounti female	5	2	40.00

(e) ABO Blood groups

The chi-square values have been calculated between both sexes and populations and presented in table 8.18. As expected three are no significant sex variations of the Bathudi and Sounti. The X^2 values at 3 d.f. between the male and female of Bathudi is 2.76 at $0.50 > P > 0.30$ probability level and between the male and females of Sounti, the chi-square value is 2.04 at 3 d.f. (Probability level $0.70 > P > 0.90$). These chi- square values indicate homogeneity of both the sexes for Bathudi and Sounti. As there are no significant sex variations the male and female data of Bathudi, male and female data of Sounti for ABO blood groups have been pooled. The Bathudi and Sounti tribes have been found to be homogeneous for ABO blood group, chi- square value ar 3 d.f between Bathudi and Sounti is 0.54 at probability level $0.95 > P > 0.90$.

Table 8.18

X^2 values for sex and inter group variations for ABO blood groups of the Bathudi and Sounti

Comparison	*X2 at 3 d.f.*	*Probability*
Bathudi male x female	2.765	0.50 > P > 0.30

(Contd.)

(Contd.)

Sounti male x female	2.047	$0.70 > P > 0.50$
Bathudi x Sounti	0.542	$0.95 > P > 0.90$

A_1 and A_2, A_1B and A_2B have been pooled for the X^2 test due to insufficient cell frequencies.

(*f*) *Colour vision deficiency*

The incidence of colour vision deficiency among the males of Bathudi and Sounti is 2.60 per cent and 4.39 per cent respectively. Though Sounti males have been found with slightly higher incidence of colour blindness as compared to the Bathudi males, but this is not statistically significant. X^2 value between the Bathudi and Sounti males at 1 d.f. for the incidence of colour vision deficiency is 0.212 at $0.70 > P > 0.50$ probability level which shows their homogeneity.

9

COMPARISON WITH OTHER POPULATIONS

In the present chapter an attempt has been made to analyse the results of the present investigations in the light of similar earlier studies. All the population groups from Orissa have not yet been investigated for all the parameters undertaken in the present study. Various authors have attempted to study the caste/tribal populations for Bio-anthropological investigations from Orissa and its neighbourhood.

9.1 MORPHOLOGICAL VARIATION

In the past various authors used different Anthroposcopic observations and somatometric characters for the purpose of studying variations among different populations. In table 9.1 the contribution of each character to the total Somatoscopic and anthropometric variability has been presented (c.f. Balakrishnan *et. al.* 1981). It may be observed that skin colour contributes about 32 per cent of the total somatoscopic variability. The skin colour, eye colour and hair colour considered together contribute about 54 per cent. Nasion depression contributes to 12 per cent to the total somatoscopic observations. Similarly, Nasal breadth and Nasal length contribution to more than 33 per cent of the total anthropometric variation. Auricular height and head breadth contributes about 10 per cent and 9 per cent each of the total anthropometric characters.

Chatterjee *et. al.* (1991) observed that "The basic characters of the majority of the Indian aborigines are as follows :

"The stature is generally short and the body is of moderate build, having dolichocephalic head. The skin colour is deep chocolate brown approaching black. The facial contours are usually

Table 9.1

Contribution of each character to the total Somatoscopic and Anthropometric Variability (c.f Balakrishnan *et. al.*, 1981)

Sl No.	*Somatoscopy Characters*	*Percentage contributions*	*Sl No.*	*Anthropometry*	*Percentage contributions*
1.	Skin colour	31.83	1.	Nasal breadth	18.44
2.	Hair colour	12.10	2.	Nasal length	14.72
3.	Nasion depression	12.00	3.	Orbital breadth	11.78
4.	Eye colour	10.07	4.	Auricular height	9.83
5.	Face shape	7.70	5.	Orbitonasal Arc	9.11
6.	Lip thickness	4.84	6.	Headbreadth	8.98
7.	Supra orbital ridge	4.53	7.	Upper facial length	4.90
8.	Earlobe size	4.40	8.	Orbitonasal breadth	4.40
9.	Earlobe types	4.35	9.	Horizontal circumference of head	3.57
10.	Body hair quantity	3.42	10.	Bizygomatic breadth	3.05
11.	Hair type	2.84	11.	Bigonial breadth	2.94
12.	Alveolar prognothism	1.92	12.	Head length	2.85
			13.	Stature	2.27
			14.	Frontal breadth	2.05
			15.	Total facial length	1.15

squarish and the superior facial height is generally short. The forehead is flat and slightly sloping backwards. Supra-orbital part of the frontal bone is straight and the supra- orbital ridges are moderately marked. Eye slits are narrow and often slightly oblique and the colour of the eyes is generally dark brown. The nasal root is often remarkably depressed and the nasal bridge is broad at the middle. The Nasal form is usually platyrrhine, except when mixed with higher types, whereas the nasal profile is generally concavo-convex. The upper and lower lips are thick and the character of the chin is either negative or neutral. Head hair is commonly straight, but the presence of wavy form of hair is also noticed. The colour of the hair is often dark brown. The body hair is generally scanty. The characteristic feature of the majority of the non-mongoloid people is the occurrence of narrow forehead with broad cheeck bones, as a result of which the facial contour is found to be remarkable in appearance. The type is recognisable even in admixture with higher types or higher caste people".

9.2 ANTHROPOMETRY

The present data of stature, cephalic index and Nasal index have been compared with the various available data of the populations of Orissa and some of the tribal populations of Bihar, West Bengal and Madhya Pradesh (Table 9.2). Bivariate distribution of mean stature and cephalic index among 77 males and 16 females are shown in Figure 9.1 and 9.2 respectively. From the figures 9.1 and 9.2 it may be observed that the Bathudi males show relatively greater affinity with the Santals, from Santal Parganas, Kharwar from Surjuga, Korwa from Lohardaga, Savara from Orissa. The Sounti males are found to show resemblance with Kodaku from Surguja, Munda from Ranchi Konda Paroja from Koraput, Asur from Ranchi, Korwa and Nagesia from Surguja, Kharia, Bhuia North from Orissa, Bhuia Pauri from Keonjhar, Saora from Ganjam, Maler from Santal Pargana and Juang from Orissa. Similarly the Sounti females are closer to the Kond from the Orissa, Asur from Bihar. The Bathudi females forms a cluster with Oraons and Santal from Bihar, Kui, Ollarogadaba, Bareng Paroja, Badogadaba from Orissa. Bivariate distribution of mean value of stature and Nasal index of 77 male and 14 female populations from Orissa, Bihar, West Bengal and Madhya Pradesh are shown in Figure 9.3 and 9.4 respectively. It may be observed from the above figures that

Table 9.2

Comparison of three Anthropometric characters of Bathudi and Sounti with other Tribal populations

A. Male Series

Sl. No.	*Populations*	*Locality*	*N*	*Stature*	*Caphalic Index*	*Nasal Index*	*Author and year*
1.	Agaria	Orissa	50	1641.76	73.84	79.07	Karve, I., 1954
2.	Bhatra	do	52	1612.75	74.67	88.20	do
3.	Bhuia (North)	do	40	1581.32	73.51	90.77	do
4.	Bhuia (South)	do	51	1602.86	77.22	86.76	do
5.	Bhuia Pauri	Keonjhar, Orissa	100	1573.10	73.29	87.93	Roy, R.C., 1935
6.	Bhuia	Mayurbhanj Orissa	81	1577.00	77.00	77.00	Basu, P.C., 1929
7.	Binjhal	Orissa	50	1570.78	77.55	91.68	Karve, I., 1954
8.	Bondo-porja	do	46	1573.52	76.04	89.17	do
9.	Brahmin Mastan	Puri, Orissa	52	1642.00	77.6	79.3	Risley, H.H., 1903
10.	Brahman Orissa	do	143	1642.92	77.31	70.46	Guha, B.S., 1954
11.	Brahman Samavodi	do	53	1663.01	77.59	77.31	Karve, I., 1954

(Contd.)

(Contd.)

12.	Chasa	do	59	1615.00	71.1	79.3	Risley, 1903
13.	Dora	Koraput, Orissa	34	1600.82	75.29	90.15	Karve, I., 1954
14	Gadaba	Orissa	52	1594.67	74.84	87.58	do
15.	Gaura	Cuttack, Orissa	41	1627.00	77.7	76.8	Resley, H.H., 1903
16.	Gond	Orissa	51	1607.18	75.30	81.27	Karve, I., 1954
17.	Guria	Puri,Orissa	40	1606.00	78.4	79.3	Risley, H.H., 1903
18.	Gwala-yadava	Orissa	50	1641.30	77.14	79.30	Karve, I., 1954
19.	Juang	Dhenkanal & Keonjhar	116	1575.70	75.29	89.96	Raj, A.K., 1958
20.	Kandra	Cuttack, Orissa	41	1625.00	78.40	79.6	Risleyt, H.H., 1903
21	Karan	Puri, Orissa	43	1638.00	76.20	81.30	do
22.	Kewat	Cuttack,Orissa	38	1611.00	77.30	82.30	do
23.	Khandayat	do	40	1645.00	73.30	78.70	do
24.	Khandayat	Cuttack, Orissa	30	1632.77	76.75	82.53	Karve, I., 1954
25.	Kharia	Orissa	28	1578.10	73.45	85.25	do

(Contd.)

(Contd.)

26.	Koya	Orissa	51	1588.66	76.51	91.81	Karve, I., 1954
27.	Kui	Khondmals, Orissa	71	1597.00	76.2	79.3	Eickstedt, E., 1933
28.	Kulta	Orissa	51	1630.96	75.82	85.25	Karve, I., 1954
29.	Kumhar	do	51	1646.86	75.74	81.70	do
30.	Meher	do	16	1614.46	75.59	78.02	do
31.	Munda	do	32	1623.68	73.44	88.95	do
32.	Niari	do	26	1611.00	76.4	80.5	Risley, H.H., 1903
33.	Nulia	do	150	1614.68	75.27	75.48	Roychoudhuri, T.C. as cited by Gupta and Dutta 1966
34.	Pan	Cuttack, Orissa	40	1607.00	77.60	82.1	Risley, H.H., 1903
35.	Pana	Orissa	50	1598.76	77.98	82.19	Karve, I., 1954
36.	Porja	do	52	1575.86	75.99	85.48	do
37.	Santal	Orissa and Bengal	100	1592.28	75.68	79.59	Roychoudhuri, I.C.
38.	Saora	Ganjam, Orissa	100	1572.8	74.5	85.2	Majumdar, D.N. 1950

(Contd.)

(Contd.)

39.	Savara	orissa	29	1604.34	73.73	89.94	Karve, I., 1954
40.	Sweeper	do	39	1603.94	77.49	83.93	do
41.	Teli	do	45	1619.00	76.50	77.4	Risley, H.H., 1903
42.	Dora	Koraput, Orissa	103	1620.00	73.94	82.55	Banerjee, M.K., 1975
43.	Khond	do	103	1587.00	76.06	78.07	do
44.	Kond	Kalahandi	53	1565.00	74.1	84.71	Sharma, K., 1979
45.	Khond	Orissa	51	1566.74	74.79	83.24	Karve, I., 1954
46.	Khond	Phulbani	100	1599.6	73.57	77.13	Ray, G.S. 1949
47.	Uraon	Orissa	39	1587.87	75.79	89.15	Karve, I., 1954
48.	Bado Gadaba	Koraput, Orissa	200	1593.9	72.2	80.8	Das, S.R. *et. al.* 1968
49.	Bareng Paroja	do	200	1587.9	75.8	82.1	do
50.	Pareng Gadaba	do	199	1594.8	72.2	81.0	do
51.	Ollaro Gadaba	Koraput, Orissa	199	1602.5	73.7	77.8	Das, S.R. *et. al.* 1968
52.	Konda Paroja	do	199	15.82.5	74.0	81.2	do

(Contd.)

(Contd.)
Bihar

53.	Asur	Ranchi, Bihar	30	1586.00	73.78	80.24	Gupta and Dutta, 1963
54.	Bhumij	Chotanagpur, Bihar	100	1592.00	75.0	86.5	Risley, H.H., 1891
55.	Chero	Seraikella	165	1600	75.0	82.9	Chatterjee, A.N. and T.C. Das 1927
56.	Kharia	Lohardaga	78	1601	74.5	88.5	Risley, H.H., 1891
57.	Kharwar	do	100	1605	75.5	89.7	Risley, H.H., 1891
58.	Korwa	do	21	1595	74.4	92.2	do
59.	Maler	Santal Parganas	100	1577	74.9	94.7	do
60.	Maler Hill	Rajmahal Hill	189	1566	74.54	84.30	Sarkar, S.S., 1935-36
61.	Malp-ahari	Santal Pargana	100	1577	75.8	93.6	Risley, H.H., 1891
62.	Munda	Ranchi, Bihar	250	1581	74.34	83.29	Basu, P.C., 1932-33
63.	Oraon	Lohardaga	250	1618	74.32	82.71	Basu, P.C., 1933-34
64.	Santal	S. Pargana	168	1596	73.85	78.46	Sarkar 1954
65.	Chero	Kolhan	165	1600	75.00	79.7	Majumdar, 1950

(Contd.)

(Contd.)

66.	Lepcha	Bengal	84	1572	81.48	67.69	Guha, 1935
67.	Lodha	Midnapur	200	1591	76.06	85.5	Bhowmick, P.K., 1956
68.	Magh	Chitta-gong hills	100	1608	81.8	82.7	Risley, H.H., 1891
69.	Bathudi	Mayurbhanj, Orissa	109	1597.33	73.86	79.89	Present Study
70.	Sounti	do	106	1578.84	74.18	85.11	Present Study
71.	Kanwar	Surguja, M.P.	109	1620.0	73.15	79.23	Ahmad,1981
72.	Kharwar	do	102	1600.3	73.5	77.6	do
73.	Kodaku	do	100	1579.5	74.2	81.5	do
74.	Korwa	do	102	1574.0	74.0	86.6	do
75.	Nagesia	do	104	1575.2	73.06	83.6	do
76.	Pandos	do	101	1594.3	72.6	79.5	do
77.	Pardhan	Mavilla, M.P.	101	1628.9	72.9	75.9	do

N = Number of individuals.

* N = for number of fingers.

1 As cited by Gupta and Dutta, 1966.

(Contd.)

B. Female Series

Sl. No.	Populations	Locality	N	Stature	Caphalic Index	Nasal Index	Author and year
1.	Lodha	Midnapur, W.Bengal	50	1494	78.4	85.79	Bhowmick, P.K., 1956
2	Asur	Netarhat, Bihar	10	1463	74.30	—	Gates, R.R., 1962
3.	Asur	do	26	1490	73.61	83.45	Gupta, P. & Dutta, P.C., 1963
4.	Birhor	Ranchi, Bihar	4	1495	73.14	—	Gates, R.R., 1959
5.	Ho	Singbhum, Bihar	50	1498	75.38	89.66	Ghosh, G.C., 1967
6.	Oraon	Ranchi, Bihar	110	1493	75.85	84.05	Banerjee, P., 1960
7.	Santal	Santal Pargana, Bihar	61	1491	77.2	73.6	Eickstedt. V., 1933
8.	Kui	Khondmals, Orissa	65	1486	76.4	78.7	do
9.	Kond	Kalahandi	11	1470	75.52	86.07	Sharma, K., 1979
10.	Bado Gadaba	Koraput, Orissa	200	1487.7	74.2	82.9	Das, S.R. *et. al.*, 1968

(Contd.)

(Contd.)

11.	Bareng Paroja	do	200	1486.4	46.1	80.7	Das, S.R. *et. al.*, 1968
12.	Pareng Gadaba	do	200	1500.7	73.3	81.9	do
13.	Ollaro Gadaba	do	198	1482.3	76.2	81.3	do
14.	Konda Paroja	do	198	1479.8	75.4	80.2	do
15.	Bathudi	Mayurbhanj,Orissa	110	1493.25	75.14	79.75	Present Study
16.	Sounti	Mayurbhanj,Orissa	105	1467.67	74.47	82.89	Present Study

the Bathudi males cluster along with the chero from Bihar, Santal and Kui from Orissa, Pandos from Madhya Pradesh, Santal from Santal Parganas, Khond from Koraput, Badogadaba, Pareng gadaba from Koraput and Asur from Ranchi, Bihar. The Sounti males cluster with Porja and Saora from Orissa, Munda from Bihar, Nagesia from Madhya Pradesh, Khond from Koraput and Kalahandi and Maler from Bihar. In case of Females, the Sounti are more close to Khond from Kalahandi and the Bathudi are comparatively akin to Kui, Bareng Paroja and Pareng gadaba from Orissa. From the above analysis it appears that the Bathudi males show affinities for anthropometric characters with Santal, Kharia, Korwa, Chero and Asur from Bihar ; Khond, Ollarogadaba, Badogadaba, Pareng-gadaba, Savara, Kui from Orissa and Kharwar and Pandos from Madhya Pradesh. The Sounti males are found to be closer to Munda and Asur from Bihar ; Kodaku, Korwa and Negasia from Madhya Pradesh and Konda Porja, Kharia, Bhuia, Saora, Maler, Juang, Porja and Khond from Orissa. Bathudi females for various anthropometric characters are found to be closer to Oraon and Santal from Bihar and Kui, Ollarogadaba, Bareng Paroja, Badogadaba and Pareng-gadaba from Orissa. The Sounti females show closer affinity with Asur from Bihar and Kond from Orissa.

9.3 DERMATOGLYPHICS

9.3.1 Papillary Patterns

The frequency of pattern types and their indices among the Tibeto-Burman speakers non-bodo, bodo, Central Dravidian speakers, Southern Dravidian speakers and Austric speaker male and female samples are compared with the present samples in Tables 9.3 and 9.4, respectively. Bivariate percentage frequency distribution of whorls and loops for the various populations are presented in Figures 9.5 and 9.6 for the male and female samples, respectively. It may be observed from Figure 9.5 that Bathudi males are relatively closer to Munda among the Austric speakers, Dhurwa, Narainpur Muria, Dorla, Ollarogadaba among the Central Dravidian speakers ; and Miri (non-bodo) and Plaingaro (Bodo) among the Tibeto Burman speakers. The Sounti males show close affinites in this regard with Juang, Sabara, Saora, and Santal among

Table 9.3

Distribution of Pattern Frequencies (in percentage) and their indices among male series

Sl. No.	Sample	N	Pattern type			Whorl/Loop index	Arch-es/ Whorl index	Pattern inten-sity value	Sources
			Whorl	Loop	Arch				
1.	Lalung	106	51.0	47.5	1.5	107.6	3.0	15.0	Chakravartti and Mukherjee, 1961
2.	Abor	147	53.2	44.3	2.5	120.2	4.7	15.1	Bhattacherjee, 1955)
3.	Angami Naga	124	52.3	47.4	0.2	110.4	0.5	15.2	Chakravartti and Mukherjee, 1962
4.	RengamaNaga	104	53.4	46.3	0.3	115.2	0.5	15.3	do
5.	Lotha Naga	106	53.8	42.8	3.4	125.5	6.3	15.0	do
6.	Sema Naga	158	54.8	44.4	0.8	123.4	1.4	15.4	do
7.	Konyak Naga	11	52.3	46.0	1.6	113.7	3.1	15.1	do
8.	Kabui Naga	164	44.3	55.6	0.1	79.6	0.3	14.4	do
9.	Mao Naga	153	55.1	44.7	0.1	123.2	0.2	15.5	do

(Contd.)

(Contd.)

10.	Galong	152	46.0	52.0	2.0	88.5	4.4	14.4	Kumar (as cited Bhatacherjee 1955
11.	Miri	100	49.3	49.6	0.9	99.4	1.8	14.8	Sharma (as cited by Sarkar 1962)
12.	Miri	10	40.3	58.6	1.1	68.7	2.7	13.9	Chakravartti and Mukherjee, 1961
13.	Rabha	132	38.3	55.0	6.7	69.7	17.4	13.2	Chakra-vartti and Mukherjee, 1961
14.	Rabha	295	50.7	47.8	1.5	106.0	3.1	14.9	Das, 1959
15.	Garo	134	41.9	55.5	2.5	75.4	6.1	13.9	Chakravartti and Mukherjee, 1961
16.	Hill Garo	76	50.8	47.5	1.7	106.9	3.4	14.9	Das, 1959
17.	Plain Garo	94	48.0	49.0	3.0	98.0	6.2	14.5	do
18.	Hajong	75	44.7	53.7	1.6	83.2	3.7	14.3	do
19.	Kach-ari	109	54.7	43.4	1.8	125.9	3.4	15.3	do
20.	Mech	72	40.3	57.2	2.5	70.4	6.2	13.8	Chakravartti and Mukherjee, 1961

(Contd.)

(Contd.)

21.	Riang	68	44.7	53.0	2.3	84.4	5.3	14.2	Basu, 1959
22.	Oroan	107	57.2	41.4	1.4	138.0	2.4	15.5	Chakravartti, 1963
23.	Oraon	27	50.4	47.0	2.6	107.0	5.3	14.7	Ghosh, 1960
24.	Khond	16	42.0	52.9	5.1	79.4	12.3	13.7	Sarkar *et. al.*, 1957
25.	Raj Gond	1221	40.06	56.7	2.7	71.7	6.7	13.8	Ghosh* (Unpublished)
26.	Pardhan	1122	36.7	59.2	4.1	62.1	11.2	13.3	do
27.	Kalam	966	37.2	57.6	5.2	64.5	13.9	13.2	do
28.	Maria of Allapally	468	52.8	45.9	1.3	114.9	2.4	15.2	do
29.	Naik Gond	1057	35.2	61.8	3.0	57.0	8.6	13.2	do
30.	Maria of Godchiroli	780	43.5	54.9	1.8	79.0	4.1	14.2	do
31.	Raja Muria	1199	50.8	48.0	1.2	105.7	2.3	15.0	do
32.	Kondogaon Muria	1089	47.4	51.2	1.4	92.5	2.9	14.6	Ghosh* (unpublished)

(Contd.)

(Contd.)

33.	Narainpur Muria	1089	48.7	50.0	1.3	97.3	2.6	14.7	do
34.	Bison-horn Miria	1098	46.1	52.2	1.7	88.3	3.8	14.5	do
35.	Dorla	1070	47.6	49.8	2.6	95.5	5.5	14.5	do
36.	Durwa	1429	48.9	49.3	1.8	99.0	3.7	14.7	do
37.	Nunkadora	1030	43.0	52.6	4.4	81.7	10.2	13.7	do
38.	Ollar Gadaba	999	49.4	50.0	0.6	99.0	5.1	15.0	do
39.	Pengo	1220	53.1	44.2	2.7	120.2	5.1	15.0	do
40.	Kond	1210	40.4	55.0	4.6	73.4	11.3	13.6	do
41.	Kadar	80	59.4	40.1	0.5	148.1	0.9	15.9	Chakravartti, 1959
42	Urali	60	53.5	46.5	–	115.1	–	15.4	Chatterjee *et.al.*, 1960
43.	Paniyan	33	58.0	40.7	1.3	142.4	2.2	15.2	Sarkar, 1954
44.	Adiyan	20	52.3	42.7	5.0	122.3	9.6	14.7	do

(Contd.)

(Contd.)

45.	Jan Kurumba	100	41.6	58.4	–	71.2	–	13.9	Chakravartti and Mukherjee, 1964
46.	Vettu Kurumba	142	36.8	60.9	2.3	60.5	6.1	13.0	do
47.	do	22	32.4	61.1	6.5	53.0	20.0	12.6	Sarkar, 1954
48.	Irula	170	43.3	55.4	1.3	78.1	3.0	14.2	Chakravartti and Mukherjee, 1964
49.	Sholaga	75	51.3	47.3	1.3	108.5	2.6	15.0	do
50.	Paniya	138	60.7	37.7	1.6	160.7	2.6	15.9	do
51.	Ulladan	162	31.2	67.3	1.5	46.4	4.8	13.0	Gupta (as cited by Chakravartti, 1959)
52.	Kollimalaialis	70	41.1	53.4	5.4	77.4	13.2	13.6	Sharma, 1962
53.	Mullu-Kurumba	134	52.8	47.0	0.2	112.4	0.3	15.3	Chakravartti and Mukherjee, 1964
54.	Santal	62	52.5	45.9	1.6	114.5	3.1	15.1	Chakra-vartti, 1960
55.	Santal	25	38.8	57.2	40.0	67.8	10.3	13.5	Biswas (as cited by Verma

(Contd.)

(Contd.)

56.	Munda	112	49.6	48.4	2.0	102.6	4.0	14.8	Chakravartti, 1963
57.	Juang	74	42.0	56.6	1.4	74.2	3.2	14.1	Sarkar *et. al.*, 1957
58.	Sabara	54	42.4	55.9	1.7	75.9	4.0	14.1	do
59.	Saora	62	37.8	55.9	6.3	67.7	16.6	13.2	Tripathy, 1967
60.	Asura	89	35.9	62.7	1.4	57.3	3.8	13.6	Dutta and Gupta, 1967
61.	Korku	100	51.2	47.0	1.7	109.0	3.4	15.0	Basu, 1969
62.	Bathudi	*1095	48.6	48.6	2.5	99.2	5.0	14.6	Present study
63.	Sounti	*1076	41.0	41.0	2.9	73.0	7.0	13.8	Present study
64.	Khasi	260	41.7	41.7	1.3	–	–	14.0	Das (cited by Sarkar, 1962)

N = Number of individuals.

*N = Number of fingers

Table 9.4

Distribution of Pattern frequencies (in per cent) and their indices among the female series

Sl No.	Sample	N	Pattern type			Whorl/ Loop index	Arch-es/ Whorl index	Patten inten-sity value	Source
			Whorl	Loop	Arch				
1.	Lalung	132	38.9	57.9	3.2	67.3	8.2	13.6	Chakravartti & Mukherjee, 1962
2.	Abor	163	45.2	52.4	2.4	86.3	5.5	14.3	Bhattacherjee, 1955
3.	Ang-ami Naga	122	45.6	52.3	2.1	87.1	4.7	14.3	Chakravartti & Mukherjee, 1962
4.	Rngama Naga	103	55.6	42.8	1.6	129.9	2.8	15.4	do
5.	Lotha Naga	108	49.3	49.5	1.2	99.4	2.4	14.8	do
6.	Sema Naga	112	53.6	46.1	0.3	116.3	0.7	15.3	do
7.	Konyak Naga	112	42.6	55.6	1.8	76.6	4.2	14.1	do
8.	Kabui Naga	118	36.4	62.7	0.9	58.1	2.3	13.6	do
9.	Mao Naga	102	51.7	48.0	0.3	107.6	0.7	15.1	do

(Contd.)

(Contd.)

10.	Galong	161	37.4	59.2	3.4	63.2	9.1	13.4	Numar (as cited by Bhattacherjee 1955)
11.	Miri	58	4.4	54.0	1.6	82.3	3.5	14.3	Sharma (as cited by Sarkar, 1962)
12.	Miri	112	40.1	56.7	3.1	70.6	7.8	13.7	Chakravartti & Mukherjee, 1961
13.	Rabha	295	45.0	50.7	4.3	88.7	9.6	14.1	Das, 1959
14.	Rabha	100	46.0	51.4	2.0	90.7	0.4	14.5	Chakravartti and Mukherjee, 1961
15.	Garo	104	48.0	50.2	1.7	95.7	3.6	14.6	do
16.	Mech	50	38.8	59.2	2.0	65.5	5.2	13.7	do
17.	Riang	23	50.0	48.7	1.3	102.7	2.6	14.9	Basu, 1959
18.	Kachari	104	47.8	49.2	3.0	97.3	6.2	14.5	Chakravartti & Mukherjee, 1961
19.	Santal	61	48.5	47.4	4.1	102.4	8.5	14.4	Chakravartti, 1960
20.	Munda	101	38.6	57.2	4.2	67.4	10.8	13.4	Chakravartti, 1963

(Contd.)

(Contd.)

21.	Juang	17	38.8	57.7	3.5	67.3	9.1	13.5	Sarkar *et. el.*, 1957
22.	Asura	43	28.7	67.6	3.7	42.4	13.0	12.7	do
23.	Kharia	13	51.5	48.5	—	106.2	—	15.2	Geipel, 1961
24.	Kadar	65	47.7	51.8	0.5	92.2	1.1	14.7	Chakravartti, & Mukherjee, 1969
25.	Jen Kurumba	100	27.0	70.8	2.2	38.1	8.2	12.0	do
26.	Vettu Kurumba	117	36.4	62.5	1.1	58.3	3.0	11.7	do
27.	Mullu Kurumba	154	45.3	53.6	1.0	84.5	2.3	14.4	do
28.	Irula	112	45.0	52.5	2.5	85.7	5.6	14.2	do
29.	Sholaga	88	61.4	38.6	—	158.8	—	16.7	do
30.	Paniya	112	53.6	45.4	1.0	117.8	1.8	15.3	do
31.	Kollimalaialis.	27	40.0	54.1	5.9	74.0	14.8	13.4	do
32.	Urali	24	44.3	54.4	1.3	81.4	2.9	14.1	do
33.	Oraon	93	54.5	42.3	3.2	129.0	5.9	15.1	Chakra-vartii, 1963
34.	Oraon	26	57.7	40.9	40.9	1.3	140.9	2.3	Ghosh, 1960

(Contd.)

(Contd.)

35.	Raj Gond	831	29.6	67.2	3.2	44.0	11.0	12.6	Ghosh*, (Unpublished
36.	Pardhan	785	36.4	60.3	3.3	60.6	9.1	13.3	do
37.	Lolam	537	32.4	65.7	1.9	49.3	5.8	13.1	do
38.	Maria of Allapally	269	48.0	50.5	1.5	94.9	3.1	14.6	do
39.	Naik Gond	758	33.4	62.9	3.7	53.0	11.1	13.0	do
40.	Maria of Gadchiroli	357	43.4	49.6	7.0	87.6	16.1	13.6	do
41.	Raja Muria	1208	46.0	50.3	3.6	91.5	7.9	14.3	do
42.	Kondagaon Muria	1047	37.1	58.4	4.5	63.5	12.4	13.3	do
43.	Narainpur	1109	38.0	56.3	5.7	67.6	14.9	13.2	do
44.	Muria Dorla	1309	42.3	54.8	2.9	77.3	6.9	14.0	do
45.	Dhurwa	1249	38.3	59.1	2.6	64.8	6.9	13.6	do
46.	Nunkadora	1049	40.7	56.3	3.0	72.3	7.3	13.8	do
47.	Ollar Gadaba	1009	46.2	52.2	1.6	88.4	3.4	14.5	do
48.	Pengo	1120	41.9	54.8	3.3	76.4	7.9	13.9	do

(Contd.)

(Contd.)

49.	Kond	1250	35.7	59.7	4.6	59.8	13.0	13.1	do
50.	Bathudi	1086	43.4	52.8	3.8	82.3	8.3	13.9	Present Study
51.	Sounti	1060	40.2	56.2	3.6	71.4	8.9	13.6	Present Study
52.	Khasi	175	42.8	53.8	3.3	—	—	13.9	Miki *et. al.*, 1960

N = Number of individuals

*N = Number of fingers

the Austric speakers, Garo, Mech, Rabha, Khasi among the Tibeto Burman (Bodo) speakers and Raj Gond and Kond among the Central Dravidian speakers.

In case of females the Bathudi show similarity with the Irula, Mullu Kurumba, Urali among the Southern Dravidian speakers, Abor, Miri, Angami Naga and Khasi among the Tibeto Burman speakers and Ollaro gadaba among the Central Dravidian speakers. The Sounti females cluster with Nunkadora, Narainpur Muria among the Central Dravidian speakers, Lalung and Miri of Tibeto Burman speakers and Munda and Juang of the Austric speakers. When the Pattern intensity indices of the Bathudi and Sounti of both sexes are compared it is observed that the Bathudi males are closely associated with Munda, while the Sounti males show similarity with Juang and Sabara among the Austric speakers. Among the Tibeto Burman speakers the Bathudi males have been found to be close in terms of Pattern intensity index with the Miri, while the Sounti males resemble the Mech, Khasi and Garo's. Among the Dravidian speakers Oraon, Narainpur Maria, and Dhurwa show affinity with the Bathudi males, while the Sounti males don't form a part of any cluster but lie between Rajgonds and Maria of Gadchiroli and Irula. Among the females of the Bathudi, the Pattern intensity index show affinity with Santals and Sounti, while the Sounti females form cluster with Juang and Munda among the Austric speakers. Among the Tibeto Burman speakers Bathudi females form cluster with Khasi, Konyak Naga, and Rabha (Das, 1959) and the Sounti with Mech and Lalung. In case of Dravidian speakers, Bathudi females are close to Dorla while as the Sounti females form cluster with Dhurwa, Maria of Gadchiroli and Nunka Dora.

9.3.2 Whorl-Loop Index

Males of the Bathudi, come very close to the Miri, Plain Garo, Tibeto-Burman speaking populations ; Dhurwa, Ollarogadaba, Narainpur Muria, Dorla the Central Dravidian speakers and among the Austric speakers. When the Sounti males are compared in this regard it is found they are very close to Khond, Rajgond among the Central Dravidian speakers ; Garo among the Tibeto-

Burman speakers the Juang and Sabara among the Austric speakers. The females of the Bathudi show similarity with the Miri, a Tibeto Burman speaker and Urali a Southern Dravidian speaking population. In case of Sounti females the Miri, a Tibeto Burman speaking population and Nunkadora forms a cluster. Narainpur Muria, Lalung, Munda and Juang also lie very close to the Sounti females.

9.3.3 Whorls and Loops on Various Digits

Bathudi males have higher frequency of whorls on digits IV, and I and are comparable with Juang and Sabara males (Sarkar and Banerjee, 1957) from Dhenkhanal Orissa. While the Bathudi females with relatively higher frequency of whorls than loops on digits IV and I are more closer to Pahira (Chakravartti, 1959) from Manbhum, Bihar, and Oraon (Chakrabartti, unpublished) from Bihar, Bathudi males and females are also identical in this regard with Vetta Kurumba (Chakrabartti *et. al.*, 1964) from Nilgiri State. The Sounti males and females have higher frequency of whorls on digit IV only and are comparable with Munda female (Chakrabartti, unpublished) from Bihar, males of Kota, Badaga, Urula and females of Toda, Vetta Kurumba (Chakravartti *et. al.*, 1964) from Nilgiri district and males of Vettu Kurumba (Sarkar, 1954) from Wynaad.

9.3.4 Monomorphic Hands

Occurrence of Similar pattern on all digits of a hand (Monomorphic) is considered to be a hereditary character (Volotzkoy, 1936). It is expected that relative incidence of monomorphic hands for whorls and those for loops will prove a better racial criteria as monomorphism seems to be a pleitropic effect of factors for different pattern types (Mukherjee *et. al.*, 1964). Bathudi males have monomorphic hands with equal frequency of whorls and loops and are comparable with Munda males and females (Chakravartti, unpublished) from Ranchi Bihar, Mullu Kurumba and Moplah males (Chakravartti *et. al.*, 1964) from Nilgiri district. The Sounti males and Bathudi and Sounti females have more monomorphic hands with loops than those with whorls and are comparable with Juang and Sabara of both sexes (Sarkar and

Banerjee, 1957) from Orissa and Toda, Kota, Badoga, Jen Kurumba, Vetta Kurumba, Irula, males (Chakravartti *et. al.*, 1964) from Nilgiri district and females of Toda, Badaga, Jen Kurumba, Mullu Kurumba, Irula, Moplah (Chakravertti *et. al.*, 1964) from Niligiri hills and Urali (Chakravartti and Gupta, 1960) from Kerala. Percentage frequency distribution of monomorphic hands for various population are presented in table 9.5.

9.3.5 Palmar Main Lines

Palmar main line D and B endings among Bathudi males and females has been mostly found to be 11.7 followed by 7.5, while among the Sounti males, and females, Palmar main lines D and B endings are mostly characterised as 7.5 followed by 11.7. "The highest frequency of 7.5.5 is a common feature in each sex of all the Mundari tribes. The Eastern Mundaris, however possess 11.9.7 in about equally high frequency. The majority of main lines in Australoid groups of Oraon (Ranchi) and Pahira have a more horizontal direction denoted by 11.9.7., and 9.7.5 formula. The Oraon of West Bengal show high frequency of longitudinal lines, which may be due to a Mundari influence among them as observed earlier. The Mongoiian people of North Eastern India have also given the highest frequency of 7.5.5 which does not contradict the hypothesis of a Mongolian element within the Mundari speakers" (Mukherjee *et. al.*, 1964).

9.3.6 Types of Palmar C Line

The present data of types of Palmar C line among the Bathudi and Sounti of both sexes have been compared with the similar studies among the various populations from Orissa state and its neighbourhood is Table 9.6. Ethnic trends in the frequencies of 4 modal types of C - lines classified according to its termination towards ulnar (U), radial (R), proximal (P) directions and by absence (O), have been emphasised by Plato (1970). Plato also observed that the ulnar and radial types of C line are also associated with longitudinal and horizontal alinements of palmar ridges respectively. R/U ratio appears to be a workable measure of transversality of ridges in a population and this ratio has been used for comparing the present data interms of C - line

Table 9.5

Percentage distribution of Monomorphic hands with loops and whorls among various populations of both sexes

Sl No.	Population	Male	Female	Author/s	Area
1.	Juang	W = 11.48 L = 18.91	W = 8.82 L = 20.58	Sarkar and Banerjee, 1957	Dhenkhanal (Orissa)
		T = 30.39	T = 29.40		
2.	Sabara	W = 12.96 L = 14.81	W = — L = 16.16	Sarkar and Banerjee, 1957	do
		T = 27.77	T = 16.16		
3.	Munda	W = 10.71 L = 10.71	W = 12.37 L = 12.37	Chakravartti as cited by Mukherjee, *et. al.*, 1964	Ranchi (Bihar)
		T = 21.42	T = 24.74		
4.	Santal	W = 10.48 L = 4.84	W = 15.57 L = 3.28	Chakravartti, 1960	Midnapure (West Bengal)
		T = 15.32	T = 18.85		

(Contd.)

(Contd.)

5.	Oroan	W = 29.00 L = 9.00 T = 38.00	W = 18.75 L = 8.75 T = 27.50	Chakravartti (Unp) As cited by Mukherjee, *et. al.*, 1964	24 Parganas (West Bengal)
6.	Oraon	W = 24.56 L = 7.01 T = 31.57	W = 18.86 L = 9.43 T = 28.29	Chakravartti (Unp) As cited by Mukherjee, *et. al.*, 1964	Ranchi (Bihar)
7.	Pahira	W = 12.12 L = 4.55 T = 16.67	W = 14.28 L = 11.90 T = 26.18	Chakravartti, 1959	Manbhum (Bihar)
8.	Toda	W = 13.71 L = 16.93 T = 30.64	W = 5.00 L = 22.00 T = 27.00	Chakra-vartti, *et. al.*, 1964	Nigiri (Madras)
9.	Kota	W = 10.00 L = 12.00 T = 22.00	W = 14.54 L = 10.90 T = 25.44	do	do

(Contd.)

(Contd.)

10.	Jenkurumba	W=3.00 L=22.00	W=4.00 L=30.00	Chakravartti, *et. al.*, 1964	Nilgiri (Madras)
		T=25.00	T=34.00		
11.	Badaga	W=9.39 L=24.24	W=8.97 L=19.87	do	do
		T=33.63	T=28.84		
12.	Vettu-kurumba	W=8.09 L=24.64	W=6.83 L=23.07	do	do
13.	Mullu-kurumba	W=13.43 L=13.43	W=8.44 L=12.99	do	do
		T=26.86	T=20.73		
14.	Irula	W=10.59 L=20.00	W=12.50 L=15.18	do	do
		T=30.59	T=27.68		
15.	Sholaga	W=20.00 L=10.00	W=20.45 L=11.36	do	do
		T=30.00	t=31.81		

(Contd.)

(Contd.)

16.	Paniya	W=22.46 L=10.00 T=30.79	W=13.39 L=8.93 T=22.32	Chakravartti, *et. al.*, 1964	Nilgiri (Madras)
17.	Moplah	W=14.95 L=14.01 T=28.01	W=13.50 L=16.00 T=29.50	do	do
18.	Vettu-kurumba	W=4.54 L=9.09 T=13.63	—	Sarkar, 1954	Wynaad
19.	Adiyan	W=20.00 L=12.50 T=13.63	—	do	do
20.	Paniyan	W=15.49 L=7.74 T=23.23	—	do	do
21.	Kadar	W=17.91 L=5.22 T=23.13	W=12.50 L=7.14 T=19.64	Chakravartti, *et. al.*,	Kerala

(Contd.)

(Contd.)

22.	Urali	W=20.83 L=12.22	W=6.26 L=22.92	Chakravartti, *et. al.*,., 1960	Kerala
		T=33.05	T=29.18		
23.	Bathudi	W=12.73 L=12.73	W=9.17 L=16.51	Present study	Orissa
		T=25.46	T=25.68		
24.	Sounti	W=8.89 L=15.28	W=4.72 L=16.98	Present study	Orissa
		T=24.17	T=21.70		

Table 9.6

Percentage frequency of modal types of palmar C line and R/U ratio among some of the Indian Populations

Male Series

Sl. No.	Popu-lation	Palace	No.of Palms	Model types of C line				R/U	Author
				U	R	P	O		
1.	Lepcha	Assam	224	79.5	5.8	12.5	2.2	0.07	Miki *et. al.*, 1961
2.	Hajong	Assam	130	76.2	11.5	6.9	5.4	0.15	Das, 1966
3.	Ollaro Gadaba	Orissa	186	65.1	25.2	5.3	4.3	0.39	Ghosh *et. al.*, 1977
4.	Khasi	Assam	484	57.8	23.3	11.4	7.4	0.40	Miki *et. al.*, 1961
5.	Khasi	do	280	63.9	27.1	4.6	4.3	0.40	Chakravartti, 1976
6.	Dorla	M.P.	212	61.3	31.6	5.6	1.4	0.51	Ghosh *et. al.*, 1977
7.	Dhurwa	do	286	58.0	33.9	3.5	4.5	0.59	do
8.	Kond	Orissa	240	57.1	33.8	4.6	4.5	0.59	do
9.	Narainpur Muria	M.P.	216	55.5	37.4	5.6	1.4	0.64	do

(Contd.)

(Contd.)

10.	Rajbansi	W.B.	234	53.6	36.1	5.7	5.4	0.67	Roychaudhury, 1962
11.	Nunkadora	Orissa	202	55.5	37.6	3.8	3.0	0.68	Ghosh *et. al.*, 1977
12.	Sounti	do	216	46.8	31.9	12.0	9.3	0.68	Present Study
13.	Pengo	do	236	53.8	37.4	4.2	4.6	0.69	Ghosh *et. al.*, 1977
14.	Mondagaon Muria	M.P.	212	51.3	37.7	8.1	2.8	0.73	Ghosh *et. al.*, 1977
15.	Munda	Orissa	130	53.1	44.6	2.3	0	0.84	Deka Mahapatra *et. al.*, 1970
16.	Raja Muria	M.P.	240	47.9	43.4	2.5	6.2	0.91	Ghosh *et. al.*, 1977
17.	Muria Godchiroli	d0	152	46.1	44.7	8.5	0.7	0.97	do
18.	Bison-horn Maria	do	220	42.3	46.3	7.7	3.6	1.09	do
19.	Lodha	W.B.	92	26.1	38.0	1.1	34.8	1.46	Ghosh *et. al.*, 1973
20.	Anglo Indian	do	90	33.7	51.5	18.4	18.4	1.50	Battacharjee, 1964
21.	Bathudi	Orissa	220	34.5	51.8	9.6	4.1	1.50	Present study

Table 9.7

Percentage frequency of modal types of palmar C line and R/U ratio among some of the Indian Populations

Female Series

Sl. No.	Population	Palace	No.of palms	Model types of C line				R/U	Author
				U	R	P	O		
1.	Lepcha	Assam	84	75.0	8.5	13.1	3.6	0.11	Miki *et. al.*, 1961
2.	Khasi	Assam	100	64	19.3	7.3	9.3	0.30	Miki *et. al.*, 1961
3.	Khasi	"	200	60.7	19.6	11.4	8.2	0.32	Chakravartti, 1976
4.	Ollaro Gadoba	Orissa	194	64.9	27.8	4.6	2.6	0.43	Ghosh *et. al.*, 1977
5.	Raja Muria	M.P.	242	61.2	23.1	5.3	5.3	0.46	do
6.	Pengo	Orissa	226	59.3	27.4	4.4	8.9	0.47	do
7.	Nunkadora	do	206	60.9	29.2	5.2	4.8	0.48	do
8.	Khond	do	244	57.4	29.1	9.8	3.6	0.51	do
9.	Dhurwa	M.P.	250	57.6	31.2	6.4	4.8	0.54	do

(Contd.)

(Contd.)

10.	Sounti	Orissa	212	54.7	31.1	6.1	8.0	0.57	Present study
11.	Narainpur Muria	M.P.	222	56.3	34.6	4.9	4.1	0.61	Ghosh *et. al.*, 1977
12.	Dorla	do	264	56.0	37.4	4.9	1.8	0.6	do
13.	Kondagaon Muria	do	206	52.3	39.8	5.8	2.0	0.76	do
14.	Lodha	W.B.	82	37.8	39.0	0	23.2	1.03	Ghosh *et. al.*, 1973
15.	Bathudi	Orissa	218	39.9	42.2	8.3	9.6	1.06	Present study
16.	Munda	Orissa	124	36.3	61.3	2.4	0	1.69	Deka Maha patra *et. al.*, 1970

variability of various populations (Ghosh and Mukherjee, 1977). Table 9.6 also presents the percentage frequency of modal types of palmar C - line along with R/U ratio among male and female populations. A close examination of the R/U ratio shows that the Sounti males form cluster with Pengo and Nunkadora, Munda from Orissa and Kondagaon Muria from Madhya Pradesh. While the Bathudi males group with Lodha and Anglo Indians of West Bengal. The Sounti females show more affinity with Dhurwa and Narainpur, Muria from Madhya Pradesh and the Bathudi females are more skin to Lodha from West Bengal than Munda from Orissa.

9.4 BLOOD GROUPS

The ABO blood groups data of the present study have been compared with some of the tribal populations from Orissa and its neighbourhood (Table 9.8). The Bathudis show their very close affinity with the Noatia from Tripura, while the Sounti are relatively closer to Pahira from Singbhum. In other words the Bathudi, Noatia, Korwa (from Palamau), Pahira and Sounti form a cluster, in respect of p, q and r gene frequencies (Figure 9.7). In respect of q gene frequency the Sounti show closeness with the Santal from Hooghly, and the Bhils from Nimar, while as the Bathudi is closely resemble the Kanwar from Bilaspur and Ollaro Gadaba from Koraput. The Bathudi and Sounti tribes have one third ratio of the p, q and r gene frequency and according to Sarkar (1954) this is a Mundari features.

Table 9.8

ABO gene frequencies among some Indian Tribal Populations

Sl. No.	Population	Area	No.	Phenotypic frequencies				Gene frequencies			Reference
				O	A	B	AB	p	q	r	
	Assam										
1.	Galong Abor		400	4.75	32.25	20.75	6.25	.22	.14	.64	Kumar, 1954
2.	Khasi	Khasi & Jaintia Hill	821	48.60	30.45	16.69	4.26	.19	.11	.70	Das, 1969
3.	Khasi	Shillong	315	31.43	36.82	24.13	7.62	.26	.17	.57	Miki *et. al.*, 1960
4.	Noatia	Tripura	142	16.20	28.87	40.84	14.09	.25	.33	.42	Kumar, 1958
5.	Riang	do	509	19.84	25.15	42.04	12.97	.22	.33	.45	Kumar & Sastry, 1961
6.	Khasi	Cherapunji	200	33.00	35.00	18.50	13.50	.28	.17	.55	Macfar-lane, 1941
7.	Lushai	Border of Burma	141	32.60	44.68	16.31	6.38	.30	.12	.58	Mitra, 1935-36

(Contd.)

(Contd.)

	Bihar										
8.	Asur	Palamau	21	38.10	57.14	0.00	4.76	.38	.02	.60	Sarkar, 1949
9.	Birhor	do	102	31.37	35.29	25.53	9.80	.26	.18	.56	Majumdar, 1950
10.	Birhor	do	39	20.51	17.95	51.28	10.26	.15	.39	.46	Sarkar, 1949
11.	Birjias	do	129	10.85	17.05	61.24	10.85	.16	.48	.36	do
12.	Bhumij Desi	Singhbhum	150	30.70	24.70	36.70	8.0	.18	.27	.55	Kumar & Mukherjee, 1968
13.	Bhumij	do	121	35.50	23.10	32.20	9.10	.18	.23	.59	Gupta, 1962
14.	Chero	Palamau	35	34.28	34.28	22.86	8.57	.24	.18	.58	Sarkar, 1949
15.	Ho	Singhbhum	200	25.00	26.00	37.00	12.00	.21	.28	.51	Kumar & Mukherjee, as cited in Kumar 1975
16.	Ho	Singhbhum	186	35.00	31.70	28.00	5.40	.21	.18	.61	Majumdar, 1950
17.	Dudhkharia	Ranchi	184	21.20	33.10	29.90	15.80	.28	.26	.46	Bhattacharjee and Kumar, 1969

(Contd.)

(Contd.)

18.	Kharwars	Palamau	53	16.98	20.75	41.51	20.75	.23	.38	.39	Sarkar, 1949
19.	Kisan	do	30	36.67	13.33	43.33	6.67	.10	.29	.61	do
20.	Korwa	do	114	19.30	27.19	32.46	21.05	.28	.31	.41	do
21.	Korwa	Mirazapur	147	32.0	35.40	20.40	12.20	.27	.18	.55	Majumdar, 1943
22.	Male Plains	S. Pargana	109	39.45	22.02	30.27	30.27	.16	.21	.62	Sarkar & Sen, 1952
23.	Male Hill	do	242	41.32	24.79	27.27	27.27	.17	.19	.69	do
24.	Mal Paharia	do	58	31.03	24.14	31.03	31.03	.21	.25	.54	do
25.	Munda	Singhbhum Keonjhar Mayurbhanj	120	33.33	30.00	29.17	29.17	.21	.21	.58	Macfarlane, 1941
26.	Munda	Ranchi	105	30.48	33.33	26.67	26.67	.25	.20	.55	Tyagi (cited by Bhattacharjee) 1969 and Kumar
27.	Munda	Ranchi	198	23.20	33.30	28.30	28.30	.28	.25	.47	Kumar and Bhattacharjee, 1970

(Contd.)

(Contd.)

28.	Oraon	Palamau	115	26.09	27.83	33.91	12.17	.22	.27	.51	Sarkar, 1949
29.	Oraon	Ranchi	125	25.60	28.80	38.40	7.20	.20	.27	.53	Kirk *et. al.*, 1962
30.	Pahira (Southern)	Singhbhum	274	22.63	40.88	25.18	11.31	.31	.20	.49	Basu, 1969
31.	Pahira	do	397	14.61	30.23	35.77	19.40	.29	.33	.38	do
32.	Santal	S. Pargana	407	31.69	21.37	35.63	1130	.18	.27	.55	Sarkar & Sen, 1952
33.	Santal	do	400	26.20	23.50	38.00	12.20	.20	.30	.50	Bhattacherjee, 1968
34.	Santal	do	199	32.00	21.00	35.00	12.00	.18	.27	.55	Sarkar, 1938
35.	Munda	Ranchi	180	27.28	22.78	29.44	20.00	.24	.28	.48	Dass Sharma, 1976
36.	Oraon	Ranchi	100	35.00	15.00	40.00	10.00	.12	.28	.60	Shukla & Tyagi, 1971
37.	Oraon	Ranchi	186	26.34	22.58	40.32	10.75	.18	.30	.52	Dass Sharma, 1976
38.	Santal Munda Oraon	Bihar Ranchi Chotanagpur	589	24.28	27.50	36.84	11.38	.22	.28	.50	Malone & Lahiri, 1929

(Contd.)

(Contd.)

39.	Santal	S. Pargana	339	33.04	20.94	34.84	11.21	.16	.25	.59	Sarkar, 1936-37
	West Bengal and Sikkim										
40.	Lepcha	Kalimpong	25	24.00	36.00	23.00	8.00	.28	.25	.47	Macfarlane, 1937
41.	Lepcha	Kalimpong	33	30.30	36.36	27.27	6.06	.26	.20	.54	Macfarlane, 1941
42.	Lepcha	Darjeeling	250	39.60	37.60	16.40	6.40	.25	.12	.63	Bhattarcharjee, 1968
43	Lepcha	Gangtok & Kalimpong	154	35.06	31.17	25.97	7.79	.22	.19	.59	Miki *et. al.*, 1960
44.	Lepcha	Sikkim	72	31.94	31.94	19.44	16.67	.28	.20	.52	Negi cited in Bhattarcherjee
45.	Lepcha	Sikkim	205	37.07	34.15	21.95	6.83	.23	.16	.61	Bhatta-charjee, 1976
46.	Bhotia	Sikkim & Darjeeling	85	36.47	27.07	21.18	15.29	.20	.16	.64	Macfarlane, 1941

(Contd.)

(Contd.)

47.	Toto	Jalpaiguri	115	2.61	28.69	53.04	15.65	.27	.47	.26	Chou-dhury *et. al.*, 1962
48.	Oraon	24 Parganas	111	24.32	27.92	36.93	10.81	.23	.28	.49	Roy, 1962
49.	Santal	Midnapur	336	25.89	27.98	36.31	9.82	.21	.27	.52	Chou-dhury *et. al.*, 1967
50.	Santal	Hooghly	115	23.43	19.13	45.22	12.17	.17	.35	.48	Mukherjee, *et. al.*, 1977
51.	Munda	24 Parganas	27	7.40	22.22	51.85	18.15	.26	.26	.48	Roy, 1962
52.	Lodha	Midnapur	130	24.60	42.30	22.30	18.80	.32	.18	.50	Nanda, 1976
	Madhya Pradesh										
53.	Bhil	Dhar	54	24.07	37.04	29.63	9.26	.27	.22	.51	Kumar, 1966
54.	Bhil	Indore	100	26.00	19.00	44.00	11.00	.16	.33	.51	do
55.	Bhil	Ratlam	88	27.28	32.95	35.23	4.45	.21	.23	.56	Kumar 1965
56.	Bhilala	Dhar	173	32.37	25.43	31.79	10.41	.20	,.24	.56	Kumar, 1966

(Contd.)

(Contd.)

57.	Gond	Bilaspur	129	28.68	26.36	34.11	10.85	.21	26	.53	Negi, 1963
58.	Kanwar	Bilaspur	91	17.58	26.37	45.06	10.99	.21	.34	.45	Negi, 1963
59.	Maria, Bison, Horn	Bastar	218	38.99	22.94	29.82	8.25	.17	.21	.62	Negi, 1963
60.	Maria Hill	Bastar	85	45.88	10.59	34.12	9.41	.10	.25	.65	Negi, 1963
61.	Muria Eastern	do	143	29.97	25.18	39.86	6.99	.18	.27	.55	Negi and Ahmad, 1952
62.	Muria Western	do	169	28.99	17.75	38.46	14.80	.18	.31	.51	do
63.	Bhils	Nimar	140	18.57	23.57	41.43	16.43	.22	.35	.43	Macfarlane, 1941
64.	Bhils	Dhar	534	34.64	28.09	28.09	9.18	.21	.21	.58	Bose, 1952
65.	Maria Gond	Bastar	123	28.45	26.02	34.15	11.38	.21	.36	.53	Macfarlane, 1940
66.	Nagesia	Surguja	138	16.67	29.71	31.88	22.74	—	—	—	Kumar, N & S Singh, (1976 unpublished)

(Contd.)

(Contd.)

67.	Koduka	Surguja	100	25.00	20.00	38.00	17.00	.20	.33	.47	Banerjee *et. al.*, 1982
68.	Pando	Surguja	100	18.00	33.00	30.00	19.00	.30	.28	.42	do
69.	Oraon	Surguja	142	19.72	35.21	32.39	12.68	.28	.26	.46	Kumar *et al.*, 1980
70.	Dhurwa	Bastar	200	29.00	31.50	29.00	10.50	.24	.22	.54	Negi &Ahmad, 1963
71.	Dhurwa	Bastar	60	23.33	30.00	36.67	10.00	.23	.27	.50	do
72.	Dorla	Bastar	200	34.00	31.50	30.50	4.00	.20	.19	.61	do
73.	Juang	do	115	21.74	21.74	47.83	8.69	.17	.39	.49	Sarkar, 1956
	Orissa										
74.	Korku	East of Berhampur	140	20.00	28.57	37.86	13.57	.24	.30	.46	Macfarlane, 1941
75.	Gadaba	Koraput	112	23.12	36.61	33.03	7.14	.26	.23	.57	Sarkar *et. al.*, 1960
76.	Khond	do	200	31.50	30.50	31.0	7.00	.21	.21	.58	Hargrave, 1963

(Contd.)

(Contd.)

77.	Porja	Koraput	108	36.11	31.48	29.62	2.78	.19	.18	.63	Sarkar *et. al.*, 1960
78.	Saora	do	249	26.51	30.91	30.50	12.05	.25	.24	.51	Hargrave, 1963
79.	Badogadaba	Koraput	225	26.22	28.44	32.89	12.44	.23	.26	.51	Das *et. al.*, 1962
80.	Bareng-paroja	do	225	27.56	24.89	36.00	11.55	.20	.28	.52	do
81.	Konda Paroja	Koraput	325	25.23	28.31	35.38	11.38	.22	.27	.51	do 1966
82.	Ollaro Gadaba	do	325	22.46	24.92	41.23	11.38	.20	.32	.48	do
83.	Pareng Gadaba	do	225	24.89	23.56	42.22	9.33	.18	.31	.51	do
84.	Bathudi	Mayurbhanj	219	16.90	26.94	39.27	16.89	.25	.34	.41	Present study
85.	Sounti	Mayurbhanj	220	15.00	26.82	37.73	20.45	.27	.36	.37	Present study

(Contd.)

10

CONCLUSION

The present study aimed at providing a comprehensive account of the Bathudi and Sounti males and females of Mayurbhanj District of Orissa. Both the Bathudi and Sounti are Scheduled Tribes. The major concentration of their distribution is in Mayurbhaj and the neighbouring district of Keonjhar of the same State. The results of the investigation have been analysed and discussed in various Chapters. About one hundred unrelated adult males and females belonging to each of the tribes mentioned here were investigated, measured, and examined for Anthroposcopic observations, Anthropometric measurements, Finger and Palmar Dermatoglyphics, Study of Morpho-genetic traits, Blood groups, and colour vision defficiency. The samples were drawn from about sixty different villages of Jashipur, Karanjia, Thakurmunda, and Sukruli blocks of Karanjia Tehasil. Data for colour blindness was gathered from the unrelated boys of various schools of Karanjia Tehasil. Demographic data from one hundred each of Bathudi and Sounti households have been collected and analysed. Bathudi are agriculturists. Most of them have their own lands. They also work on others land as wage labourers. The majority of the Sountis are concentrated in remote villages situated on either side of the Baitarni river separating the districts of Mayurbhanj and Keonjhar. The Sountis mostly work as agricultural or daily wage labourers.

The Bathudi and Sounti live in separate wards in villages which are known as Bathudisahi and Sountisahi, respectively. Both these tribes have different titles (*Khili*) awarded to their ancestors by the rulers or Zamindars in appreciation of services rendered to them. Fifty Bathudi and 36 Sounti titles have found place in the samples of the present study. Out of them 14 titles are commonly shared by them. According to Census of Mayurbhanj 1931, the inter-relationship among the Bathudi, Sounti, and Bhuiya were intimate. Presently the Bathudi and Sounti are endogamous populations. Village endogamy is also practised. According to the people, in certain cases even clan endogamy is permissible. But no such occurrence has come to our record yet. Boys and girls get married, when they attain adulthood mostly around 22 years and 18 years respectively. Marriage relations are usually restricted within a radius of about twenty kilometers. Bathudis have been found to be economically better off than the Sountis, more educated, and concentrated in places having easy access to medical facilities. In contrast, the Sountis are poor, non-literate, and have their settlements in relatively remote and inhospitable localities practically lacking any medical facility. The incidence of non-literacy is the highest among the women. Number of pregnancies, birth wastage, and mortality among the Sountis are more than among the Bathudis. The overall impact of all these factors seem to have resulted in a slightly higher family size among the Bathudi (5.25 individuals) than that of the Sounti (5.03 individuals). The Bathudis consider themselves superior to the Sountis and hence claim a higher position in the social hierarchy. It may be due to their better awareness about the various high yielding seeds improved techniques of agriculture, or better education and economic status. This receives further support from the views that the Bathudis, as compared to the Bhuiyas and Sountis, are more intelligent and industrious (Census of Mayurbhanj, 1931).

Most of the Bathudis and Sountis have dark skin complexion, dark brown eyes, and black hair. Head hair are mostly straight, thick with medium texture. Beard and moustache are scanty. Eyes are small, straight with thin eye brows and imperceptible supra-orbital ridges. Nose is concave with medium depression and horizontal septum. Slope, width, and height of the forehead is medium. Face has round chin, prominent check bones, and medium lips. Body is muscular and athletic. The Bathudis and Sountis have short stature, dolichocephalic heads and mesorrhine nose, except the Sounti males who have platyrrhine nose types. Euryen type upper faces are most common among the Sounti males and females and Bathudi females ; and the Mesen type is mostly found among the Bathudi males. Bathudi and Sounti males have preponderance of Euryprosopic and their females are characterised by the higher frequency of Hypereuryprosopic face types. Except nasal breadth, thoracic circumference, and weight, Bathudi males have higher mean values for all the anthropometric characters as compared to the Sounti males. However, the Bathudi females except foot breadth and weight have greater mean values for all the anthropometric characters than the Sounti females. Females of both the populations have comparatively less mean value for all the characters than their respective males. Right type of hand clasping, handedness and left type of arm folding are most frequent in the present samples of the Bathudis and Sountis. Incidence of tongue rollers, single clockwise occipital hair whorl, completely free ear lobes and Digital formulas 2 < 4 occurs in relatively higher frequencies in the present series of Bathudis and Sountis.

Loops followed by whorls and arches occur in highest frequency among the Bathudis and Sountis. Whorls and radial loops show preponderance among the male series, while the ulnar loops and arches occur in higher frequency among the female series. Bathudis have relatively higher values of Pattern intensity and Furuhata indices. The Sountis have more value for Dankmeijer index. Whorls and loops occur in equal proportion as monomorphic patterns among the Bathudi males but loops have been found in preponderance over whorls as monomorphic pattern in case of Bathudi females and Sountis of both sexes. Incidences of monomorphic patterns on fingers are higher among the Bathudis than among the Sountis.

D and B line ending 11 and 7 is frequent among the Bathudis. Among Sountis 7 followed by 11 D line ending and 5′ + 5" followed by 7 B line ending are in preponderance. Bathudis have higher frequency of radial C line type but Sountis have relatively greater occurrence of ulnar C line type. Radial C line type has greater frequency among the males of Bathudi. But ulnar C line type have preponderance among the Sounti females. Axial triraddi t′ occurs relatively in greater frequency among the Bathudis and Sountis of the present series, having its greater frequency among the females than among the males. It may also be observed that Sountis have a higher frequency of t′ than Bathudis. Patterns on palmar area occur more frequently at IV inter-digital area among the males and females of both populations, except Bathudi males among whom the patterns have preponderance at III interdigital palmar area. Palmar pattern at IV interdigital area have preponderance among the Sountis than among the Bathudi. Bathudi have more mean value than Sountis for Total finger ridge count, Triradii on palm, Triradii on finger, 'a-b' ridge count and Main line index. Males of both populations have relatively greater mean values than female for all the five quantitative dermatoglyphic characters except Triradii on palm and 'a'b' ridge count.

Blood group B followed by A has the maximum frequency in the present samples. A B blood group has been reported both among the Bathudis and Sountis but A among Bathudis in the present samples. Incidence of colour blindness is greater among Sounti (4.39%) than the Bathudi (2.60%). The greater incidence of colour blindness seem primarily due to higher proportion of deutan to proton among Sounti (4 : 1) as compared to Bathudi (3 : 1).

In the male series maximum differences have been found to be significant statistically for dermatoglyphic qualitative characters (64.28%) followed by Anthroposcopic observations (40.91%), quantitative dermatoglyphic characters (40%), and anthropometric measurements (33.33%). Differences in the female series are found to be statistically significant, maximum for anthropometric characters (58.82%), followed by dermatoglyphic characters (qualitative 42.86%, and quantitative 40.0%) and Anthroposcopic observations (22.73%). The trends of variations as observed in male series for dermatoglyphic character and female series for anthropometric characters support and are in agreement with the views of Ghosh (1977 & 1981) and Das *et. al.* (1968) respectively. There are no statistically significant differences for ABO blood groups, colour vision deficiency, and the differences are least for morphogenetic characters (9.09%) among the Bathudis and Sountis. Sex differences among the Bathudis are significant statistically for all the anthropometric characters, followed by quantitative dermatoglyphic characters (40%), Anthroposcopic observations (35%), and quantitative dermatoglyphic characters (28.57%). Sex differences among the Bathudis are significant statistically for all the anthropometric characters, followed by quantitative dermatoglyphic characters (40%), somatoscopic observations (35%), and quantitative dermatoglyphic characters (28.57%). As observed incase of Bathudis, like wise the Sounti males and females show statistically significant differences for all the anthropometric characters followed by Anthroposcopic observations (40%) and dermatoglyphic characters (Qualitative 28.57% and quantitative 20%). There are statistically significant sex differences for 9.09% Morphogenetic characters among the Sounti. Nevertheless, there are no statistically significant sex differences for ABO blood groups among the Bathudis and Sountis, and morpho-genetic traits among Bathudis.

Though there are variations among the Bathudis and Sountis for different attributes, it may be observed that both these populations have much in common in respect of their marriage pattern, ecology, demographic aspects, anthroposcopic and anthropometric characters. Results of dermatoglyphic characters show closeness for quantitative characters specially in the female series. Bathudis and Sountis have maximum similarities for Morpho-genetic traits, blood groups, and colour-vision deficiency. According to Census of Mayurbhanj (1931), Bathudis and Sountis are branches of the Bhuiya. In anthroposcopic characters and anthropometric measurements, Sountis appear closer to the Bhuiyas than the Bathudis do, Sountis have their distribution very near to the Bhuiya-pirth and Juang-pirth in Keonjhar districts. Bathudi males have been found to be closer in respect of stature and cephalic index to the Santal, while the Sounti males show their affinities with the Kodaku and Munda. The Bathudi females occupy a position near to Birhor and Oraon, and the Sounti females are closer to Asur and Khond, when compared for the Stature and cephalic index.

When the results of dermatoglyphic characters are compared, it is found that Bathudis show resemblance with Mundas, Khasi and Irula in respect of pattern types whorls and loops ; Oraon and Khasi for Pattern intensity index ; whorls occur more on I and IV digits than loops and hence they are closer to Juang and Sabara ; Bathudi males are closer with Munda and Mullu Kurumba as the proportions of monomorphic patterns as whorls and loops are in equal proportion and Bathudi females with Juang and Sabara ; Main line D and B endings 11 and 7 indicate their closeness with Oraon. Sounti males and females are closer to Juang, Sabara Nankadara and Miri for whorl and loop pattern types ; Mech, Rajgond and Miri for pattern intensity index ; Vettu Kurumsa, Munda (female) and Kota, Badaga and Irula (males) for patterns whorls and loops on different digits ; Juang and Sabara for monomorphic patterns ; and Juang, Sabara and Munda for the D and B line endings. Bathudis show resemblance with Noatia, while the Sountis appear closer to Pahira ; However, Bathudi, Sounti, Pahira, Noatia, and Korwa form a cluster in respect of p, q and r gene frequencies. In respect of q gene frequency Bathudi show resemblance with Kanwar and Juang, while the Sounti are closer to Santal and Bhils. The Comparison of Bathudis and Sountis with other populations in respect of Stature and cephalic index, dermatoglyphic characters and blood groups indicate their closeness with the Juang, Sabara, Santal, Munda, Birhor, Asur, Kanwar, Korwa (Mundari speaking), the relationship with Oraon, Khond, Irula, Mullukurumba Nunkadara, Vettu Kurumba, Kota Badaga, Pahira specially among the females may indicate about the inter mixture with the neighbouring Dravidian populations. It gathers support from the argument as according to Risley (1915), "there are 9 hybrid combinations of Mundas including (a) Khangar-Munda (b) Kharia-Munda (c) Kankpat-Munda (d) Karanga- Munda (e) Mahili-Munda (f) Nagbansi Munda (g) Oraon Munda (h) Sad-Munda (i) Savar-Munda". Sarkar (1954) has added 2 more names to this list of Munda-Bhuiya and Munda-Chamar. Risley (1915) has further observed that "the Munda are hybrid and descended from inter marriage between the Munda men and women of other tribes". The closeness with Khasi, Miri, Mech, Noatia may indicate about the mongoloid admixture among both the populations. Bathudis and Sountis have nearly equal one third ratio of p, q and r genes and it further supports the argument of their Mundari character (Sarkar, 1954).

According to Roy (1935) "I am led to the conclusion that the Sountis, like the Bathudia form a branch of the great Bhuiya tribe. In physical features, they exhibit no marked differences from the Bhuiyas. In characteristic cultural traits too, they resemble the Bhuiyas. Both the Sountis and Bathudis have the same changu nat or characteristic dances to the tunes of the changu drum as the Bhuiyas have. Sounti and Bathudi maidens, like their Pauri Bhuiya sisters, go to neighbouring villages to dance with the young of those villages. The Sountis and the Bathudis like the Pauris are fond of eating the small flying insects locally called Kaloi Pok" The present account supports that the Bathudis and Sountis are closely related to Bhuiyas and they by and large are more close to the Mundari speakers than the Dravidian speakers. When compared naturally the Sountis appear to be closer to the Bhuiyas than the Bathudis. On the basis of pigmentation, stature, cephalic index and nasal index, we may find that the Bathudis and Sountis of both the sexes can be described as of dark pigmentation, short stature dolichocephalic index and mesorrhine nose types except the Sounti males, who have platyrrhine nose types. Accordingly, we may classify the Bathudi of both sexes and Sounti females as of Palae-Mediterranean, while as the Sounti males of Proto-Australoid racial types according to Guha (1944). The Hill Bhuiyas were classified by Roy (1935) as of Proto-Australoid type. It may indicate relative closeness of Sountis with the Bhuiyas than with the Bathudis. There could be two possible interpretations for this. Either the Bathudis branched out earlier than the Sountis or the former have had a higher degree of hybridization than the latter. The present exercise established with evidence the apparently close relationship of the Bhuiyas with the Bathudi as well as Sounti. Between the two, however, the Sounti resemble the Bhuiya more than the Bathudi. This substantive observation apart, the exercise also throws light on the possible mechanism of fission or fusion as well as the nature of migration that together have developed the contemporary population composition of the region inhabited by the Bathudis as well as the Sountis. From the methodological stand point also the present study demonstrates an improvement as, for the first time comparisons of populations have been made on the basis of data gathered from both the sexes having more or less the same proportion. Throughout our analysis of data, therefore, comparison has been across populations and sexes. Although in the present study this does not make any major difference in the overall conclusions drawn, the advantage of such rigorous comparison is evident as the same makes the researcher draw generalizations with a relatively higher degree of confidence. Whatever conclusions have been drawn, therefore, have a higher degree of validity.

REFERENCES

ABEL, W. 1934 : As cited in Verma, 1952.

AHMAD, S.H. 1975 : "ABO Blood Groups and Sickle Cell Trait Among the Kondh and Nuka Dora of Koraput District." In *Bio-Anthropological Research in India* (Ed) H.K. Rakshit, Anthropological Survey of India, Calcutta.

-------- 1981 : "*Anthropometric Measurements and Ethnic Affinities of Chattisgarh Tribes*", Anthropological Survey of India, Calcutta.

ALBINUS 1764 : As cited in Cummins and Midlo 1943.

ANNET, M. 1964 : "A Model of the Inheritance of Handedness and Cerebral Dominance, *Nature*, 204 : 59-60.

--------- 1973 : "Handedness in Families", *Ann. Hum. Genet.*, 37 : 93-105.

BALAKRISHNAN, V. and L.D. SANGHVI 1981 : "Morphological and Genetical Distances in Tamil Nadu", pp.103-143. In, *Biology of the People of Tamil Nadu* by Sanghvi *et. al.*, (Eds.), The Indian Society of Human genetics : Pune. The Indian Anthropological Society : Calcutta.

BANERJEE, A.R. 1956 : "Hair Character of the Juang and Other Tribes of Orissa". *Man In India*, 13 : 195-198.

BANERJEE, M.K. 1975 : "Anthropometry, Phalangeal Hair and Red Green Colour Vision Among the Kondh and Nuka Dora of Koraput", In *Bio-Anthropological Research In India*, H.K. Rakshit (Ed). Anthropological Survey of India, Calcutta.

BANERJEE, M.K and P. DHAR 1982 : "Distribution of A_1 A_2 BO Blood Groups Among the Kadaku and pando of Surgaja District, Madhya Pradesh", *J. Ind. Anthrop. Soc.*, 17 ; 1 : 75- 77.

BANERJEE, P. 1960 : "A Comparative Study of Oraon Physical Characters", *Bull. Anth. Surv. India*, 9 : 2.

BANSAL, I.J.S. 1966 : "Frequency of a-b ridge Counting Among the Maharashtrian of India", *The East. Anthrop.* 19; 2 : 117-122.

BARUA, S. 1982 : "Biodemographic Factors Associated with Offspring Mortality Among the Hajongs of Meghalaya", *J.Ind. Anthrop. Soc.*, 17 ; 2 : 143-146.

BASU, A. 1969 : "The Pahira : A Population Genetical Study", *Amer. J. Phys. Anthrop.*, 31 : 399-416.

------- "Finger Prints of the Korku", *Man In India*, 49; 1 : 95-101.

------- 1972 : "A Demographic Study of the Kota of Nilgiri Hills", *J.Ind. Anth. Soc.*, 7 : 29-47.

BASU, M.P. 1967 : "A Demographic Profile of the Irula", *Bull. Anth. Surv. Ind.*, 16 ; 3-4 : 267-289.

BASU, M.P. and D.K. GUHA 1973 : "Some Demographic Aspects of the Teli", *J. Ind. Anth. Soc.*, 8 : 61-76.

BASU, P.C. 1929 : "The Anthropometry of the Bhuiyas of Mayurbhanj", *J. Asiatic. Soc. Bengal*, N.S. 25 : 157-163.

------ 1932-33 : "The Racial Affinities of the Mundas", *Trans. Bose. Research, Inst.*, 8 : 211-247.

------- 1933-34 : "Racial Affinities of Oraon", *Trans. Bose. Research Inst.*, 9 : 132-176.

BASU, S. 1959 : Finger Dermatoglyphic Study of the Riang of Tripura", *J. Asiatic. Soc. Bengal*, 1; 2 : 161-168.

BATESON 1909 : As cited in Race and Sanger, 1975.

BECKMAN, L. and J.A. BOOK 1959 : "Distribution and Inheritance of Mid-digital Hair in Sweden", *Hereditas*, 45 : 215- 220.

------- 1960 : "An Evolution of Some Anthropological Traits Used in Patternity Test", *Hereditas*, 46 : 543-569.

BERNSTEIN, F. 1925 : As Cited in Race and Sanger, 1975.

BERNSTEIN, M. B.S. BURKS 1942 : "The Incidence and Mendelian Transmission of Mid Digital Hair in Man", *J. Hered.*, 33 : 45-53.

BERNSTEIN, M.M. 1949 : "The Mid-digital Hair Genes, Their Inheritance and Distribution Among White Races", *J. Hered.*, 40 : 127-131.

BELL, 1833 : As Cited in Cummins and Midlo, 1943.

BHALLA, V. 1966 : "Blood Group Distribution Pertaining to ABO, MNSs and RH-Hr System in the Indian Sub-Continent", *Anthropologie*, 4 : 67-86.

BHALE, R.B. 1970 : "Maximum Likelihood Estimation of A_1 A_2 BO Gene Frequencies", *Eastern Anthrop.*, 23 : 75-85.

BHATTACHARJEE, D.K. 1964 : "The Palmar Dermatoglyphics of the Anglo-Indians of India", *Z. Morph. Anthrop.*, 55 ; 3 : 357-367

BHATTACHARJEE, P.N. 1954 : "Blood Group Investigations in the Abor Tribe", *Bull. Dept. Anthrop.*, Govt. of India, 3; 1 : 51-54.

-------- 1955 : "Dermatoglyphics of the Abor People in Assam", *Anthropologist* 2 ; 2 : 22-35.

-------- 1957 : "ABO Blood Group of the Angami Naga", *East Anthrop.*, 11 : 42-47.

-------- 1968 : Sero-Genetical Variations in the Lepcha of Darjeeling District with Special Reference to the Indian Mongoloid", *Bull. Anthrop. Surv. India*, 17 : 382-92.

-------- 1976 : As Cited in Piplai *et. al.* 1979.

BHATTACHARJEE P.N. and N. KUMAR 1969 : "A Blood Group Genetical Survey in the Dudh Kharias of the Randhi District (Bihar, India)", *Hum. Hered.*, 19 : 385-397.

BHOWMIK, P.K. 1956 : "Physical Affinities of the Lodhas of Midnapore", *Man in India*, 36 : 110-131.

BIDLOO 1685 : As Cited in Cummins and Midlo, 1943.

BIRD, G.W.G. 1951 : "Specific Agglutinating Activity for Human Red Blood Corpuscles in Extracts of Dolichos Biflorus", *Curr. Sci.*, 20 : 298-299.

-------- 1952 : "Relationship of Blood Sub-Group, A_1, A_2 and A_1 B and A_2 B to Haemagglutinins Present in the Seeds of Dolichos Biflorus", *Nature*, 170 : 674.

BISWAS, P.C. 1936 : "Uber Hand and Finger Leisten Von Indien," *Z. Morph. Anthrop.*, 35 : 519-550. As Cited in Chakravartti, 1963.

BISWAS, P.S. 1968 : "Recent Advances in and Further Scope of Dermatoglyphics, In *Proceeding of International Symposium on Dermatoglyphics*. P.C.Biswas and A. Sharma (Eds). Department of Anthropology, University of Delhi, Delhi, pp. 4-6.

BOHNER, K. and F. HARREN 1939 : As Cited in Cummins and Midlo, 1943.

BONNEVIC, K. 1924 : "Studies on papillary pattern On Human Fingers", *J. Genetics*, 15 : 1-111.

-------- 1929 : As Cited in Holt, 1968.

-------- 1931 : do

BOPEGAMAGE, A. 1959 : "India's Population Grows Young", *Soc. Bull.*, 8 ; 71.

BOSE, UMA, 1952 : "Blood Group of the Bhils", *Bull. Dept. Anthrop. Govt. of India*, 1 : 14-18.

BOYD, W.C. 1939 : *"Blood Groups"*, Tabul. Biol. Haque.

-------- 1940 : "Critique of Method of Classifying Man Kind", *Am. J. Phys. Anthrop.*, 27 : 333.

-------- 1950 : *"Genetics and Races of Man"*, Little Brown and Co., Boston.

Census of Mayurbhanj State 1931 : No. 1 : Report, Calcutta.

Census of India 1961 : *"District Census Hand Book Mayurbhanj"*, Superintendent, Govt. Press : Orissa.

Census of India 1971 : *"Scheduled Castes and Scheduled Tribes"*, Series I, Paper 1, Registrar General and Census Commissioner of India.

Census of India 1981 : Primary Census Abstract Scheduled Tribes, Series 1, India, Part II B [111]. Registrar General and Census Commissioner, India.

Census of India 1981 : "Series 16, Orissa, Paper 1, Direction of Census Operation, Orissa.

CHAKLADAR, H.C. 1936 : "Problems of the Racial Composition of Indian Peoples". Presidential Address Section of Anthropology and Archaeology, *Proceeding of the 23rd Indian Science Congress*, Part II : 359-390.

CHAKRAWORTY, A. 1973 : "Certain Consideration on the Genetics of Hand Clasping in Human Population", *Hum. Pop. Genet.*, Proc. 1st Conferences, 28 ; 1 : 277-288.

CHAKRAVARTTI, M.R. 1959 : *"Dermatoglyphics: A Physical Survey of the Kadar of Kerala*, Memoir No.6. *Dept. Anthrop. Govt. of India*, 1-119.

--------- 1960 : "Dermatoglyphics of the Santal of West Bengal", *Bull. Dept. Anthrop. Govt. of India*, 9; 1 : 41-52.

-------- 1963 : "Ethnic Bearing of the Dermatoglyphic Studies in India", *Acta, Genet. Med. Gemel*, 12; 4 : 374-404.

CHAKRABORTY, M. 1965 : "ABO Blood Group of the Zeliang Naga", *Man in India*, 45 : 311-315.

CHAKRAVARTTI, M.R. and D.P. MUKHERJEE, 1961 : "Dermatoglyphic Study of Tribes and Castes of the State of Assam", *Science and Culture*, 27 : 584.

--------- 1962 : "Dermatoglyphic Studies on the Tribes and Castes of Nagaland and Manipur State", *Bull. Anthrop. Surv. India*, 11 : 233-234.

---------	1964 :	"Dermatoglyphic Affinities of the Tribes and Castes of Nilgiri Bills (India)," *Z. Morph. Anthrop.*, 55; 3 : 335-356.
CHAKRAVARTY, S.K.	1976 :	"Variation in the Termination of Polymorphous C-line in Palmar Dermatoglyphics of the Khynriam of Shillong", *J. Ind. Anthrop. Soc.*, 11 : 117-120.
CHAMBER, E.G.	1955 :	"*Statistical Calculations For Beginners*". University Press : Cambridge.
CHATTERJEE, A.N.	1948 :	"The Variation in Stature and Cephalic Index among Bangalee College Students". Presidential Address, Section of Anthropology and Archaeology, *Proc. 35th Indian Science Congress*, Part II : 153-176.
CHATTERJEE, A.N. and T.C. DAS	1927 :	"The Hos of Seraikella", Anthropological Papers, University of Calcutta, Part 1, N.S.I : 63-75.
CHATTERJEE, B.K.	1929 :	"The Marriage Ceremonies of the Bathuria of Mayurbhanj State", *Man In India*, 2 & 3 : 157-163.
CHATTERJEE, B.K., M.R. CHAKRAVARTI and P. GUPTA,	1960 :	"Dermatoglyphics of the Uralis of Kerla", *Man in India*, 40; 1 : 36-51.
CHATTERJEE, B.K. and G.D. KUMAR	1950 :	"Dermatoglyphic Study of Some Tribal Groups of Travancore", (Unp.)
CHATTERJEE, B.K. and G.D. KUMAR	1977 :	"A Genetical Approach to the Morphological Variations Among Indian Tribes". Paper presented in the *Seminar on Human Variation in India*, Organised by the Anthropological Survey of India, Calcutta.
CHATTERJEE, S.	1975 :	"Dermatoglyphic Statement on the Santals of Three Villages in Santal Parganas". In *Bio-Anthropological Research in India*, Calcutta by H.K. Rakshit (Ed.).
CHAUDHURI, S., M.R. CHAKRAVARTTI, B. MUKHERJEE, S.N. SEN, J. GHOSE and A. MAITRA	1962 :	"A Study of Haematological Factors, Blood Groups, Anthropometric Measurements and Genetics of some of the Tribal and Caste Groups of 1. South India-Kerala, Nilgiris and Andhra Pradesh, 2. North Eastern India (Indo-Bhutan Border) Totopara, *9th Cong. Inst.* Soc. Blood Transfus. Mexico. Bibl. Haemat. 1964 ; 14 : 196-205.
CHOWDHURY, BHAGIRATHI	1963-64:	"Bathudi", *Adivasi*, 3 : 137-138.
COON, C.S.	1963 :	"*The Origin of Races*, Jonathan Cape : London.

CUMMINS, H. 1936 : "Methodology in Palmar Dermatoglyphics", *Middle American Research Series, Tulane, Univ. Publication*, 7 : 23-81.

CUMMINS, H. and C. MIDLO 1926 : "Palmar and Planter Epidermal Configurations (Dermatoglyphics.) in European Americans", *Amer. J. Phys. Anthrop.*, 9 : 471-502.

-------- 1943 : "Finger Prints Palms and Soles", Blakiston Co. : Philadelphia.

CUMMINS, H. and M. STEGGERDA 1935 : "Finger Prints in a Dutch Family Series", *Am. J. Phys. Anthrop.*, 20 : 19-41.

CUMMINS, R; S. LECHE and K. MECLUBE 1931 : "Bimanual Variation in Palmar Dermatoglyphics", *Am. J. Anat.*, 48 : 199-230.

CURSTERN 1955 : "Principles of Human Genetics", W.H. Freeman and Co. Sanfransisco : California.

DAS, B.M. 1959 : "Finger Prints of the Hajong", *Man in India*, 39; 1 : 20-27.

DAS, B.M. 1969 : "ABO Blood Group in the Tribal Population of North-East India with Special Reference to the Khasi", *Anthropologist*, Sp. Vol : 85-92.

DALTON, E.T. 1872 : "*Descriptive Ethnology of Bengal*", London.

DANFORTH, C.H. 1921 : "Distribution of Hairs on the Digits in Man", *Am. J. Phys. Anthrop.*, 4 : 18-204.

DANKMEIJER, J. 1934 : As Cited in Cummins and Midlo, 1943.

DANKMEIJER, J. 1938 : do

DAS, S.R., D.B. SASTRY, and D.P. MUKHERJEE 1966 : "Blood Groups (A_1 A_2 BO, MN, Rh) ABH Secretion in Pareng Gadaba, the Ollaro Gadaba and Konda Paroja of Koraput District of Orissa", *Acta. Genet.*, 16 : 169-183.

DAS, S.R., D.P. MUKHERJEE and D.B. SASTRY 1968 : "A Somatological Survey of Five Tribes in the Koraput District, Orissa", *Bull. Anthrop. Surv. India*, 17 ; 4 : 400-422.

DAS, S.R., P.N. BHATTACHARJEE D.B. SASTRY and D.P. MUKHERJEE 1962 : "Blood Groups (ABO, MN, Rh) ABH Secretion, Sickle Cell Trait and Colour Blindness in Bado gadaba and Bareng Paroja of Koraput District in Orissa", *Bull. Anthrop. Surv. India*, 11 ; 3-4 : 145-151.

DASHSHARMA, P. 1966 : "A Note of the Palmar Dermatoglyphics of the Ladhaki Males", *The Eastern Anthropologist*, 19; 1 : 75-80.

--------- 1976 : "Physical Anthropology of Oraons", Mudas and Dusadhs of Bihar", *J. Ind. Anthrop. Soc.*, 11: 121-124.

DATTA BANIK, N.D. and K. SAHA — 1975 : "Factors Related to Prenatal Mortality" *Ind.J.Pediat*, 42 : 310-315.

DE, B. — 1967 : "A Short Note on Middle Phalangeal Hair Among the Khond", *Bull. Anth. Surv. India*, 16; 1 and 2 : 133-137.

DEKA MAHAPATRA, U. and P. BEHRA — 1970 : "Palmar Dermatoglyphics of the Munda `of Orissa", *Man in India*, 50 : 121-134.

DEKA MAHAPATRA, U. — 1991 : "Finger and Palmar Dermatoglyphics Study Among Some Tribal Populations of Koraput, Orissa", Paper presented in the Seminar on "*Human Variation in India*, Organised by the Anth. Surv. of India, Calcutta.

DEKA, U. — 1991 : "Genetic Variations in the Populations of Koraput District", Paper Presented in the Seminar on "*Human Variation in India*", Organised by the Anthropological Survey of India, Calcutta.

DEKA, U. — 1980 : "Diversity in Population Groups in Orissa, Presidential Address, Section of Anthropology and Archaeology, *67th Annual Session of the Indian Science Congress.*

DEKA, U., P.N. SAHU and P. PATOJOSHI, — 1991 : "Variation in Defective Colour Vision in Some Populations of Orissa", in Seminar on "*Human Variation in India*, Organised by the Anthropological Survey of India, Calcutta.

DEVI, B. — 1975 : "A Note on the Reproductive Life of Kond Women", In Rakshit, H.K. (Ed), *Bio-Anthropological Research in India*, Anthropological Survey of India, Calcutta, pp. 225-231.

DIXON, R.B. — 1923 : "*The Racial History of Man*", Charles Scribneas: New York.

DOWBEY, J.E. — 1926 : "Further Observation on the Manner of Clasping of the Hands", *Am.Nat.*, 60 : 387-390.

DRAKE-BROCKMAN — 1896 : "In *the Tribes and castes of the North-West Provinces and Oudh*", 1 : XXVII-XLII.

DUNGERN E.V. and HIRSZFELD L. — 1910 : As Cited in Race and Sanger, 1975.

-------- — 1911 : do

DUTTA, P.C. — 1966 : "A Review of Inherited Defective Colourvision Variability and Selection Relaxation Among the Indian", *Acta. Genet.*, 16 : 327-339.

DUTTA, P.C. and P. GUPTA. — 1967 : "Finger Print Patterns of the Asura Tribe of Chotanagpur, India", *Acta. Genet.*, 17:248-259.

EICKSTEDT, E.V. 1930 : "Reisen in Suddra Widischen Landern", *Ethnologischer Anzeiger*, 2 : 133-40.

------- 1933 : "Die Rassengeschichite Indian Mit Besonderer Berucksichtigung Von Mysore", Z. *Morph. Anthrop*, 32 : 77-124.

------- 1939 : "The History of Anthropological Research in India", In L.A. Krishna Iyers, *The Travancore Tribes and Castes*". Vol.2, Trivandrum.

EICKSTEDT, E.F. VON 1934 : "Ressen Kunde Und Rassengeschickte der Menschheit", Stuttgart.

EPSTEIN, A.A. and OTTENBERG, R. 1908 : "Simple Method of Performing Serum Reactions", *Proc. N.Y. Path. Soc.*, 8 : 117-123 (As Cited in Race and Sanger 1975).

ELDERTON, E.M. 1920 : "On the Inheritance of the Finger Print", *Biometrika*, 13 : 57-91.

ESSEN-MOLAR, E 1941 : As Cited in Holt, 1961.

FANG, T.C. 1950 : As Cited in Holt, 1968.

FAULD, H. 1880 : As Cited in Cummins and Midlo, 1943.

FREIRE-MAIA, A. *et. al*. 1960 : "Genetic Analysis in Russian Immigrants", *Am. J.Phys. Anthrop.*, 18 : 135- 140.

FREIRE-MAIA, A. and J.D.E .ALMEIDA 1966 : "Hand Clasping and Arm Folding Among African Negroes", *Hum.Bio.*, 38:175-179.

FORGOET 1892 : As Cited in Cummins and Midlo, 1943.

FRIEDENREICH 1931 : As Cited in Race and Sanger, 1975.

FRIEDENREICH, V. and ZACHO, A. 1931 : As Cited in Race and Sanger, 1975.

FURUHATA, T. 1927 : The Difference of the Index of Finger Prints According to Race. *Japan Med. World*, 7 : 162-164.

GALTON, F. 1892 : "*Finger Prints*", Macmillon : London.

------- 1895 : *Finger Print Directories*, Macmillon : London.

GANGULY, P. 1976 : *Physical Anthropology of the Nicobarese* Anthropological Survey of India, Calcutta.

GARN, S.M. 1961 : "*Human Races*" Charles C. Thomas : Illinois.

GATES, R.R. 1952 : "*Human Genetics*", The Macmillon : New York.

------- 1962 : "The Asurs and Birhors of Chotanagpur", In *Indian Anthropology* (Eds.) T.N. Madan and Gopala Sarana, pp. 163-184.

GEIPEL, G. 1942 : As Cited in Cummins and Midlo, 1943.

------- 1961 : "Das Test leistensystem der Hande bei Vorderindern", *Z. Morph. Anthrop*. 51 : 181.

GHOSH, G.C. 1967 : "Anthropometry of the Ho of Seraikella, Srighbhuas", *Man in India*, 47 ; 2 : 127-132.

--------- 1976 : "The Finger and Palm Prints of Twelve Central Indian Dravidian Speaking Tribes : A comparative Study of the Raj Gond, Pardhan, Kolam, Muria, Maria, Dhurwa, Dorla, Naik Gond, Nunkadora, Ollaro Godaba, Pengo and Kond", Unpublished Ph. D. Thesis, University of Calcutta : Calcutta.

------- 1981 : "Dermatoglyphics of the Kond, Pengo, Ollaro Godaba and Nuukadora", *Bull. Anth. Surv. India*, 3 & 4 : 6 - 13.

GHOSH, G.C. and D.P. MUKHERJEE 1977 : "Variation of the Types of Palmar C-line in Indian Population", *Bull. Anthrop. Surv. India*, 26; 1 & 2 : 83-101.

GHOSH, R.R. 1960 : "Finger Print of the Oraon of Nazat, West Bengal", *Bull. dept. Anthrop.* 9; 2 : 39-42.

GREW, N. 1684 : As Cited in Penrose, 1968.

GRIERSON, W.V. 1931 : Census of India, Vol. 1, Part III, pp. 91- 92.

GOUD, J.D. and P.R. RAO 1979 : "The Colourblindness and Taste Sensitivity of Phenylthiocarbamide in Tribal Population of Andhra Pradesh", *J. Ind. Anthrop. Soc.*, 14 : 269-274.

GRUNEBERG, H., 1928 : As Cited in Cummins and Midlo, 1943.

GHUA, B.S. 1935 : *"The Racial Affinities of the People of India"*, Census of India, 1931, Vol.1., Part III, A.

--------- 1944 : *"Racial Elements in the Population"*, Bombay, Oxford University Press : Oxford. Pamphlets on Indian Affairs, No.22.

GHUA, U. 1960-61: "Fertility Behaviour of Rural Bengali Woman", Unp.

--------- 1962-63: "Fertility, Behaviour of South Indian Woman", Unp.

GULATI, R.K., K.C. MALHOTRA and J.V. UNDEVA 1981 : "Field Work". In, *Biology of the People of Tamil Nadu"* (Eds.) L.D. Sanghvi, V. Balakrishnan and I. Karve, Society of Human Genet : Pune, Indian Anth. Soc. : Calcutta.

GUPTA, P. and P.C. DUTTA 1963 : *Man in India*, 43; 2 : 114- 118.

GUPTA, P. and P.C. DUTTA 1966 : *"Anthropometry in India, 1868-1961"*, Anth. Surv. India : Calcutta.

GUPTA, S.P. 1962 : "Analysis of Some Aspects of Human Biology of Bhumij, Bathudi and Savara of

		Dalbhum", *Bull. Bihar Tribal Research Institute*, 4 : 69-76.
HADDON, A.C.	1924 :	*"The Races of Man and their Distribution"*, University Press : Cambridge.
HARGRAVE	1963 :	As Cited in Mourant A.E. *et. al.*, 1976.
HENRY, E.R.	1901 :	"Classification and Uses of Finger Prints", Routledge : London.
HILDEN, K.	1922 :	As Cited in Gates, 1952.
HINTZE	1747 :	As Cited in Cummins and Midlo, 1943.
HIRSZFEID, L. and HIRSZFEID, H.	1919 :	"Serological Difference Between the Blood of Different Races, the Result of Researches on the Macedonian Front", *Lancet*, 2 : 675-9.
HOLT, S.B.	1949 :	"A Qualitative Survey of the Finger Prints of a Small Sample of the British Population", *Ann. Eugen.*, 14 : 329-335.
--------	1951 :	"The Correlation Between Ridge Counts on Different Finger", *Ann. Eugen.*, 16 : 287-291.
--------	1954 :	"Genetics of Dermal Ridges : Bilateral Asymmetry in Finger Ridge Count", *Ann. Eugen.*, 18 : 211-231.
--------	1961 :	*"Dermatoglyphic Pattern: Genetical Variation in Human Population"* (Ed.) Harrison, G.A. Pergamon Press : Oxford.
--------	1968 :	*"The Genetics of Dermal Ridges"*, Charles, C. Thomas : Illinois.
ISHIARA, S.	1968 :	*"Tests for Colour-blindness"*, Kanchara Shuppan Co. Ltd., Japan.
KARL, E.	1934 :	As Cited in Cummins and Midlo, 1943.
KARVE, I.	1954 :	"Anthropometric Measurements in Karnataka and Orissa and a comparison of these two Regions with Maharashtra", *J. Anthrop. Soc. Bombay*, 8 ; 1 : 45-75.
KARVE, I. and V.M. DANDEKAR	1951 :	"Anthropometric Measurements of Maharashtra", *Decean College Monograph*, Series No.8 : Poona.
KIRK, R.L., LAI, L.Y.C., VOS, G.H. and VIDYARTHI, L.P.	1962 :	"A Genetical Study of the Oraons of the Chotanagpur Plateau (Bihar, India)", *Am. J.Phys. Anthrop.*, 20 : 375-385.
KLOEPFER, H.W.	1946 :	"An Investigation of 171 Possible Linkage. Relationship in Man", *Ann. Eugen.*, 13 ; 35- 71.
KOPEC, ADA C.	1970 :	The Distribution of the Blood groups in the United Kingdom", Oxford University Press : London, New York.

KUMAR, N. 1954 : "Blood Group and Secretor Frequency Among the Galong", *Bull. dept. Anthrop., Govt. of India*, 3; 1 : 55-64.

------- 1958 : "ABO Blood Group and Secretor Factor Distribution Among the Noatia : A Mongoloid Tribe of Tripura State", *Anthropologist*, 5 ; 1 & 2 : 42-46.

------- 1965 : "ABO Blood Groups and Sickle Cell Trait Investigations in Madhya Pradesh, Ratlam and Adjoining Districts (Central India)", *Bull. Anthrop. Surv. India*, 14 : 40- 44.

------- 1966 : "ABO Blood groups and Sickle Cell Trait Investigations in Madhya Pradesh, Indore District (India), *Act. Genet. Med. Gamell.*, 15 : 404-408.

------- 1966 : "ABO Blood Groups and Sickle Cell Distribution in Malwa, Western Madhya Pradesh", *J. Ind. Anth. Soc.* 1 : 129-139.

------- 1968 : "A genetic Survey Among the Rana Tharu of Nainital District in Uttar Pradesh", *J. Ind. Anthrop. Soc.*, 3 : 39-55.

------- 1970 : "Demographic Characters of Sauria Paharia of Santal Parganas District, Bihar", (Unp.).

------- 1975 : "Intra-Affiliations of the Munda People of Bihar", pp. 90-98, In, *Bio-Anthropological Researches in India.* (Ed.). H.K. Rakshit. Anthropological Survey of India, Calcutta.

KUMAR, N. and P.N. BHATTACHARJEE 1970, As Cited in Kumar, 1975.

KUMAR, N., M.K. BANARJEE and L.P. GANDHI 1980 : "Distribution of A_1 A_2 BO Blood Groups, ABH Secretion in Saliva and Sickle Cell Trait Among the Oraon of Madhya Pradesh", *J. Ind. Anthrop. Soc.*, 15 : 211-213.

KUMAR, N. and A. MAITRA 1965-66: "Demographic Characteristics of the Rana Tharu of Nainital District, Uttar Pradesh", (Unp.).

KUMAR, N. and D.P. MUKHERJEE 1968 : "A Genetic Survey Among the Desi Bhumij of Chotanagpur in Bihar", *Anthropologist*, Sp. Vol. : 75-83.

KUMAR, N. and D.B. SASTRY 1961 : "A Genetic Survey Among the Riang : A Mongoloid Tribe of Tripura", *Z. Morph. Anthrop.*, 51 : 346-355.

KUMAR, N., and S. SINGH 1976 : "ABO Blood Group Investigations Among the Nagesia Tribe of Chattisgarh (Unp.).

LAL. P. 1968-70: "Demographic Characteristics of Gallong, Minyong, Pasi and Mijo-Mishi of NEFA" (Unp.).

LANDSTEINER, K. 1900 : As Cited in Race and Sanger, 1975.

LECHE, S.M. 1933 : "Handedness and Bimanual Dermatoglyphic Differences", *Am. J. Anat.*, 53 : 1-53.

LIU,T.T. and T.C. HSU 1949 : "Tongue Folding and Tongue Rolling in a Sample of Chinese Population", *J. Hered.*, 40 : 19-21.

LOCARD, E. 1906 : An Cited in Cummins and Midlo, 1943.

LUTZ, F.E. 1908 : "The Inheritance of the Manner of Clasping the Hands", *Am. Nat.*, 42 : 195-196.

MACFARLANE EILEEN W.E. 1937 : As Cited in Mourant, A.E. *et. al.*, 1976.

MAHALANOBIS, P.S., D.N. MAJUMDAR and C.R. RAO 1949 : "Anthropometric Survey of the United Provinces 1941, A Statistical Study", *Sankhya*, 9 : 89 - 324.

MAJUMDAR, D.N. 1943 : "Blood Groups of Tribes and Castes of the Uttar Pradesh with special Reference to the Korwa", *J. Asiatic. Soc. Beng.*, 9 : 81-84.

------- 1949 : "Anthropometry and Crime", *Man in India*, 29 : 46-58.

------- 1950 : *The Affairs of a Tribe*, pp. 18-42, Universal Publishers : Lucknow.

MAJUMDAR, D.N. and C.R. RAO 1960 : "*Race Elements in Bengal*", Asia Publishing House : Calcutta.

MALHOTRA, K.C., V.BALAKRISHNAN and I. KARVE. 1981 : "Anthropometric Variation in Tamil Nadu. In· *Biology of the People of Tamil Nadu* (Eds.) Sanghvi *et al.* The Indian Soc. Hum. Genet. Pune and The Indian Anth. Soc : Calcutta.

MALHOTRA, K.C. B. KARMAKAR, B.M. REDDY and M.VIJAY KUMAR 1980 : "Ulner Triradius (t"), Border Triradius (t^b) and Extra Limited Triradius (test), the neglected Triradii on Human Palm". Technical Report No. Anth/7/1980. Indian Statistical Institute : Calcutta.

MALHOTRA, K.C., G.S. MALLIK, B.Y. BHANU and S.L. TATE and P.M. FULMALI 1974 : "Incidence of Colourblindness Among Four Endogamous Nomadic Groups : An Example of Natural Selection", *Heredity*, 32 : 145-149.

MALONE, R.H. and LAHIRI, M.N. 1929 : As Cited in Mourent A.E. *et al.*, 1976.

MALPIGHI, M., 1686 : As Cited in Cummins and Midlo, 1943.

MARTIN, R. 1928 : Lehrbuch Der Anthropologie, Band 1, Verlag Von Gustay Fisher, Jena.

MAVALWALA, J. 1963 : Quantitative Analysis of Finger Ridge Counts of the Parsi Community in India", *Ann. Hum. Genet.*, 26 : 305-313.

MAYER, J.C.A. 1783 : As Cited in Cummins and Midlo, 1943.

METZNEK, I. 1939 : do

MIKI, T. and H. HAYATE 1961 : On the Palm Patterns of the Lepchas and the Khasis, *J. Anth. Soc. Nippon.*, 63 : 67-91.

MIKI, T; T. TANAKA; H. HASEKURA and T. FURUHATA 1960 : "Investigations on the Finger Prints of the Lepchas and Khasis", *Proc. Jap. Acad*; 36.6.

MITRA, P.N. 1935-36: As Cited in Mourant, A.E. *et. al.*, 1976.

------- 1936 : "Blood Group of the Angomi Naga and Lushai Tribe", *Ind. J. Med. Res.*, 23 : 685-686.

MOURANT, A.E. 1954 : *The Distribution of Human Blood Groups*, Oxford : Blackwell.

------- 1958 : *"The ABO Blood Groups"*, Oxford : Blackwell.

MOURANT, A.E. ADA C. KOPEC and KAZIMIERA DOMANIESSKA-SOBCZAK 1976 : *"The Distribution of the Human Groups and Other Polymorphisms"*, Oxford University Press : London.

MUKHERJEE, B.N., K.C. MALHOTRA, S.K. DAS, P.P. MAJUMDAR, MANAMI ROY, S.L. KATE and G.S. SAINANI 1977 : "Serological and Bio-Chemical Variation Among Santals of West Bengal", Ms. as Cited in Piplai, C. and D.P. Mukherjee (1979).

MUKHERJEE, D.P. 1962 : "Mahar Hand Prints - A Prelimintry Report", *Current Science*, 31; 2 : 66-67.

------- 1963 : "Variation in Defective Colour vision Among Some Tribes of Assam", *Bull. Anthrop. Surv. India*, 12 : 39-42.

------- 1963 : "A Brief Note on use of Dermatoglyphics in Medical Genetic :s", *J. Soc. Res.* 6; 1 & 2 : 130-1330.

------- 1965 : "Anthropological Observations on Toe Print Patterns Among the Hill Tribes of North East India", *Z.Morph.Anthrop.*, 56; 3 : 217-231.

------- 1966 : "Inheritance of Total Number of Triradii on Fingers, Palms and Soles", *Ann. Hum. Genet.* 29 : 349-353.

------- 1967 : "Quantitative Genetics of Dermal Ridges with Special Reference to an Indian Population", (Unp.)

-------- 1974 : "New Approaches to Dermatoglyphic Methodology", in *Human Polpulation Genetics in India* (Eds.) Sanghvi *et. al.*, 1 : 262-268.

-------- 1975 : "Dermatoglyphic Variation Among the Austro-Asiatic and Tibeto-Burman Speaking Polpulation", Proc. 2nd Annual conference, Ind. Soc. Hum. Genet. Calcutta, Memeographed.

MUKHERJEE, D.P. and M.P. CHAKRAVARTTI 1964 : "A Dermatoglyphic Approach to the Mundari Ethnic Problem", *Z. Morph. Anthrop.*

MUKHERJEE, D.P., P.CHANGAL REDDY and M.LAKSHMANADU 1980 : "Dermatoglyphic Effects of Inbreeding", *J. India. Anthrop. Soc.*, 15 : 67-79.

MUKHERJEE, D.P., INDRANI SARKAR AND G.C. GHOSH 1980 : "A Proposal Formation of Palmar Patterns with Special Reference to Jataba and other Indian Populations", *Acta.Anthropogenetica.*, 4; 1 & 2 : 71-84.

MUKHERJEE, D.P., and S.M.SIRAJUDDIN 1974 : "Genetics of Palmar Patterns in a Triputi Sample", *Bull. Anthrop. Surv. India*, 23; 3 & 4 : 69.

NAG,M.K. 1954 : "A Dermatoglyphic Study of the Danikkar of Travancore", *Bull.Anth.Surv.India*, 3; 2 : 95-116.

NANDA, D.K. 1976 : A note on ABO and MN Blood Groups of the Lodha of Midnapur, West Bengal - As Cited by Piplai, C. and D.P. Mukharjee, 1979.

NEEL, J.V. and R.H.POST 1963 : "Transitory Positive Selection for colour Blindness", *Eug. Quat.*, 10 : 33-35.

NEGI, R.S. 1963 : "ABO Blood Groups, Sickle Cell Trait and Colour-blindness in the Maria of Bastar, Gond and Kanwar of Bilaspur", *Bull. Anth. Surv. India*, 12 : 149-153.

NEGI, R.S., and B.N. SAHAY 1991 : "Incidence to Colourblindess in North Western India with Special Reference to Dehra Dun City", Paper presented in the *Seminar on Human Variation in India*, Organised by the Anthropological Survey of India, Calcutta.

NEGI, R.S. and S.H. AHMAD 1962 : "The Bhatra, Muria and Mahra of Bastar : A Blood Group Genetic Study", *Bull. Anth. Surv. India*, 11 : 221-231.

-------- 1963 : "A Study of A_1 A_2 BO, MN, Rh Blood Groups, ABH Secretion in Saliva and Colourblindness in the Dorla and Dhurwa of Bastar", *Bull. Anthrop. Surv. India*, 12; 1 & 2 : 21-29.

NEWMANN, H.H. 1930 : "This Finger Prints of Twins", *J. Genetics*, 23 : 415-446.

O'MALLEY, L.S.S. 1913 : "*Census of India 1911*", pp. 504, Vol.V, Part.1. Bihar, Bengal, Orissa and Sikkim. Calcutta.

PENROSE, L.S. 1965 : "Dermatoglyphic Topology", *Nature*, 205-544.

-------- 1968 : "Medical Significance of Finger Prints and Related Phenomenon", *Brit. Med. Journ.* 2 : 321-325.

PHELPS, R. 1952 : "Relative Index Finger as a Sex Influenced Trait in Man", *Am. J. Phys.Anthrop.*, 4 : 72.

PICKFORD, R.W. 1963 : "Natural Selection and Colourblindness", *Eug. Rev.*, 55 : 97-101.

PIPLAI, C. and D.P.MUKHERJEE 1979 : "Distribution of Blood Groups Among the Tribal Population of West Bengal", *J. Ind. Anthrop. Soc.*, 14; 2 : 157-165.

PLATO, C.C. 1970 : "Polymorphism of the C-line of Palmar Dermatoglyphics With a New Classification of the C-Line Termination", *Am. J. Phys. Anthrop.*, 33 : 413-420.

PODDAR, S. 1975 : "Effects of Birth Order and Mother's Age On Reproductive Wastage", in *Bio-anthropological Research* in India, (Ed.) H.K.Rakshit, Anthropological Survey of India : Calcutta.

POLL, H. 1937 : As Cited in Cummins and Midlo, 1943.

PONS, J. 1959 : "Quantitative Genetics of Palmar Dermatoglyphics", *J. Hum. Genet.*, 11 : 252.

-------- 1964 : "Genetics of the a-b Ridge Court On Human Palm", *Ann. Hum. Genet.*, 27 : 273-277.

POST, R.H. 1962 : "Population differences in Red and Green Colour Vision deficiency : A Review and a Querry on Selection Relaxation", *Eug. Quart.*, 9 : 131-46.

PRASAD, N. 1961 : Bathudi. Land and People of Tribal Bihar, Ranchi : *Tribal Research Institute*, pp. 237-243.

PURKINJE, J.E. 1823 : As cited in Cummins and Midlo, 1943.

QUELPRUD,T. 1934 : As Cited in Gates, 1952.

RACE,R.R. and R. SANGER. 1954 : "*Blood Groups in Man*, 2nd Edition, Oxford : Blackwell.

-------- 1975 : *Blood Groups in Man*, 6th Edition, Blackwell Scientific Publication : Oxford, London.

RAKSHIT, H.K. 1959 : "A Demographic profile of two Bastar Tribes", As Cited by Devi, B., 1975.

--------	1972 :	"The Dorla and Dhurwa of Bastar : A Demographic Profile", *J. India Anth.Soc.*, 7 115-128.
--------	1975 :	*Bio-anthropological Research in India*, Anthropological Survey of India : Calcutta.
RAKSHIT, H. and J. DASGUPTA,	1971 :	"Aspects of Marriage Pattern in Nine Population Groups of Maharashtra", *Man in India*, 51 : 83-91.
RAO, C.R.	1948 :	"The Utilisation of Multiple Measurements in Problems of Biological Classification", *J. Royal Statistical Society*, Series B, 10 : 2.
RAO,P.D. PRASAD and K.C.TRIPATHY	1963 :	"The Physical Anthropology of the Saoras", *Proc. 50th.i.s.c.a., part* III (Abstract).
RAY, A.K.	1954 :	"Reproductive Life of Pahira Women", *Man in India*, 34 : 151-160.
--------	1958 :	"A Note on Juang Anthropometry", *Man in India*, 38 : 56-59.
RAY, ANIMA	1965 :	"Household and Fertility Survey of the Nulia of Puri (Unpublished).
RAY, GAUTAM SANKAR	1949 :	"A Study of the Physical characters of the Khonds", *Eastern Anthropologist*, 2; 3 : 138-144.
RIFE,D.C.	1940 :	"Handedness with Special Reference to Twin", *Genetics*, 25 : 178-186.
RIFE,D.C.	1943 :	"Handedness and Dermatoglyphics in Twins", *Human Biology*, 15; 1 : 46-54.
--------	1954 :	"Dermatoglyphics on Ethic Criteria", *Am. J. Hum. Genet.*, 6: 3 : 319-327.
RISLEY, H.H.	1891 :	*The Tribes and Castes of Bengal*. Anthropometric Measurements : Calcutta, vol.1 and 2.
--------	1903 :	*Census of India 1901, Report on Ethnographic appendices, Vol.1, Part 1.*
--------	1915 :	*"People of India"*, Calcutta.
ROUT, S.P.	1948 :	"Notes on Juang", *Modern India*, 28; 1 and 2 : 1-146.
--------	1969/70:	"Hand Book on Juang", *Modern India*, 28; 1 & 2 : 1- 92.
ROY	1968 :	As Cited in Piplai, C. and D.P. Mukherjee, 1979.
ROY, R.C.	1935 :	"Anthropometric Data on Hill Bhuiya", In *The Hill Bhuiya of Orissa* by S. C. Roy, App. A. pp. 321.

ROY, S.C. 1935 : "The Hill Bhuiyas of Orissa, with Comparative Notes on Plain Bhuiyas", *Man in India*, Ranchi.

ROYCHOUDHURI, D. 1962 : "Palmar Dermatoglyphics of Rajbansi of Midnapore", *The Anthropologist*, 9; 31-38.

ROYCHOUDHURI,T.C. As Cited in Gupta and Dutta, 1966.

ROYCHOUDHURI,T.C. 1952 : "The Racial Problems of Bengal", *Man in India*, 32 : 52-63.

RUSSELL, R.V. and HIRALAL 1916 : *"The Tribes and Castes of the Central Provinces of India"*, 1 : 374, London.

SALLER, K. 1930 : Leitfaden der Anthroplogie, Verlag Von Julius Springer, Berlin.

SANGHVI, L.D., V .BALAKRISHNAN and I. KARVE 1981 : *"Biology of the People of Tamil Nadu"*; The Indian Soc. Human Genet : Pune and The Indian Anthrop. Soc. : Calcutta.

SARKAR, S.S. 1935-36: "Racial Affinities of the Inhabitants of Rajmahal Hills", *Trans. Bose,Res. Inst.*,11 : 123-153.

-------- 1936-37: "Blood Grouping Investigation in India with Special Reference to Santal Parganas, Bihar", *Trans. Bose. Res. Ins.*, 12 :89.

-------- 1938 : "Preliminary Note on the Blood groups of the Aborigines of Bihar", *Current Science*, 6 : 7.

-------- 1944 : "The Reproductive Life of Maler Women" *Man in India*, 24 : 29-32.

-------- 1949 : As Cited in Mourant, A.E. *et. al.*, 1976.

-------- 1953 : "The Origin and Migration of the Andamanese in the Andaman Islands", *Man in India*, 33 : 165-274.

-------- 1954 : *"The Aboriginal Races of India"*, Bookland : Calcutta.

-------- 1956 : As Cited in Mourant, A.E. *et. al.*, 1976.

-------- 1956/57: "Blood Groups From Orissa", *Science and Culture*, 22 : 180-1.

-------- 1959 : "Blood Groups and colourblindness Among Kotas", *Science and Culture*, 25 : 379.

-------- 1962 : *"Dermatoglyphics in India:Indian Anthropology"* (Eds.) Madan and Saran, Asia Publishing House : Bombay.

SARKAR, S.S and A.R. BANERJEE 1957 : "Finger Prints of Orissan Aborigines", *Man in India*, 37, 3 : 182-191.

-------- 1959/60: "Further Studies on ABO Blood Group From Orissa", *Science and Culture*, 25 : 294-295.

SARKAR, S.S., A.R.BANERJEE, P.BHATTACHARJEE and A.K. ROY 1960 : "Further Studies on ABO Blood Groups From Orissa", *Science and Culture*, 25 : 694-5.

SARKAR, S.S., and D.K. SEN 1952 : As Cited in Mourant, A.E. *ét. al.*, 1976.

SARMA, A.V.N. 1962 : "A Note on Papillary Patterns of Kollimalaialis of Salem District", *Bull. Anthrop. Sur. India*, 11 : 143.

SATPATHY, G.N. and P.S.DASPATNAIK 1968 : "Living conditions of Tribals of Simlipal Hills", *Adibasi*, 10; 2 : 1-69.

SEN, TULIKA 1953 : "Reproductive Life of Some Indian Women", *Man in India*, 33 : 31-54.

SENET 1906 : As Cited in Cummins and Midlo, 1943.

SETH, P.K. 1963 : "The a-b ridge count in Palmar Dermatoglyphics of the Indians of Punjab", *Man*, 242 : 189-190.

SCHROTER 1814 : As Cite in Cummins and Midlo, 1943.

SHARM, A.A. 1957 : "Notes on Palmar Main Line Index and Transversality", *Anthropologist*, 4; 1 : 20-25.

-------- 1964 : "A Methodological Study on Angle atd (t, t′, t″) distribution on the Palmar Prints" *Z.Morph.Anthrop.*, 55; 1 : 24- 31.

SHARMA, J.C. 1968a : "A Study of Dermatoglyphics of Hands and Feet of the Lahulis, In : *Proceeding Volume of International Symposium on Dermatoglypics*, P.C. Biswas and A. Sharma (Eds.) Department of Anthropology, University of Delhi, pp.153-164.

-------- 1968b : "Convergent Evolution in the Tribes of Baster", *Am. J. Phys. Anthrop.*, 28; 2 : 113-118.

-------- 1970 : "Convergence and Divergence of Dermatoglyphic Traits in Human Population; based on a study of the four Tribal Groups of Baster", *Eastern Anthropologist*, 23; 1 : 17-35.

SHARMA, K. 1979 : *The Konds of Orissa*, Concept Publishing Co. : New Delhi.

SHOOBERT, W.H. 1933 : "*Census of India 1931*, Vol.XII, Part I, Govt. Press : Nagpur.

SHUKLA, B.R.K. and D.TYAGI 1971 : As Cited in Piplai and Mukherjee, 1979.

SINGH, I.P. and M.K. BASIN 1968 : "*Anthropometry*", Bharti Bhawan, Delhi, Jallandhar city, Ambala Cantt.

SINGH, K.S. 1982 : "Incidence of colourblindness Among the Tangkhul Naga of Manipur", *J. Ind. Anth. Soc.*, 17 : 79-81.

SINGH, SWARAN 1984 : Finger and Palmar Dermatoglyphic Study among the Bathudi and Sounti of Mayurbhanj District of Orissa, *Human Science*, 33 (3) : 248-256.

-do- 1985 : Demo-genetic Study among the Bathudi and Sounti Tribes of Mayurbhanj District of Orissa. Paper presented in the Seminar on Small population and Genetic Demography, Organised by the Anthropological Survey of India, Calcutta.

-d0- 1986 : Anthropometric Study Among the Bathudi and Sounti of Mayurbhanj, Orissa, *Human Science*, 35 (1) : 50-59.

-do- 1987 : Incidence of Colourblindness Among Some Ethnic Groups of Mayurbhanj District, Orissa, *Human Science*, 36(3) : 248- 259.

-do- 1989 : Morphological and Genetical Investigation of the Bathudi and Sounti Tribes of Mayurbhanj. District, *Human Science*. 38 (1) : 61-68.

-do- 1989 : A_1A_2BO Blood Groups of the Bathudi and Sounti Tribes of Mayurbhanj District, Orissa, *Human Science*, 38 (1) : 205- 209.

-do- Anthroposcopic Study Among the Bathudi and Sounti Tries of Mayurbhanj district of Orissa. *J. Anth. Sur. India* (in the press).

SRIVASTAVA, R.P. 1965 : "Blood Groups in the Tharus of Uttar Pradesh and on their Ethnic and Genetic relationships", *Hum. Hio.*, 37 : 1- 12.

SRIVASTAVA, R.P. and B.R.K. SHUKLA "A Quantitative Study of Dermatoglyphics of Purabia Chamars and Gujar Pasis of U.P.", *Anthropologist*, 13; 1 & 2 : 69-70.

STOKIS, E. 1908 : As Cited in Cummins & Midlo, 1943.

STURTEVANT, A.H. 1940 : "A New Inherited Character in Man", *Proc. Nat. Acad. Sci.*, 26 : 100-102.

THOMSEN, O. FRIEDENREICH, V. and WORSAAE, E. 1930 : As Cited in Race and Sanger, 1975.

THURSTON, EDGAR 1909 : *"Casts and Tribes of Southern India"*, Vol.1 (A & B), Madras.

TIWARI, S.C. 1952 : "The Distribution of Blood Groups Among the Bhotias of Almora District, U.P.", *Man in India*, 32 : 148-151.

TRIPATHY, K.C. 1963 : "Dermatoglyphics Studies of the Sa-ara, Orissa", *The Eastern Anthropologist*, 18 :152-158.

-------- 1967 : "A Note on Finger Prints of the Saora (Lanjia) of Orissa", *The Eastern Anthropologist*, 20; 1 : 69-70.

UNDEVIA, J.V., 1981 : "Genetic Variation in Tamil Nadu", pp. 75-102.

VALLOIS, H.V. 1965 : "Anthropometric Technique", *Current Anthropology*, 6; 2.

VERMA, B.B 1952 : "Dermatoglyphic Study of Fingers Among Uraons of Chotanagpur", *Man in India*, 35; 3 : 134-152.

VERSCHUER, O. 1934 : As Cited in Cummins and Midlo, 1943.

VOLOTZKOY, M.V. As Cited in Cummins and Midlo, 1943.

VUCETICH. J. 1904 : As Cited in Cummins and Midlo, 1943.

WEINER, A.S.P. 1937 : "Complications in Ear Genetics", *J. Hered.*, 28 : 425-426.

-------- 1943 : *Blood Groups and Transfusion*, Springfield.

WENINGER, M. 1937 : As Cited in Cummins and Midlo, 1943.

WILDER, H.H. 1897 : As Cited in Cummins and Midlo, 1943.

-------- 1904 : "Racial Differences in Palm and Sole Configuration", *Amer. Anthrop.*, 6 : 244-292.

R.K. GULATI, P.K. SUKUMARAN, H.M. HATIA, H.R. MASTERN, V. BALAKRISHNAN and L.D. SANGHVI 1981 : In, "*Biology of the People of Tamil Nadu* by L.D. Sanghvi, V.Balakrishnan and I.Karve (Eds.), The Indian Society of Human Genetics : Pune and the Indian Anthropological Society : Calcutta.

Index

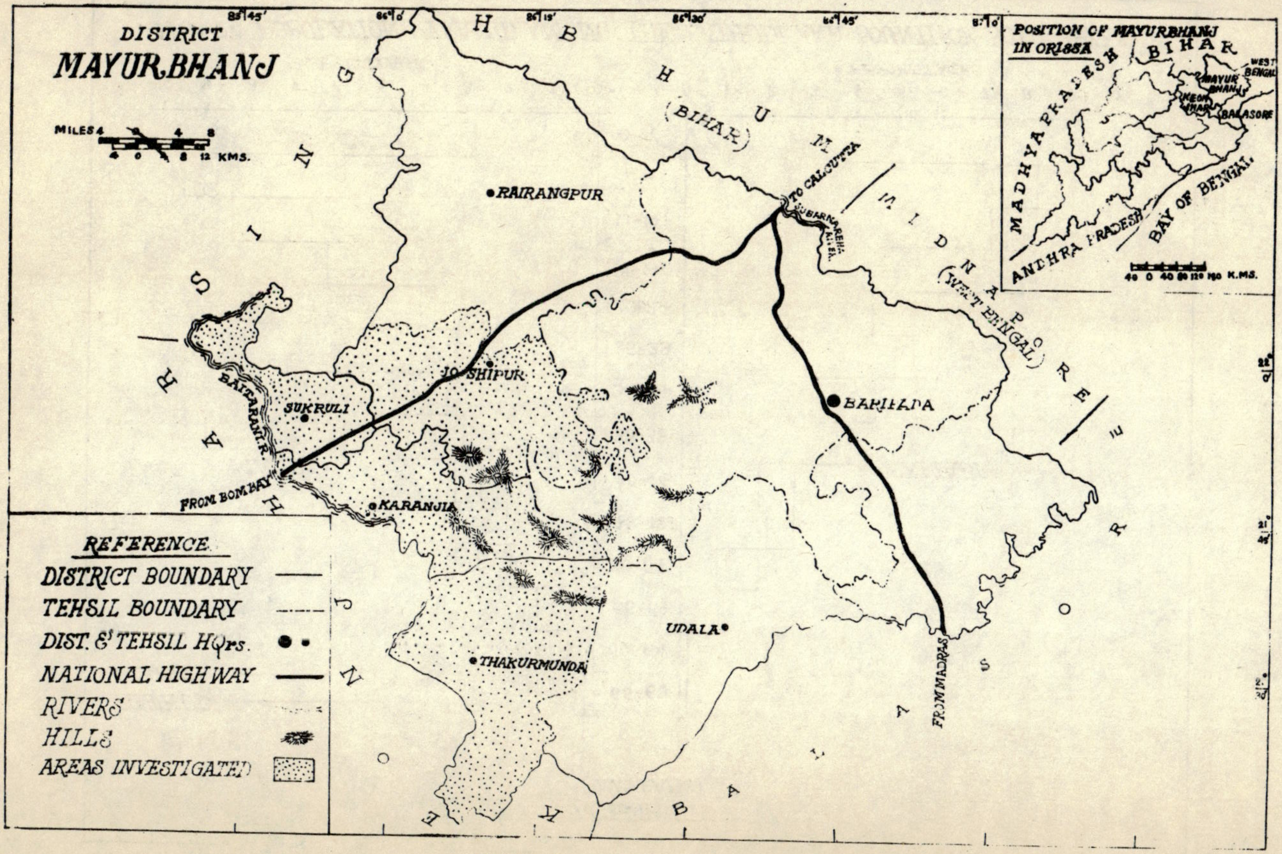

FIG.-1.2 MAP OF MAYURBHANJ

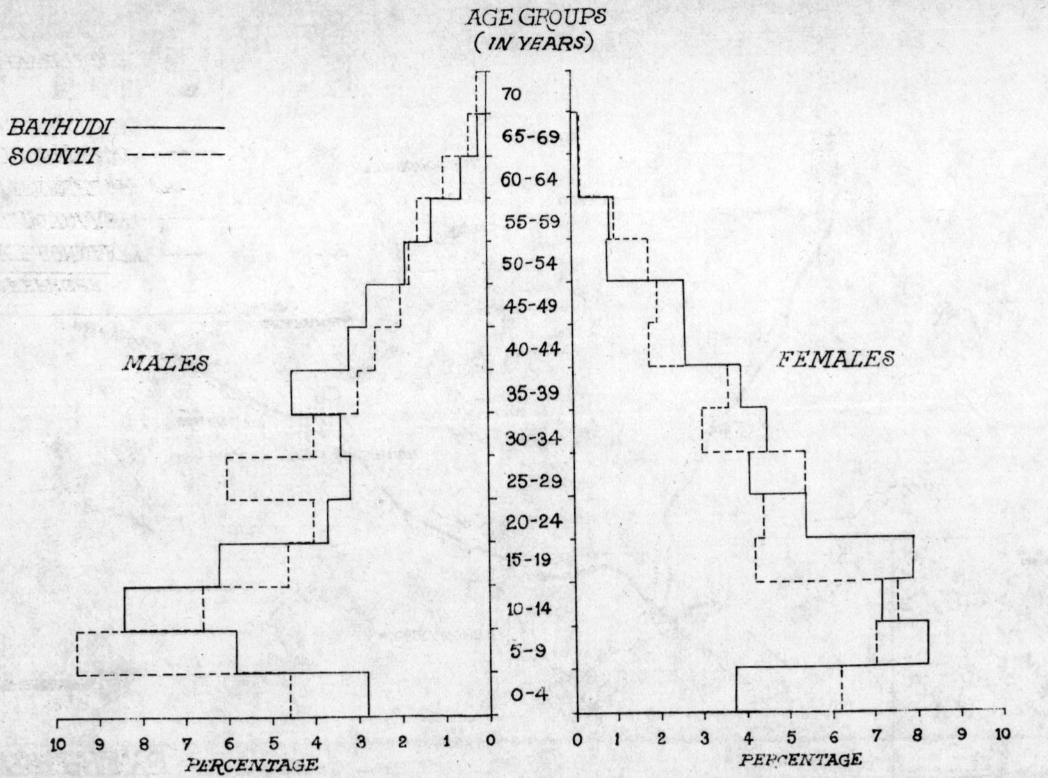

FIG:-2·1 POPULATION PYRAMID AMONG THE BATHUDI AND SOUNTI OF BOTH SEXES.

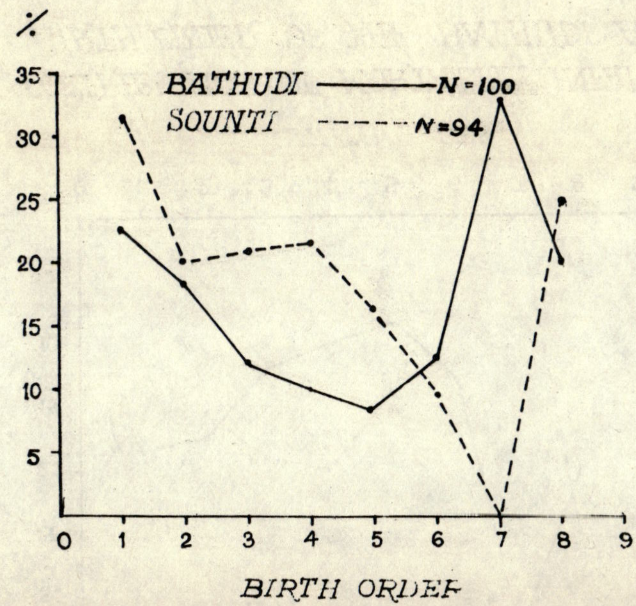

FIG:-2.2 DISTRIBUTION OF MORTALITY (PRENATAL & INFANT) ACCORDING TO BIRTH ORDER OF THE BATHUDI & SOUNTI

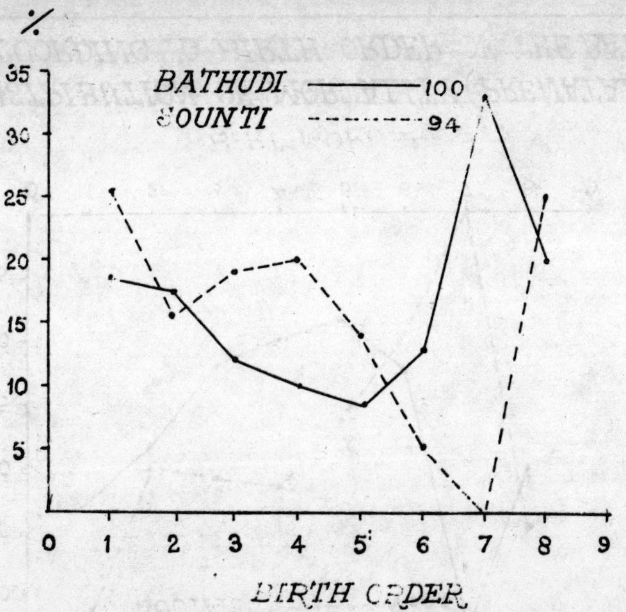

FIG:-2·3 DISTRIBUTION OF MORTALITY (INFANT) ACCORDING TO BIRTH ORDER OF THE BATHUDI AND SOUNTI

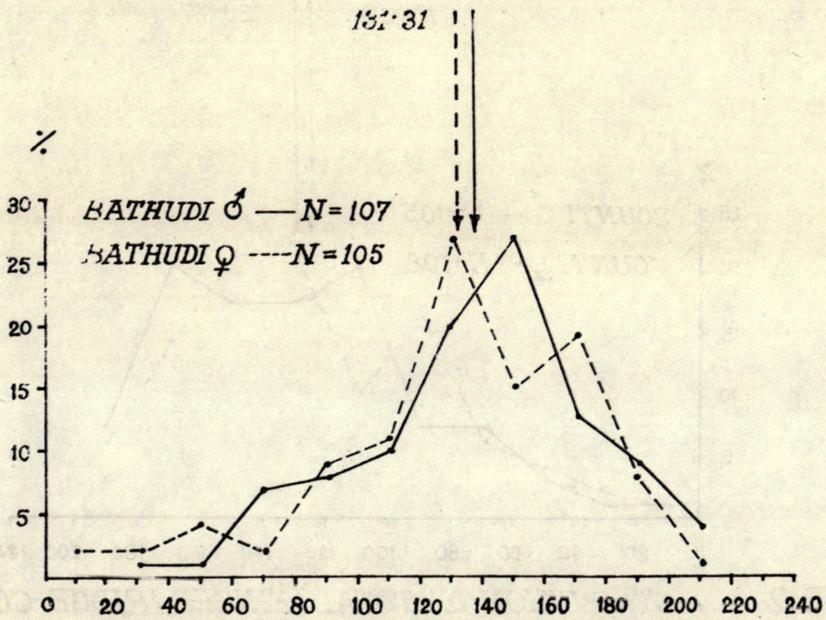

FIG:-5·1 DISTRIBUTION OF TOTAL FINGER RIDGE-COUNT OF BATHUDI MALE AND FEMALE

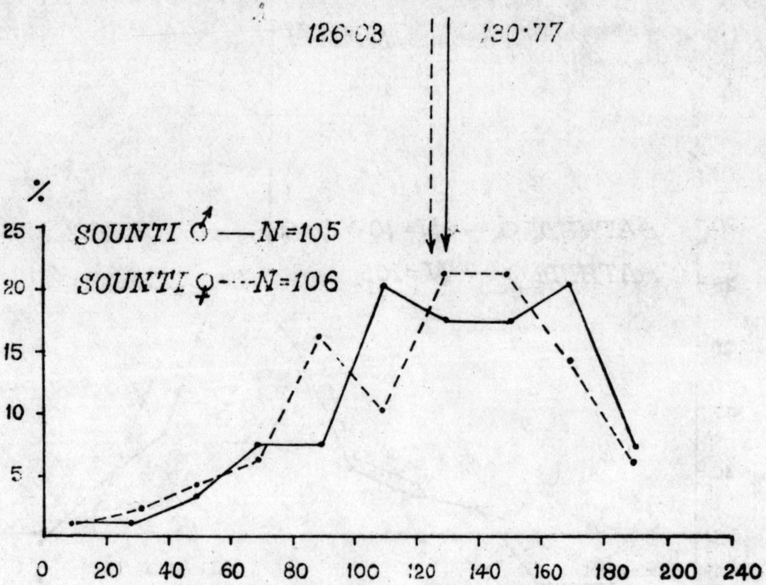

FIG:-5·2 DISTRIBUTION OF TOTAL FINGER RIDGE-COUNT OF SOUNTI MALE AND SOUNTI FEMALE

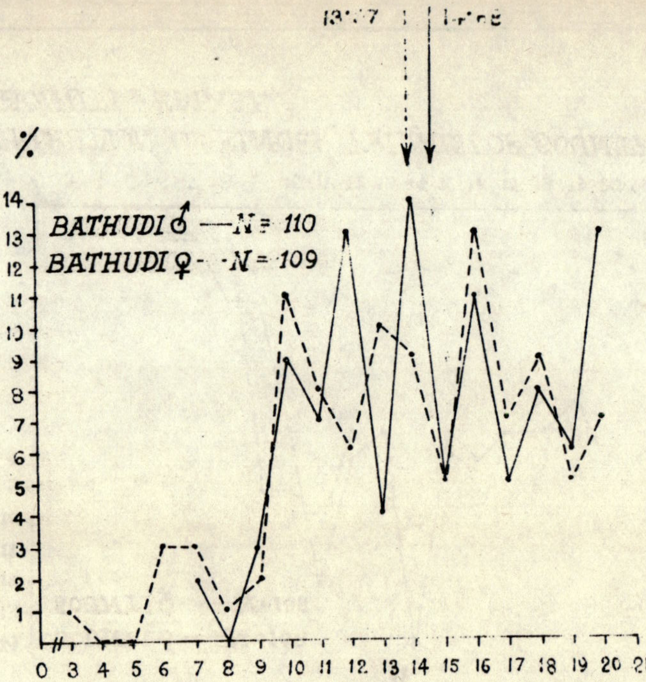

FIGURE:-5.3 DISTRIBUTION OF FINGER TRIRADII OF BATHUD MALE AND BATHUDI FEMALE.

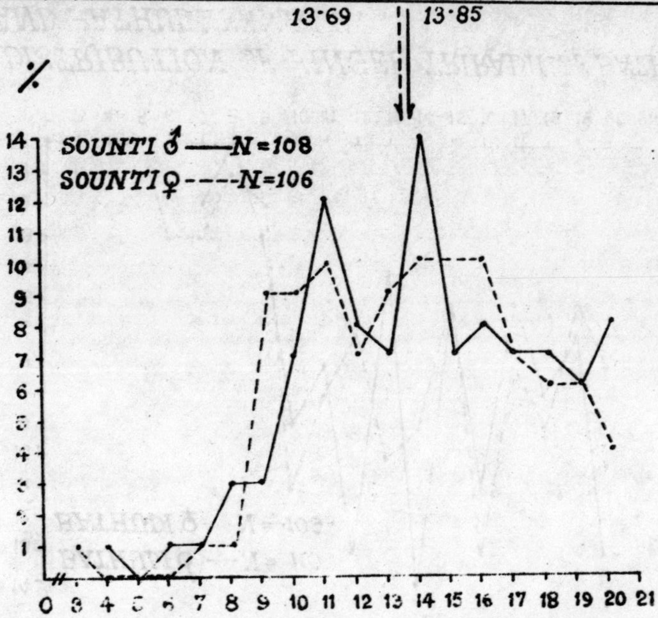

FIGURE :-5·4 DISTRIBUTION OF FINGER TRIRADII OF SOUNTI MALE AND SONUTI FEMALE.

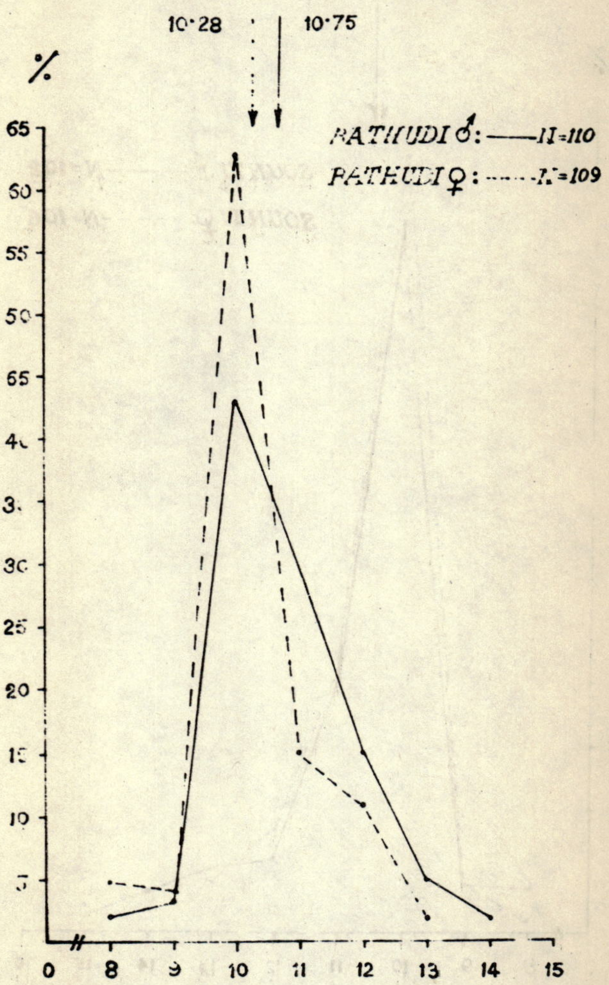

FIG.-5·5 DISTRIBUTION OF PALMAR TRIRADII OF BATHUDI MALE AND BATHUDI FEMALE

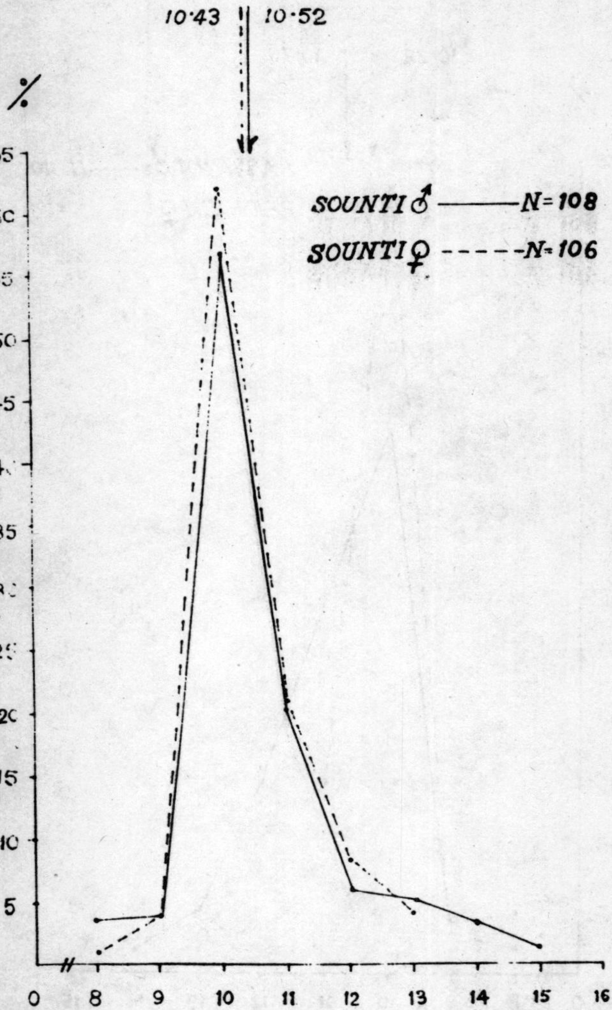

FIG.- 5.6 DISTRIBUTION OF PALMAR TRIRADII OF SOUNTI MALE AND SOUNTI FEMALE

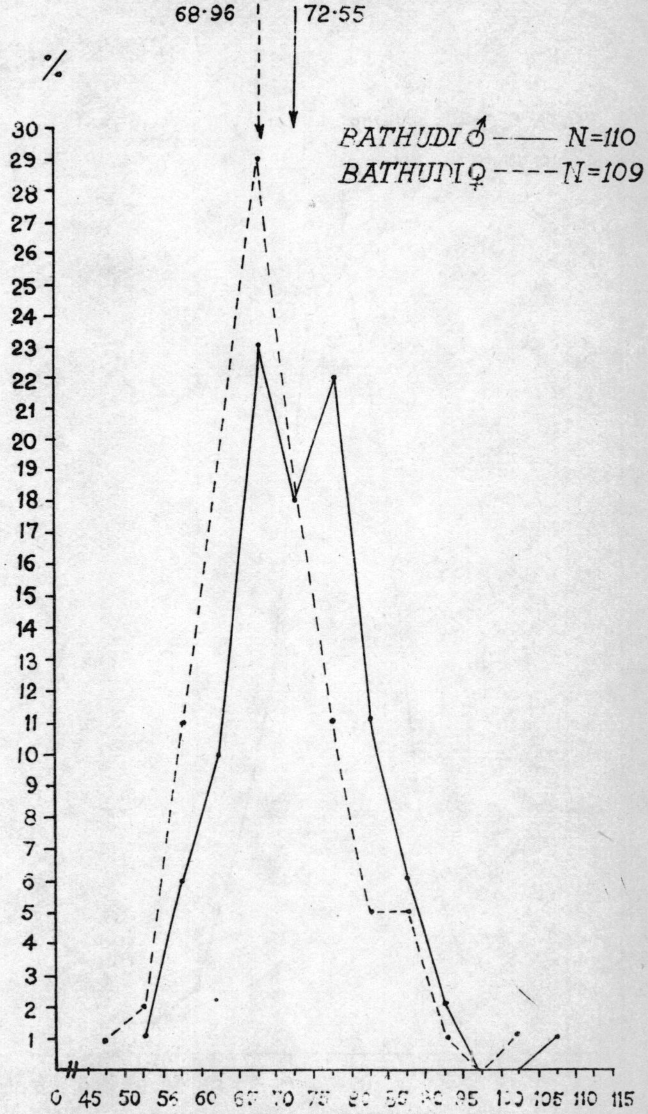

FIG.-5·7 DISTRIBUTION OF a-b RIDGE COUNT OF BATHUDI MALE & BATHUDI FEMALES.

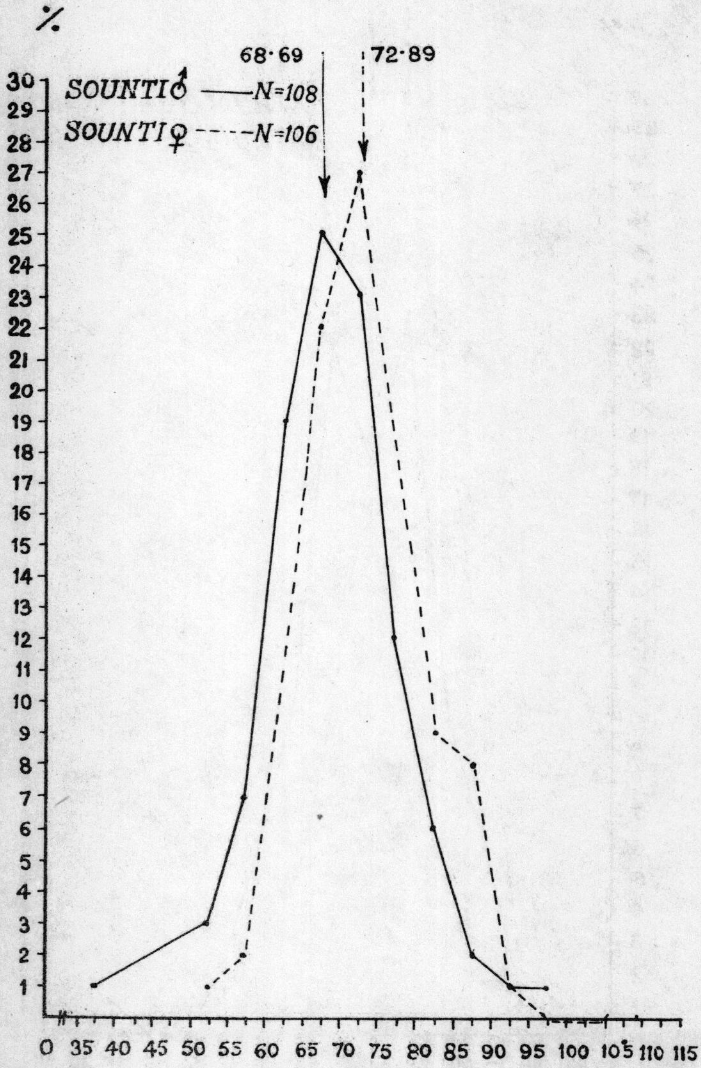

FIG.-5·8 DISTRIBUTION OF a-b RIDGE COUNT OF SOUNTI MALE & SOUNTI FEMALE

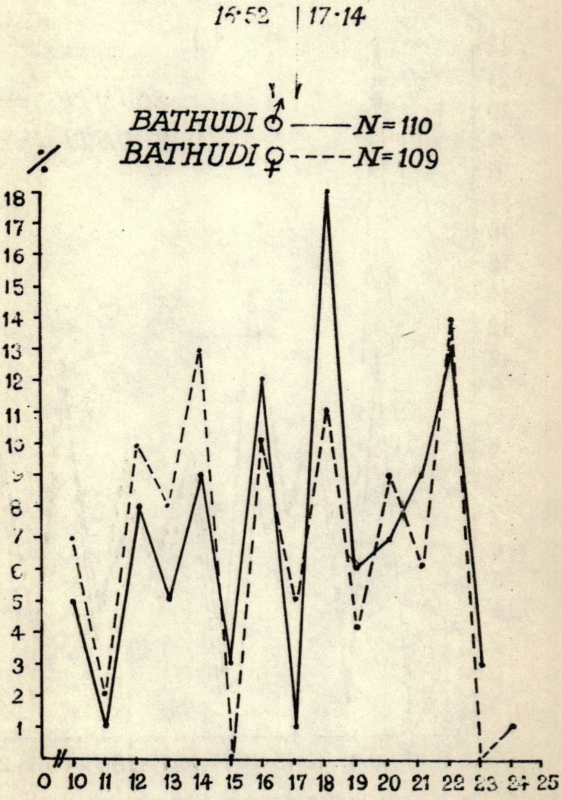

FIG.- 5·9 *DISTRIBUTION OF MAIN LINE INDEX OF BATHUDI MALE AND BATHUDI FEMALE*

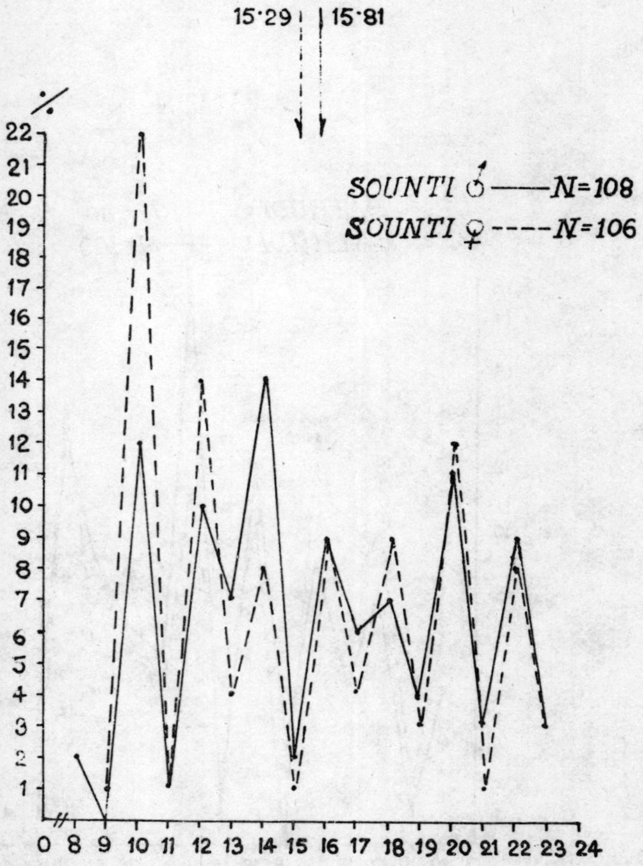

FIG.-5·10 DISTRIBUTION OF MAIN LINE INDEX OF SOUNTI MALE AND SOUNTI FEMALE

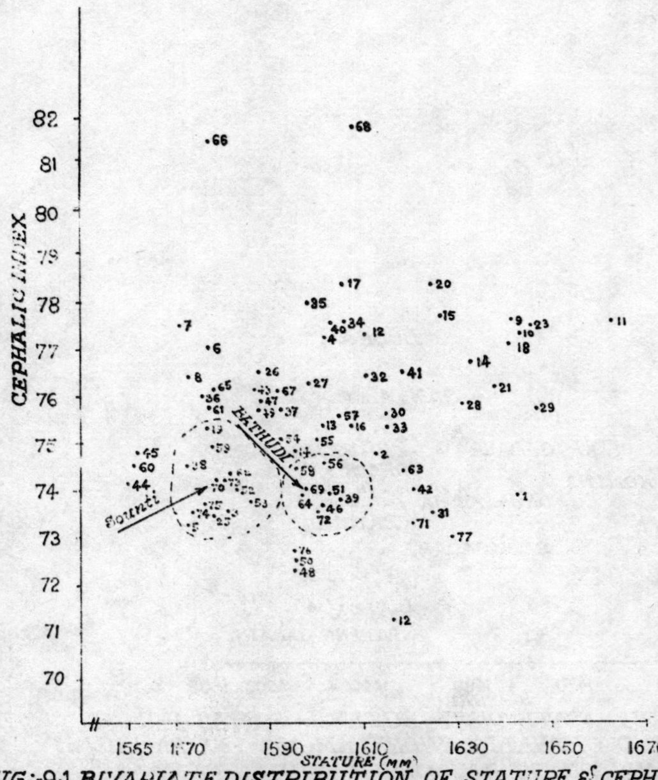

FIG:-9·1 BIVARIATE DISTRIBUTION OF STATURE & CEPHALIC INDEX AMONG THE BATHUDI & SOUNTI MALES & OTHER TRIBALS

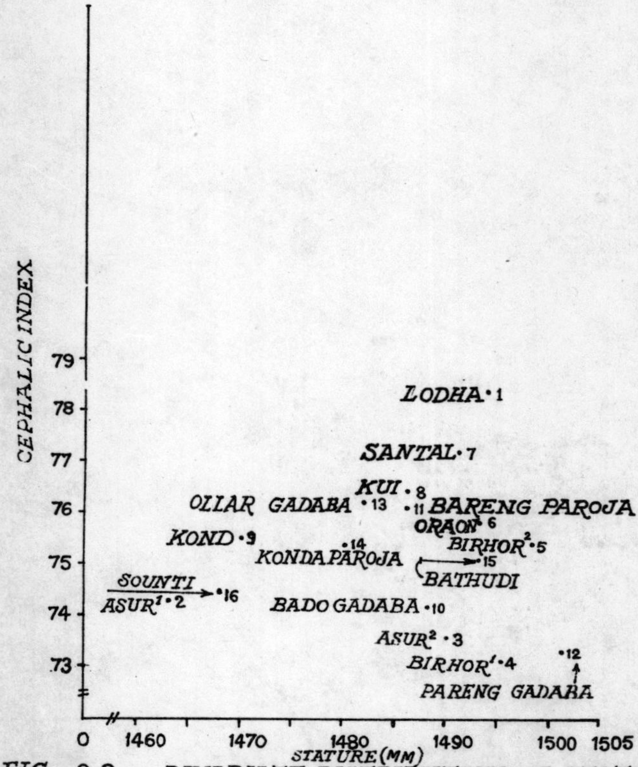

FIG.- 9·2 BIVARIATE DISTRIBUTION OF STATURE AND CEPHALIC INDEX AMONG THE BATHUDI AND SOUNTI AND OTHER TRIBAL FEMALES

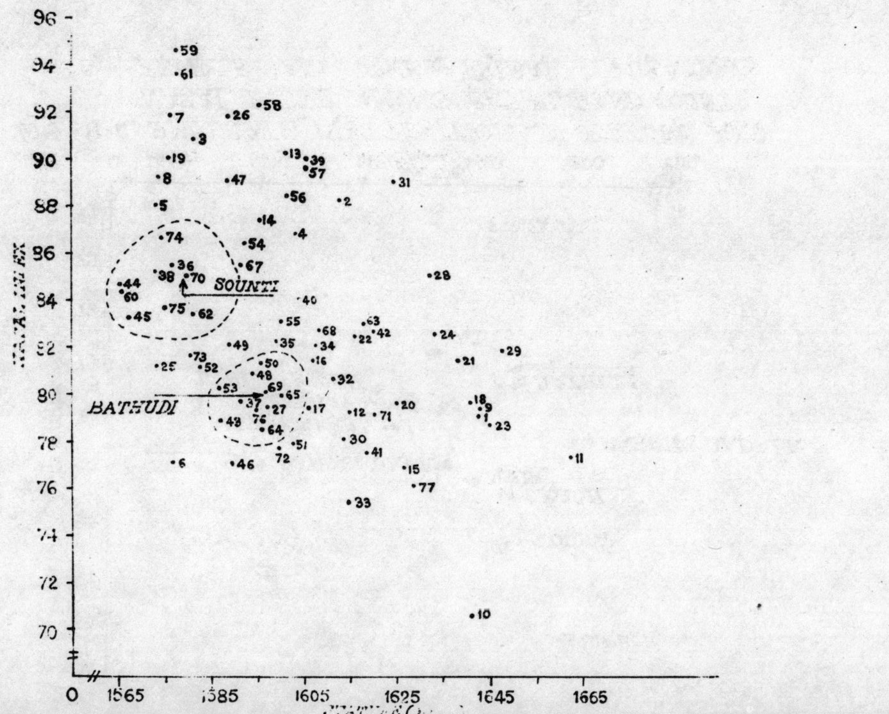

FIG.-9·3 BIVARIATE DISTRIBUTION OF STATURE AND NASAL INDEX AMONG BATHUDI AND SOUNTI MALES AND OTHER TRIBAL POPULATIONS.

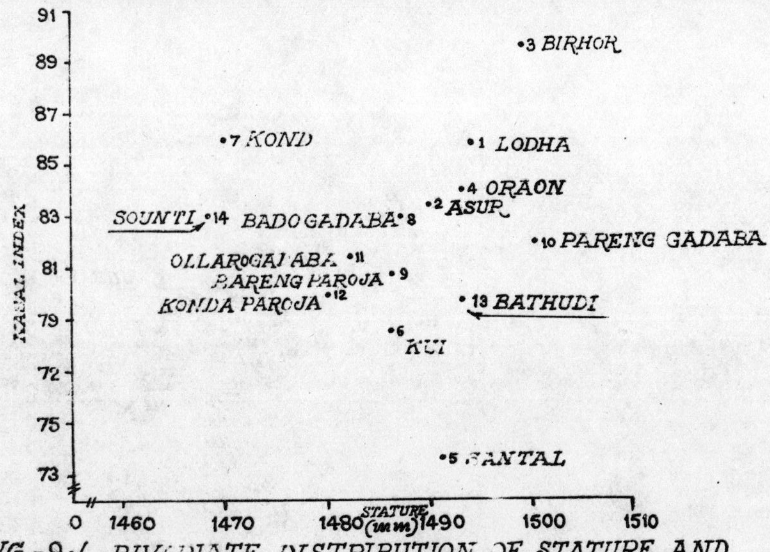

FIG.-9·4. BIVARIATE DISTRIBUTION OF STATURE AND NASAL INDEX AMONG BATHUDI AND SOUNTI FEMALES AND OTHER TRIBAL POPULATIONS

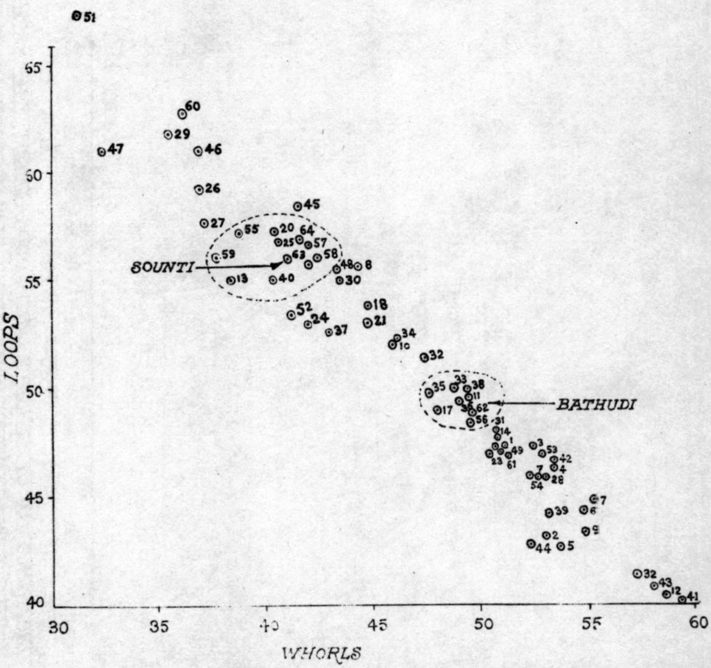

FIG.-9·5 DISTRIBUTIONS OF WHORLS AND LOOPS AMONG BATHUDI, SOUNTI AND SOME OTHER INDIAN TRIBAL POPULATIONS (MALE SERIES)

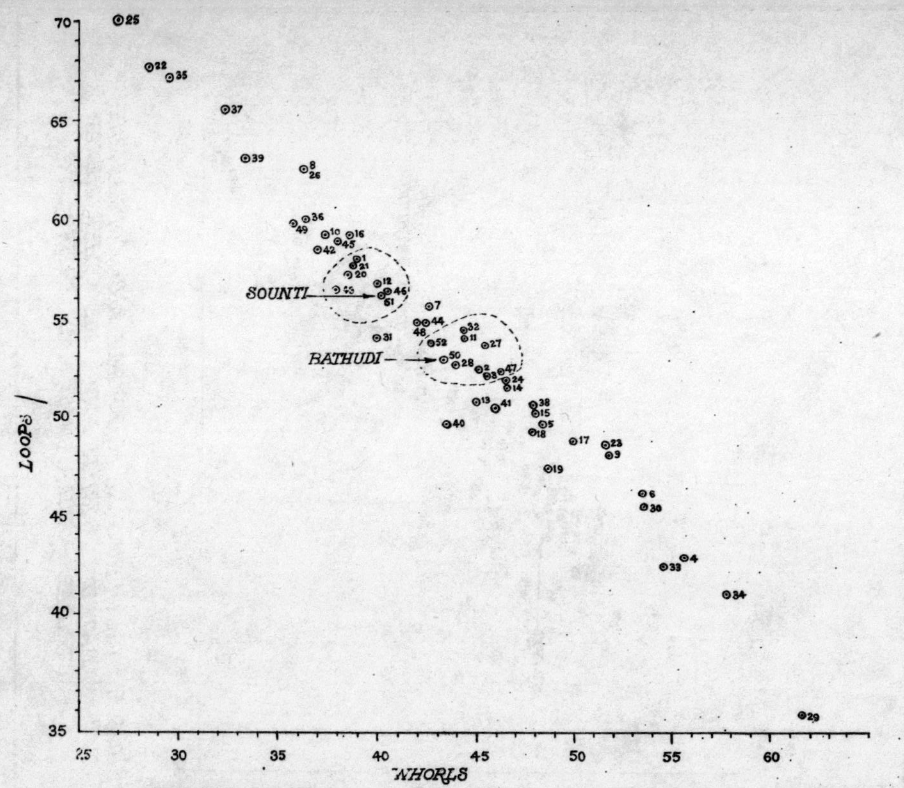

FIG.- 9.6 DISTRIBUTION OF WHORLS AND LOOPS AMONG THE BATHUDI AND SOUNTI FEMALES AND SOME OTHER INDIAN TRIBAL POPULATION

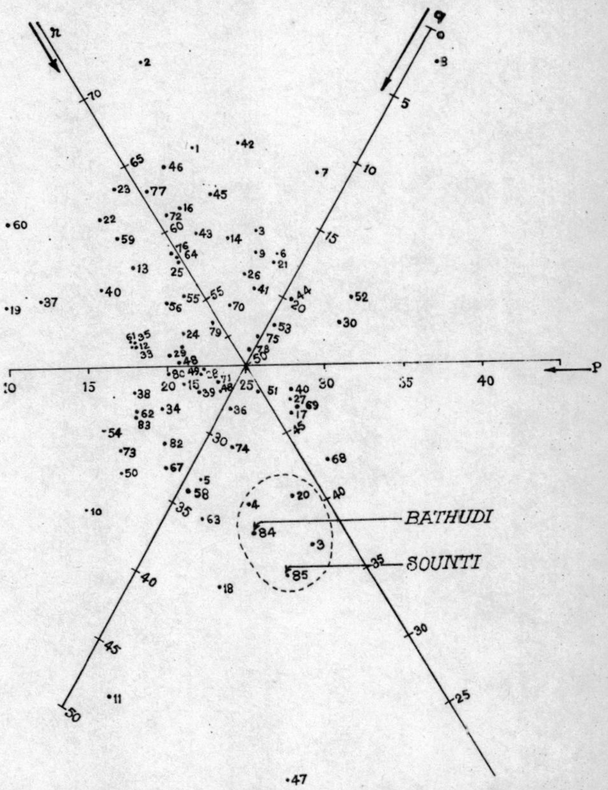

FIG:-9·7 DISTRIBUTION OF P, q, r. GENE FREQUENCIES AMONG SOME OF THE INDIAN TRIBAL POPULATIONS.